A Time To
LOOK
BACK

Growing up during the
Cuban revolution

A memoir by
ANTHONY TIMIRAOS

A Time to Look Back is a work of nonfiction.
Some names and identifying details have been changed.

Published by Anthony Timiraos Photography, LLC

Copyright © 2021 by Anthony Timiraos

Permission requests, questions, and/or error notifications relating to this book should be communicated to the author at tony@atimetolookback.com

Website: www.atimetolookback.com

ISBN: 978-0-578-98001-0 (Hardcover)
ISBN: 978-0-578-98004-1 (ePub)

Cover photography by Anthony Timiraos
Cover design by Arthur Crispino
Editor - Ashley Sweren
Book Layout - Saravanan Ponnaiyan

Table of Contents

Acknowledgment

The U.S. is built largely by immigrants from all over the world who have made significant contributions in science, medicine, arts, economy, education and every other field imaginable. Immigrants seeking a better and safer homeland were welcomed to this country with open arms. Networks of religious organizations, the non-profit community, the corporate community and local citizens worked hand in hand to help those in need get settled, begin a new life, join and contribute back to our society. Leaving your country of birth is not an easy decision to make and too often their only other choice was to risk their lives and the lives of their family.

The recent debates over immigration issues has escalated to unnecessary levels. False and unbalanced claims about the negative effects of immigration reform by a small vociferous group of individuals and politicians seems to have infected many others who once believed in empathy for those seeking to live in a free world. I am a proud immigrant and grateful for the help and support my family and I received during the early 1960s. I witnessed many other families during the same period transition from nothing to success. Blanket endorsement in support of closing our borders to those in need is contrary to the basic principles that have made the United States a place that many emulate. Yes, there has to be controls and a legal process that one must follow to emigrate. As we all look back in our family history we will find a distant relative who arrived here from a foreign land, was welcomed onto our shores and supported so they could experience a better life for themselves and for their future families.

****

I am grateful to many friends who knew my story and encouraged me to write this book.

* * * * * * * * * * * *

Writing my story of a brief five-year period in my life was more challenging than I had originally expected. Going through old family photos, notes and personal records brought me back vividly to a crucial time in my life which I found strenuous to describe on paper. I was fortunate and grateful to get help from my niece and professional editor, Ashley Sweren who took the time from her busy schedule to review and edit my words to create a visual format that painted the picture of those five years. I could not have finished this book without her feedback. Thank you.

* * * * * * * * * * * *

This book would not have been possible if our close friends Stephen Draft and Allen Peterson had not convinced us to join them on a cruise to Cuba during the Christmas holidays of 2018. I enjoyed sharing my childhood experiences with them during our cruise. Thank you.

* * * * * * * * * * * *

And last but not least, the day to day encouragement, support, edits and sounding board came from my husband Arthur Crispino. I am grateful for his love and countless contributions to this book.

Acknowledgment

Dedication

To the 14,048 Pedro Pan children
who experienced a similar story.

To thousands of other children who were forced
to leave their country of birth for a better life.

To my husband

About the Author

Anthony Timiraos was born in Havana, Cuba and currently resides in South Florida with his husband Arthur who has been by his side for 51 years. He began his professional career as a Certified Public Accountant in Hartford, Connecticut. Various career advancement moves for both brought them to Boston, New York City and back to Connecticut.

A retirement to South Florida in 2003 was shortened when he accepted the position of Chief Financial Officer for the county's community foundation. After five years, he co-founded, with four other local philanthropists, Our Fund, Inc, a new community foundation serving LGBTQ+ non-profit organizations providing services in South Florida. He became their first Chief Executive Office and President in 2011 and retired in 2016 to enjoy travel and photography. Our Fund, Inc. is currently one of the largest LGBTQ+ community foundations in the country.

His love for travel and photography began in his early college years, Today, Anthony has traveled the globe extensively and enjoys capturing portraits of the people he meets and the architecture of places he visits. He is also known for his focus of the male form, which has led to the creation of a captivating body of work displayed in four books. His photography from global travels also bespeak a truly perceptive eye for ambiance and character.

Other books published:

Expose - a collection of classical nude photographs
Expose More - the continuing collection of classical nude photographs
Expose Love - photographic essay of male couples in classical nude poses
Expose Art - male nude photography at a virtual art exhibit
The Faces of Cuba - a photographic view of life in the island.
Journey to India - a photographic collection

A child on the other side of the border is no less worthy of love and compassion than my own child.

- PRESIDENT BARACK OBAMA

Operation Pedro Pan

A mass exodus of 14,048 unaccompanied Cuban minors ages 6 to 18 to the United States between January 1960 and October 1962.

This book is 1 of 14,048 stories of Pedro Pan children and one of many other thousands of untold stories by immigrant minors from other countries whose parents only wanted freedom and a new life for their families.

Prologue

A cruise to Cuba during the Christmas holidays of 2018 brought me back 60 years to a critical period of my life between December 31, 1958, in La Habana, Cuba, and December 31, 1963, in Waterbury, Connecticut.

My story begins as a five-year-old child when my family was forced to adapt to Fidel Castro's revolution. I felt their crushing disappointment when a political revolt to return democracy to Cuba failed. I experienced a military raid of our home by government officials and armed militia. I saw the look on my mother's face when we heard my father was sent to jail without cause.

I was being taught in school that capitalism was evil and the only solution was living in a socialistic and communistic society. A constant parade of military vehicles, political assassination attempts, bombings, and gunfire in my neighborhood became the norm.

In 1962, when I was 8, my parents sent my brother and me to the U.S. as part of Operation Pedro Pan, the largest exodus of children in the Western Hemisphere. They wanted us to escape the indoctrination of communism and live in a free democratic land in hopes that the rest of the family could soon follow. I was welcomed to my new homeland by a generous religious organization and a country that had empathy for families seeking asylum from restricted and dangerous societies.

At an age when most boys were playing cowboys and watching "Lassie," I was living in another country, apart from my parents. To no fault of my sponsors, I had to live in numerous locations when I arrived in America, including a regretful stay in an orphanage for troubled young boys from broken families who could not be placed in foster homes. I watched the horrors of a close encounter with nuclear war.

What I learned and experienced between the ages of 5 and 10 were remarkable lessons that shaped my life, personality, disposition, and attitudes. I witnessed the positions my parents were placed in and the decisions they were forced to make to survive. I learned a lot about life from their brave example.

Prologue

PART ONE

There are risks and costs to a program of action. But they are far less than the long-range risk and costs of comfortable inaction.

- JOHN F. KENNEDY

CHAPTER 1

Happy New Year
1959

In the early morning hours of January 1, 1959, Cuba's dictator, Fulgencio Batista, decided quickly and hastily to gather a group of family and loyal friends for an elegant but brief New Year's Eve celebration at Camp Columbia, a military station outside of La Habana in the Marianao neighborhood.

But, instead of pouring champagne, Batista and his cohorts boarded a plane and fled Cuba for political asylum in the Dominican Republic. A second plane left La Habana later that night carrying ministers, officers, and the governor of La Habana.

A crook, murderer, and thief, Batista didn't just bring his friends along for his escape. He also took more than $300 million amassed through graft and payoffs as well as fine art worth a substantial fortune.

Happy New Year - 1959

Batista had previously been elected President of Cuba in 1940 for a four-year term. After he lost re-election, he moved to Florida, but later returned to Cuba to run for president again in 1952. It began to look like that effort was doomed. So, what does a politician who is a crook, murderer, and thief do when he faces imminent defeat? He preempts the election by organizing a successful military coup against the current president! From 1952 to that early morning of January 1, 1959, Batista was the U.S.-backed military dictator of the island.

He lost his political popularity with the Cuban people because of his corruption, payoffs, suspension of constitutional rights, and attempts to frighten the people through open displays of brutality against his political enemies. His army, though substantial, was undermined by a popular movement led by the young charismatic Fidel Castro that started to brew in Cuba's eastern mountain range, moving westward across the island to La Habana.

There was chaos inside Batista's administration. Many of his generals and other military personnel were beginning to defect and join the new revolution. As Castro's army kept moving closer and closer to La Habana, Batista had no choice but to orchestrate his last-minute dramatic exit from the island with as many valuable possessions as he could take on the plane.

****

A few hours earlier, in my home in the Santo Suarez neighborhood of La Habana, less than 5 miles east of Camp Columbia, I was getting ready to go to bed. It was New Year's Eve 1958, and my parents, Segundo and Rosa, were leaving to attend a formal party with several friends at the well-known Rancho Luna Restaurant in the Wajay neighborhood. It was less than 10 miles south of Camp Columbia where Batista was scheduled to have his own private party.

Both of my parents were dressed in formal attire as if they were going to attend the Academy Awards. They kissed their three young boys, Segundito (8), Jorge (3), and me, Antonio (5), goodnight for the third time. As most mothers do, Rosa verbally repeated her written list of instructions to the sitter who was hired to watch us that night until they returned home sometime after midnight.

We were not allowed to stay up late. But that night, after midnight, I was awakened by loud noises out in the street, glass breaking, people running, and screaming. I couldn't tell if the people were celebrating or demonstrating. There was chaos outside and I did not want to get out of bed to look out the window, if there were any problems, I felt the sitter would protect us. Soon after the noise quieted down, my parents returned home. I could overhear them tell the sitter that they left their swanky party earlier than expected because of the street demonstrations and concerns that the protesters would invade the restaurant while the patrons were inside enjoying the New Year's celebration.

On their way home, they witnessed groups rioting on the main streets, shooting randomly at government buildings and other properties known to be occupied by loyal supporters of Batista. People were celebrating his rumored departure from Cuba, and the eventual control of the country by Fidel Castro. My parents were afraid for their lives but managed to circumvent the obstacles to arrive home safely.

The political unrest continued for about a week into the New Year. We were not allowed to go to school or to play outside during that time for fear of the demonstrators' violence. All day long during this unsettling time, we were forced to keep the doors and windows facing the street closed, draw the curtains, and keep minimal lights on at night. We could hear the constant roar of military vehicles traveling at a high rate of speed outside of our home and occasional gun shots. My father still went to work every day but was careful about which route he would take to avoid the protesters and the remains of Batista's army which, by this time, began to shift their allegiance to Fidel Castro.

On January 7, 1959, a week after Batista fled the country, Castro and his army of guerrilla fighters entered the city of La

Happy New Year - 1959

Habana in a triumphant parade just like Julius Caesar had done in Egypt. But this time there was no Cleopatra, elephants, camels, or lions. Just a bunch of bearded men lacking soap, water, and basic personal hygiene in military trucks.

This is when my life began to change. I felt that I had begun my adult years at the age of 5.

****

I was raised by very conservative Cuban parents who were madly in love. My father, Segundo, was an accountant/office manager for Jose Arechabala, a large company with headquarters in the La Habana Vieja neighborhood across from the Catedral Colon (Cathedral of San Cristóbal de la Habana). My mother, Rosa, was a housewife who raised my brothers and me.

Our house was a simple classic Spanish-style home. Our neighborhood was home to many middle-class families and a short 10-minute ride to the downtown and La Habana Vieja neighborhoods.

Life for me as a child during the 1950s was safe and predictable. A real-life Cuban "Leave It to Beaver," I spent weekdays in school and late afternoons playing with neighborhood kids at a local playground. Later in the evening, it was homework followed by dinner with the entire family. My father would arrive from work and after some social interaction with the neighborhood adults on the front porch, the five of us would go inside and sit together for dinner.

My brother Segundito always felt he had to play the conservative, serious role and do everything in his power to protect his younger brothers. At the same time, he had a bit of a devilish prankster personality and liked to use it to tease us and friends in the neighborhood. Jorge was the youngest with more energy inside his small body than Segundito and I had combined. He needed to be watched 24 hours a day. My mother would always say to us, *"Cuida a Jorge, el es muy joven y chiquito."* (Take care of Jorge, he

Happy New Year - 1959

is too young and small.) That left us with a lot of guilt if we did not watch him all the time.

The dinner conversations at home varied. My finicky brothers and I would always complain about something on our dinner plate even though my mother was an excellent cook. Her common response was, *"No puedes moverte de esa silla hasta que tu plato esté vacío."* (You can't move from that chair until your plate is empty.) Today, I realize that she was no different than most mothers trying to raise three boys.

My parents were very discreet at the table with their adult conversations, especially when they talked politics in front of us. I did practice the study of eavesdropping during their dinner talks which was mostly in what I call, "Cuban Code," because they assumed we would not understand. That's when I began to develop a political opinion at my tender age based on my parents coded comments.

Sundays included mornings at church and afternoon lunches at one of my two grandmothers' houses. Abuela Balbina was my father's widowed mother. She was frail with very thick and wavy shoulder-length hair that was pure snow-white. She always dressed in a three-quarter-length black dress with beige nylons that were pulled up just below her knees and would many times roll down to her ankles. The pair of slippers always on her feet seemed to be at least 200 years old.

Living in the same house with Abuela Balbina was her older sister, Esperansa, who was never married and always dressed like Abuela Balbina. Esperansa suffered from a tooth ailment as a teenager that left her jaw and the lower part of her face deformed. Her mental state was questionable when I knew her, so we were always afraid to go near her because she wanted to kiss us all the time. *"Mira, mira, mira. Besitos para todos."* (Look, look, look. Kisses for everyone.)

Abuela Balbina had three children. My father was the oldest followed by her only daughter, Tia Nena, who also lived in the same household. She was born only 13 months after my father. Tio

Happy New Year - 1959

Orlando was the youngest of the three and lived near us with his wife and two daughters.

Tia Nena was single at that time, a socialite who was well known in elite circles of La Habana. She was very attractive, always wearing heavy makeup and the latest Cuban fashions. Her bold perfume, bright red lipstick, red fingernails and toenails combined in a distinct style and attitude to match was her trademark. Later in life, she told us about many of her boyfriends and how she kept them a secret from her mother and my father. Abuela Balbina, Esperansa and Tia Nena lived in a beautiful old Spanish-style townhouse on Calle Amargura in the center of the La Habana Vieja neighborhood.

Abuela Teresa, my mother's mother, had five children. Tia Vivina was the youngest, preceded by Tio Alberto, Tio Yayo, my mother Rosa, and Tia Maria Luisa, the eldest. Abuela Teresa was also a widow and lived with her sister a few minutes from our home. She seemed to be younger to me and had more energy than Abuela Balbina.

Abuela Teresa's clothing style and physical looks were not as dark, gloomy, and "scary widow looking." She was more into traditional greys, neutrals, and softer colors. She always slapped too much talcum powder all over her body. Her sister dressed the same, except that she was much quieter and did most of the cooking on Sundays. That is why her dresses always had food stains. Abuela Teresa liked to take the credit for the excellent food, but everyone knew who the real cook in that household was. They both lived in a simple ground-level apartment with a large patio facing the front sidewalk.

So, every Sunday, it was either Balbina or Teresa's home for lunch after church. At each home, other aunts and uncles would join us and, depending on which abuela we visited, the subject of politics became either heated or agreeable based on who was present that day. It was fun as a child to see your relatives argue quite strongly at times about something I thought back then to be unimportant. These useless political issues seemed to me like a waste of time and energy. Who cares?

Happy New Year - 1959

****

We were the typical, middle-class Cuban family living in La Habana. But on that New Year's Eve of 1958, I started to realize there was more going on outside my comfortable reality. Military vehicles racing past the front door was not something anyone would see on "Father Knows Best" or "The Adventures of Ozzie and Harriet." Things were happening outside of our control that would change our lives and the lives of thousands of Cubans forever.

Happy New Year - 1959

CHAPTER 2

Welcome to La Habana 2018

I was awakened by my own internal clock with an alarm that seemed to know the precise time we would be approaching the port. My eyes opened at exactly 5:00 a.m. on December 20, 2018, almost 60 years to the day after that famous New Year's Eve celebration in 1958 that took place not far from where I was now.

I leapt out of bed, opened the sliding glass doors of our suite, and stepped out onto our cabin's verandah. Out on the dark horizon, I saw that famous castle, the Castillo de los Tres Reyes del Morro, known to us when we were kids as "*El Morro*", with some spotlights on the stone walls protecting the entrance to the port.

I woke up my husband Arthur who was sharing this trip with me, dressed quickly, and grabbed my camera as we raced upstairs to the sun deck to experience our entrance into the harbor. A place

I had not seen for almost 56 years. The harbor of a city I used to call home.

My heart was beating louder than a drum line at a college football game. I could not determine if the rapid beating was due to the excitement and anticipation of what was to come over the next several hours or perhaps the three flights of stairs we just ran. I hoped it was the excitement and anticipation and not a sign of an upcoming heart attack.

The ship slowly sailed into the harbor as I jumped back and forth from the port side to the starboard side several times because I couldn't determine which side of the ship had the best views to capture on camera. As we got closer to the port entrance and docks, our long-time friends and travel-mates Stephen and Allen arrived on the deck. There, we saw the dome of El Capitolio in the distance, a public edifice similar in design to the U.S. Capitol building and one of the most visited sites in Havana commissioned by a former Cuban president and built during the mid 1920's.

Both Stephen and Allen are avid world travelers who we have known for more than 15 years. This was their first time in Cuba, and it was at their suggestion that Arthur and I found ourselves on this cruise with them, circling the island during the Christmas holidays in 2018.

I initially hesitated about returning to Cuba more than a half century after leaving. But after some discussions with Arthur, we both thought it would be a great opportunity for me to return to my roots and for Arthur to finally see my country of birth. Earlier that year, Arthur and I celebrated our 48th anniversary together, so he was awfully familiar with my childhood stories of Cuba. He knew my family well and was just as anxious as I was to visit.

The docks and warehouses at the port were now in full view as the ship turned. Most of what we saw was in dilapidated condition. Just on the right was a beautiful church with a stone façade that was very dark, almost black, most likely due to years of pollution and lack of maintenance. It was the Convento de San Francisco de Asis where we occasionally attended mass with Abuela Balbina back in the late 1950s and early 1960s.

Welcome to La Habana - 2018

I saw cars traveling in both directions as the ship slowly prepared to dock and the crew threw ashore their light throwline with a linesman's line attached to secure the ship to the dock. My mind immediately took me back to my youth, riding in the back seat of my father's 1954 Buick, looking out the car window at a frenzy of activities between the freighters loading and unloading cargo, trucks pulling in and out of the port, and people crossing the streets everywhere. It was a common route to Abuela Balbina's house in a neighborhood adjacent to the port.

As I stood on one of the top decks of the ship with my camera, I found myself overwhelmed by the darkness and unable to take any photos. The sky at dawn was indeed dark, but so was the city in a way I can't explain. I let my mind wander back to a life before I left Cuba at the age of eight – I don't recall the view being so dark.

My memories were bright and clear, a stark contrast to what I was experiencing. The car rides through the old neighborhoods, the strolls on the Malecon, the music on the streets, and the chatter of people socializing with their families and neighbors were coming back to me vividly as we got closer and closer to the dock.

I could see in my mind the corner grocery store where I was always sent to get leche, arroz, or a last-minute grocery item needed for dinner in the days when food and basic necessities were available without having to stand in line for hours. I could also visualize the small, privately owned shops in La Habana Vieja, especially a store I loved to visit because they sold magic toys for children.

Suddenly, I noticed a smile across my face and wondered if what I was going to witness today would be somewhat similar or substantially different. Perhaps I should prepare myself to be disappointed. Did I really believe that it would be the same as it was back in the 1950s? Was I prepared if what I experienced today was the opposite of my memories?

The excitement of getting off the ship was overwhelming, and I did not allow much time to consider the "what-if" scenarios of potential disappointment or whether I would even be allowed to enter the country. In a couple of hours, I hoped to be out on the streets following the footsteps I took many years ago.

The ship was departing at 5:00 p.m. the same day we arrived, so our day had to be efficient with an early start if we wanted to visit all the key locations I planned. We met for breakfast at the buffet stations. It was a rather quick breakfast for all of us as my anxiety of getting out onto the streets of La Habana became contagious.

We quickly returned to our cabin to grab my camera and an envelope containing copies of street maps and specific addresses to find. Then we took a brisk walk to the ship's exit and down the gangway to the terminal where we were required to go through a passport/visa checkpoint.

The fear of not being allowed to enter the country hit me like a lightning strike and I began to panic. Between the four of us, I was the only person originally born in Cuba, and therefore I required a special visa to enter the country. A few minutes of delays at the checkpoint seemed like hours as the young guard, who was not much older than 18, took his time looking back and forth between my documents and my face several times. All clear! I was allowed to enter the country! My husband and friends who were waiting on the other side of the transom erupted in applause – They must have sensed my fear of being denied entrance. We were now out of the terminal and on the streets of La Habana.

It took us less than five minutes to find a cab. It wasn't just an ordinary cab you would see on the streets of any major city in the world, it was a 1959 Chevy Impala convertible. We negotiated an hourly fee with the driver, Ramon, who agreed to take us to the specific addresses I had listed, including some tourist sights. Ramon was wearing a ski jacket and knit cap because he said he felt a cold chill in the air. The temperature was in the low 70s that morning, and the skies were clear. We Floridians would consider the temperature perfect for t-shirts and shorts, not ski jackets and knit caps.

Once we got inside his car, we were convinced that at some point we would be asked to push the Impala, as Ramon struggled to get sufficient momentum to drive up just the slightest inclines. All four of us were terrified the car would break down and we would be stranded in the middle of La Habana. I was grateful that didn't happen and we were not asked to get out and push at any time during our tour. Meanwhile, Ramon did not waste any time whistling and blowing the horn at every female that walked by close enough to hear his very public admiration of them. It was embarrassing and made the four of us slump down in our seats so we were not seen or accused of being chauvinistic pigs by anyone. Our defense would have been to admit the four of us were gay. Finally, I felt we were nearing our first stop – My childhood home at Calle J.H. Goss #177.

Ramon was having unexpected difficulties finding the Santo Suarez neighborhood, let alone Calle J.H. Goss. He was not familiar with the name of the street even though he acknowledged he knew the location during our initial negotiations. It did not matter; we were in the car and I was not getting out to find another cab in the middle of a residential neighborhood in La Habana. After several stops to ask for directions, we were on our way. Can you visualize a 1959 Chevy Impala convertible with five men asking for directions in the middle of La Habana?

On our way to my childhood home, we could see the deterioration of homes. Some needed substantial repairs, some property lots were just piles of rubble from a collapsed house, and some were fairly well maintained. Each street was an eclectic view of the conditions in which the residents were accustomed to living. This was not my recollection of the neighborhood.

The look of the street pavement was not any better. There were potholes as far as the eye could see, remains of traffic lights that did not light up, and sidewalks that were not suitable for pedestrian traffic. Ramon took extra precaution to drive around the potholes. Some of the streets were so bad that they resembled dirt roads rather than actual paved streets. Any one of those potholes could have caused substantial damage to this 1959 Impala that was already on life support. The thought of getting stuck with a broken-down car and a driver that whistled at every female that passed by within 20 yards was terrifying! We were not going to let it happen.

I began to imagine getting stuck in an unknown neighborhood and trying to find transportation back to the port. What would we do standing in the middle of a street somewhere in La Habana, no Uber or Lyft, no GPS, no cellphone service, and no other cabs since this was a residential neighborhood and not a tourist area? All we could do was continue to sit back and try to enjoy the view, the sun, and the Cuban breezes.

I assumed the role of the navigator in the front passenger seat. Someone had to take the lead since Ramon was too busy admiring all the pretty girls on the streets. I asked him to continue onto Santo Suarez, figuring once we reached the neighborhood, we would find the main street. At that point, I felt my memory would click in and I could lead us to the house.

I remember the main street that crossed Calle J.H. Goss and knew that at the corner was a tall church, San Juan Bosco on Avenida de Santa Catalina, where Tia Vivina and Frank were married. We finally entered the neighborhood of Santo Suarez and headed north on Avenida de Santa Catalina where I could see the tall steeple of a church a few miles ahead. As soon as we got close to the front entrance, we confirmed it was San Juan Bosco Church, and directly in front of us was Calle J.H. Goss on the right.

By this time, my husband and friends had somewhat frightened looks on their faces sitting quietly in the back seat. They were quite impressed with my directional ability, memory, and control of Ramon. The challenge now was to find #177.

We drove down Calle J.H. Goss and everyone in the car was looking for house numbers. It was rare to see any house displaying their street number, so instead I was looking for a façade that matched what I pictured in my mind. I knew exactly the shape and style of the outside of my house and the surrounding homes. After a couple of short blocks, there it was. Not in great condition, but it was all there. It took me a couple of minutes to decide to exit the car and get closer to the outside of the house and the surrounding neighbors' homes. So much of my view was the same, so much was different.

We were posing for pictures and selfies outside on the sidewalk when Ramon asked me if we wanted to go inside. I thought he was kidding. Surprised he would even bother to ask me, I responded by saying, *"Sí, ¿Y cómo piensa hacernos entrar sin ir a la cárcel?"* (Yes, and how do you plan to get us inside without going to jail?) *"Fácil"* (easy), he shrugged. He approached the front gate, knocked, and after a few minutes, a middle-aged lady came out onto the front porch. Ramon explained to her who we were and that I lived in this house when I was a child. A huge smile came across her face. She introduced herself as Consuela, looked at me, opened the gated front entrance, and invited all of us inside, including Ramon. That was his *"fácil"* plan to get us inside. He simply knocked on the door and asked to be invited inside. Brilliant! Why didn't I think of that obvious strategy? Ramon looked at me with a huge Cuban smile. I think he felt a significant tip was earned.

CHAPTER 3

Church and Lunch
1959

Driving towards San Juan Bosco Church on our way to Calle J.H. Goss reminded me of an exceptional Sunday in 1959 several months after Castro took over.

We got out of bed, ate a quick breakfast, and dressed up in our Sunday best. All five of us got in the car for our weekly pilgrimage and drove to church as usual. During the ride, we acknowledged our usual warning from my mother to behave during mass or else we would all return home and skip lunch at Abuela Teresa's home. We arrived on time, as always, and sat in a pew close to the altar. Segundito always sat by the aisle, my father to his right, Jorge in the middle, my mother next, and I was last. It was obvious that the seating arrangement was strategic. The three boys were prevented from even looking at each other with either Segundo or Rosa in between. It was a time to pray, not to play or make fun of others. Making fun of others in church was a great pastime for us.

Just before Communion was served, a group of Castro's devout supporters disrupted the service and walked down the main aisle of the church to declare, in front of the priest and the congregation, that Catholicism was no longer welcomed in Cuba. I am certain you would not have been surprised by the Cuban Catholic tempers that erupted from the pews.

Arguments flared up in the middle of the service and fist fights broke out in front of the altar between the Castro supporters and various parishioners. Women began to get involved in these fights also. Lots of hair was pulled, faces slapped, veils ripped off ladies' heads, and clothes torn. The men were more conservative; they just threw punches at each other (most of the time missing a hit) creating a scene like a Saturday night boxing match on television. The women were the most vulgar during the fight – *"Tu eres una gran puta. ¿Cómo puedes entrar en la casa de Dios?"* (You are a big whore. How could you enter the house of God?) hollered a lady sitting across from us as she held her Bible and rosary beads with her left hand and slapped a lady demonstrator on the face with her right hand.

The priest in the middle of the altar attempted to calm down the group with a message that only a few could hear, *"Esta es la casa de Dios. Deben respetar su hogar."* (This is the house of God. You should respect his home.) My terrified parents ushered the three of us out of the church via a side door, Jorge being carried by my mother because he was too young to run, my older brother and me holding my father's hands on either side.

Not unlike many other kids, I was always bored during religious services, so this was the most excitement I had ever witnessed in church. Front row seats at the Saturday night fights, but on Sunday morning in church. What could be better for a boy my age?

Visibly shaken, my parents tried to relax and not show fear in front of us as we all raced to the car – Typical Cuban parents, *"Todo está bien, hijos. No se preocupen ... "* (All is good my sons. Do not

Church and Lunch - 1959

worry ...) We were told to keep the windows up, lock the doors, and put up with the heat from the Cuban sun for a few minutes until we were clearly out of harm's way.

The ignition started, and as we were backing up from our parking space to drive away, the fist fights moved outside and all around our car. I continued to see women getting involved and physically fighting with other women and men who were supporters of Castro, even beating each other over the head with their handbags. The word *"puta"* (whore) was now used equally by the demonstrators and parishioners. Everyone was a *"puta."* I continued to see a lot of hair pulling and veils used as weapons by some angry women, many of them now wearing torn clothing and nylons with runs. It looked like a scene from a comedic movie. Hollywood could not have staged this scene better. My parents did not think it was funny at all. I thought it was hysterical. My father managed to drive around the chaos and head for Abuela Teresa's home earlier than expected.

Well, that was certainly the most excitement I experienced in church, and it was the last time we were able to attend due to my parents' fear of continued harassment and violence. That was fine with me; most of the time I was terribly bored in church.

****

Castro saw the Catholic Church as an enemy. He was angered by the Church's support of a free and democratic Cuba and its denunciation of communism. In addition to nationalizing many foreign- and domestic-owned companies, he nationalized all the Catholic schools, revised their curriculum, and restricted any Church publications. Demonstrations during Sunday services were common for several years, and eventually services were eliminated due to security issues. In 1961, Castro expelled more than 130 priests who were rounded up in one night and shipped to Spain on a freighter. The Vatican responded by ex-communicating Castro, who was originally raised and baptized Catholic. He did not care

Church and Lunch - 1959

about being ex-communicated. His strategy to remain the country's dictator was to eliminate anyone who opposed his policies. That's how dictators retain their majority support.

****

We arrived at Abuela Teresa's home earlier than usual on that Sunday, and I could sense a strong feeling of discomfort from my parents as they explained to my grandmother what just happened in church. Yes, they tried to tell her the story in Cuban Code so we would not understand and be upset. I had already graduated from "Cuban Code College" by the time I was 6, so they should have just let me be part of the conversation instead of trying to ignore me.

Later that afternoon, as was the case on previous Sundays, the aunts, uncles, cousins, boyfriends, and girlfriends came to see Abuela Teresa and to eat her cooking (which her sister made but she took credit as always).

Once again, just a couple of hours after the church fights, the talk of politics at Abuela Teresa's home flared up some angry emotions between Tio Yayo and Frank who was Tia Vivina's soon-to-be husband and a strong supporter of Fidel Castro. Tio Yayo, my mother's younger brother, was a young, handsome, opinioned Cuban playboy with very thick eyebrows and a thick mustache the shape of an upside-down "U" surrounding his mouth from which a lit Cuban cigar was always bouncing up and down. It would stink up the entire room, not to mention our Sunday clothing.

Frank was a slightly overweight, quiet, conservative, non-smoking Cuban of German descent who always had a very short, tight, German-looking crew cut hairstyle and wore terribly boring and unmatched tight-fitting clothing. Tia Vivina was in her early 20s, young with a look of angelic purity and innocence, and used too much talcum powder (just like her mother, Abuela Teresa) all over her body. She could pass for a Catholic nun if she had a white cardboard headdress, matching full-length black and white dress, funky black shoes, and a paddle for anyone who misbehaved.

Church and Lunch - 1959

On this Sunday, Yayo and Frank's argument was much more heated than those of previous Sundays. They were screaming at each other with only one inch of airspace between their faces. At one point, the screaming was loud enough that you could probably hear them very clearly down the street. Tio Yayo would say to Frank, *"Eres una vergüenza para el pueblo Cubano y una gran decepción para nuestra familia."* ("You are a disgrace to the Cuban people and a huge disappointment to our family.") Frank would respond, *"No me importa lo que pienses, tú eres una desgracia para tu país."* (I don't care what you think, you are a disgrace to your country.) This continued, and nobody could separate them. Before I realized what was happening, all five of us exited out the side door of Abuela Teresa's kitchen while Frank and Tio Yayo continued with their verbal accusations. We got back in the car for a quiet ride home, except for some Cuban Code coming out of my parents' mouths.

The church fist fights and Abuela Teresa's family revolution on the same day. I could not wait to tell my friends about my Sunday experiences! But as if she were reading my mind, the way most mothers do, I was threatened with early bedtime for an entire month if I ever disclosed any of my day's experiences to anyone else, ever! I thought it was an exciting day and something interesting to share with friends, but I played it safe and kept my thoughts to myself. Do other families have political fights like ours? Will future Sundays be the same? What should I expect?

Over time, emotions settled down between Frank and the family. Still, nobody liked Frank. But because Tia Vivina was in love with him, the family was gracious to tolerate his presence if he did not talk about his political views. Notice I said "tolerate" and not "accept." Tia Vivina did marry Frank and I was the ring bearer for the ceremony held near our home at San Juan Bosco. The reception was held at Jose Arechabala's headquarters. It was a beautiful and elegant evening. My first time in a full-tails tuxedo – I got a lot of attention and felt important among family and friends.

****

Church and Lunch - 1959

Many in my family (Tio Frank not included) were convinced that Fidel Castro's revolution and policies would be a short-term diversion of Cuban politics and democracy. History confirms that Frank was correct in his vision of the political future of Cuba. Unfortunately, Frank did not consider the economic effect of how Castro's policies would tie a noose around the necks of the Cuban people. In the late 1950s and early 1960s, many Cubans sensed a serious problem in the country and decided to begin considering emigrating to The United States or other countries that would take them.

My parents were brave. They became part of that group and started evaluating several options of how and when to leave Cuba. That meant leaving behind for the government's coffers all our possessions, including cars, cash, bank accounts, jewelry, clothing, our home, and all its contents. But those are only material things. What I think hurt the most was the thought of leaving many family members behind who wanted to gamble. Many felt that this was only going to be a temporary hiccup in their lives. Sadly, history proved them wrong.

Church and Lunch - 1959

CHAPTER 4

Calle J.H. Goss
2018

Imagine how I felt when Consuela invited us inside our old home at Calle J.H. Goss. I was shocked and visibly nervous as I walked in through the front door. It was hard to believe that Ramon, with his charm, convinced Consuela, a total stranger, to allow us inside of her house. My heart began to beat faster than a jackhammer on concrete.

As I walked through the front door, my initial reaction was that all the rooms seemed smaller. Yes, I am bigger now, perhaps that was why every room looked half the size. I gave Arthur, Stephen, Allen, and Ramon a tour of the interior and courtyard. I could still see every room in my mind, the living room where we always decorated our Christmas tree in December, the dining room where we all sat down for dinner together and celebrated birthdays, the courtyard where we played, the bedroom where all three of us slept, the tiles in the bathroom, and the hallway where I learned to walk. I also showed them old family pictures I had scanned and loaded on my iPhone. Pictures of birthday parties, family on the front porch, and Christmas morning with all the toys under the tree.

Even after spending a few minutes inside, it was still difficult to believe I was there and inside my house. I was having an "out of body" experience and had to pinch myself to make sure it was not a dream. Ramon was very proud of himself and kept a big smile on his face during the house tour. Still confident he was going to get a big tip when he dropped us off at the end of the tour.

It's very easy to recall your childhood memories when you visit the home you were raised in during your early years. Being there brought back many more memories I had forgotten. Walking from room to room and describing the rooms as I remembered them to my husband, friends, Ramon, and Consuela was an emotional experience I still find difficult to share. I guess you could say it was a "feel-good" moment as I explained to them the layout of our bedroom – bunk beds in the corner of the room, a smaller bed for Jorge, a dresser, and a wardrobe for all our clothes. The furniture was custom-made to fit in the room. The window in our bedroom was opened all the time to allow for cross-ventilation of those Cuban breezes from the courtyard to the hallway to the bedroom.

Now I looked in that same bedroom and saw an unpleasant room in desperate need of multiple coats of plaster and paint. It was dark with a musty, mildew odor, windows closed, and half-full of boxes. The furniture needed repair and a major dusting. There was a small desk with a chair missing its back and one armrest, and a dirty blanket on the dusty floor for a dog that was fenced inside the room. This used to be our bedroom.

Walking around the house, I shared with them my memories of birthday parties around the dining room with family, neighborhood friends, and plenty of gifts. It was fun back in those days to be the center of attention at my age. Every birthday I was dressed in a new outfit and my hair was perfectly combed as my parents insisted that

I stand with them to greet everyone at the front door. There was nothing worse for a child than the slobbering of lipstick on your forehead, cheeks, ears, and everywhere on your head from all the adult ladies attending your party. I am sure they came just to be social and chat with the other adults. I still feel that my birthday was their secondary purpose for being there.

After the usual kissing scene between me and my female adult relatives and a few minutes with my mother in the bathroom cleaning up my face from all that shocking red Cuban lipstick, I was usually ignored by all the adults and sent to the courtyard to play with cousins and friends my age. This gave them a chance to socialize and mingle with the others, using Cuban Code to chat about politics or subjects they claimed were not suitable for children. They did not really care about my birthday or my birthday cake, but they all ran into the dining room to sing *"Feliz Cumpleaño"* (Happy Birthday) and pose like overacting movie stars for pictures as I blew out the candles on the cake.

Today, I looked at that dining room and the large table we had was gone, replaced by a small folding table and three mismatched chairs that I would have considered unsafe for human (or animal) use. A small bedroom dresser in the corner replaced our dining room buffet cabinet with a large mirror hanging on the wall. The plaster on the wall showed signs of mold. There were orange stains from roof leaks in one corner and missing plaster in the other corner and on the ceiling. The walls had not been painted for many years. No draperies on the windows.

I got the feeling that this room and perhaps all the rooms in the house hadn't been painted since I left. I'm not suggesting that Consuela and her husband are to blame for the lack of basic repairs, maintenance, and the overall poor condition of my house. Basic materials and resources to maintain any house in Cuba are often not available or difficult to afford. Given the choice between putting food on the table or attempting to find and afford materials to maintain the house, who could blame them when their priority was obviously to make sure their family was fed.

Calle J.H. Goss - 2018

As I walked from my parents' bedroom to our bedroom, I passed the only bathroom inside the house that had been completely covered in those famous baby blue tiles of the 1950s. The matching baby blue toilet, baby blue vanity, and baby blue bathtub and shower we had back in those days gave the bathroom that classic 1950s Cuban retro look. All those same fixtures and tiles were still there today, some of them cracked, stained, and discolored. The lack of consistent running water in Cuba today was difficult to imagine. City water was only turned on twice a week, so the cistern on the roof needed to be filled immediately during the short time water was available. The original plumbing for the bathtub and shower (which used to be behind the tiles and inside the walls) was replaced by new plumbing positioned over the tiles. The original shower and tub plumbing fixtures were still there, but now their function was to hang wet towels. The ceiling was missing chunks of plaster. And just above the bathroom window was a huge mold stain from rain seeping inside.

Consuela was impressed I remembered so much and asked me many questions about the house. I knew from the look on her face and her questions, she appreciated the short history lesson I lectured while walking into each room. A part of me did not want to leave so quickly, the other part was ready to say goodbye, one last time. I wasn't sure if I should be upset at the conditions of the house or happy that I didn't live there anymore. The somber look of the interior due to the lack of basic maintenance and obvious plumbing and structural issues was somewhat distressing to witness. I could see that Consuela and her husband, who was not at home at the time, were trying hard with the resources they had available to them. Once a maintenance issue gets out of hand, it is difficult to catch up when you have limited resources.

Parting ways was melancholy, even though we just met for the first time less than an hour earlier. Consuela hugged me and thanked me for the history of the house. We were all so grateful and honored that she invited us, complete strangers, inside her home. I wanted to give her a small monetary gift for her generous hospitality and the invitation to tour the inside, but she adamantly refused to accept it. I was determined for her to have it, so after she went inside and closed her door, I slipped several bills under the front door before we drove away.

Once again, Ramon was in the driver's seat whistling at the women walking down the street. I was in the front seat next to Ramon looking at the house, remembering an early morning ride to the airport in the back seat of my father's 1954 Buick. Segundito and I were scheduled to fly to Miami by ourselves. Looking out through the window that morning, I never believed I would ever see our house again. Here I was today, in 2018, looking at the same view I experienced so many years ago.

We toured the neighboring streets and the neighborhood playground, which was empty of people but filled with what seemed to be the remains of the original swings and other playground fixtures. It looked like a dumping ground for a construction site or a movie set with the remains of a World War II battle. Not surprisingly, there were no children playing. Our next stop was my school campus, which was originally a private school named Valmaña. Back in the early 1960s, the school was taken over by the Cuban government and turned into a government-run school with a specific government-created curriculum. The property included several 1940s-style buildings surrounded by a beautiful old Spanish baroque colonial building that had recently partially collapsed.

Our old schoolyard and outbuildings were the same, except for that distressed look of deterioration and some hopelessness on the faces of the children outside in the schoolyard. The kids were not dressed in uniforms as we were required to wear when we attended. Today, their school clothing looked worn and dirty. After spending a couple of minutes watching the kids playing, I looked around inside the car and noticed some anguish on everyone's faces, including Ramon's. Watching these kids play turned into a quiet moment for us as we drove away to our next sight to visit. I am sure the four of us were all processing what we had just seen

Calle J.H. Goss - 2018

and grateful for what we have today. I wondered what was going through Ramon's mind. Did he feel the same way we did?

****

"What does all this mean to me?" I asked myself as my mind wandered after that quick drive by my old schoolyard. Did my early life experiences as a child in Cuba shape my life as an adult in The United States? What did I learn as a child, besides the Cuban Code used by most Cuban parents in front of their children? What did my parents teach me that has stayed with me and will remain with me for the rest of my life? Perhaps if my parents decided to stay in Cuba, those kids playing there could have been my kids or my grandchildren. Would I have been satisfied with my life today if I had remained in Cuba? I have learned that the decisions we make, or others make for us, early in our lives could have dramatic long-term effects on our future, our personality, and our reactions.

Our parents play the role of architects, designers, and contractors of our lives, personality, and temperament. We look up to them in early childhood when their hands are under our armpits as we try to navigate and learn to walk down the main hallway in our homes. We place our trust in them that they will not let us fall. As we grow, we see the look on their faces when they see us cry. We feel their bodies holding ours tightly when we are hurt. When we are adults, we see the joy in their hearts when we are happy and when we make them proud. Their decisions, what they do, what they say, and how they react in front of us leave a permanent engraving on our lives. We learn from their actions. We are young and impressionable, and as we grow up, we look to them and their past actions for answers. Their responses are tattooed on our spirit.

****

We were now leaving behind the Santo Suarez neighborhood as I was realizing that much of what my parents taught me back

Calle J.H. Goss - 2018

in the 1950s helped me survive many of the difficult moments of my adult years. So much history for me continued to flash through my mind while riding around the streets of La Habana. It was impossible to concentrate on any one memory. I had many questions to ask myself – Some had obvious answers, some did not. I saw what was in view from the front seat of the 1959 Impala: a neighborhood left behind. Not just left behind by me, but also left behind by the passage of time.

As we began to drive away from Santo Suarez, my memories of leaving the country alone with Segundito continued to radiate through my mind. Now, I was re-living that time in a short, several-hours visit many years later. I couldn't get out of my head the memory of looking at our home from the back seat of my father's 1954 Buick as we rode to the airport on that early morning in 1962. Today, I saw another vision of the same house. This time from the front seat of a 1959 Impala. Lots of changes in my life, much of the same here in my neighborhood.

I have no regrets. I did not cry when my father pulled away from our driveway back on that early morning of February 17, 1962 and I did not cry on December 20, 2018, when Ramon turned the ignition on and drove down Calle J.H. Goss and on to our next stop.

Calle J.H. Goss - 2018

CHAPTER 5

Keep to Yourself
1959

"No abras la boca. No le digas una palabra a nadie." (Don't open your mouth. Don't say a word to anyone.) Those directions were constantly repeated to us whenever we walked out the front door. After a while, I became terrified to engage in conversations with anyone. Could I say something to someone that would jeopardize my family? I did not want to be responsible for saying something that would send my parents to jail.

Shortly after that famous New Year's Eve of 1958 when Batista fled and Castro then took control as dictator of the island the following week, it was apparent that everyone was trying too hard to act normal and not draw any notice. Everyone avoided being singled out in public. It became critically important to keep your political opinions to yourself and refrain from engaging in political conversations with anyone you did not know or trust. Participating in talks that could lead into a political discussion and be interpreted as critical of the Castro regime was an extremely dangerous dialog. Everyone seemed to be afraid of political retribution backed by stories and rumors being spread around of people missing or hurt because of their anti-Castro open opinions or actions.

There were still a lot of discussions between trusted family and friends focused on someone somebody knew who spoke out against the government in front of their neighbors or friends and later went missing, disappeared into the thin air. Perhaps those were just rumors, or maybe true stories. Nobody could confirm or really wanted to confirm. The radio and television media were now controlled by the government, so any news issued that could be perceived as anti-Castro news was never released. Castro also controlled the print media, anything printed in newspapers or magazines was always favorable to him and his regime. There was no "fake news," only Castro's version of the news. It was better to play it safe and not cause any unnecessary controversies. *"No te metas en eso, mantén la boca cerrada y ocúpate de tus propios asuntos."* (Don't get involved, keep your mouth shut, and mind your own business.) That seemed to be a common phrase of advice for many Cubans during that time.

Those social moments my parents had with neighbors in the late afternoon and early evening on the front porch ceased. Although we still had some minimal "play time" allowed after school with neighborhood kids, the adults did not congregate while the kids played, as they did in the past, unless they were truly trusted friends. If parents of playmates that were not well known happened to meet on the sidewalk, it was always cordial, non-threatening, non-political, and extremely limited. After a short time on the sidewalk or playground, we were told to go inside the house where my mother would close the front door and the window facing the street so any conversations inside the house could not be heard out on the street. It was easy enough for anyone walking up and down our sidewalk to hear discussions going on inside the

Keep to Yourself - 1959

house in our living room while the front window and main door was open. Most homes would keep them open to ventilate and cool down the interiors during the late afternoons because, in those days, air conditioning was not common in residential homes.

What used to be a very social time for my family, whether it was in the playground, on the sidewalk, or at the front porch, became shortened and quickly turned into quiet time inside the house. If there was a knock on the door, nobody except my parents was allowed to open it. And unless it was someone we knew and trusted, they were usually not invited inside. My parents warned us not to invite friends over to the house unless it was previously approved by my them. The fear of any casual comments overheard by one of my friends and repeated when they got home would terrify them.

I can still hear my parents giving us lessons on what to say if by any chance we were confronted by anyone – whether it was a family member, neighbor, or stranger – asking if my family supported Castro or U.S. policies (which, by the way, did happen to me several times). We were taught to say, *"No, no somos politicos,"* (No, we are non-political,) nothing more, nothing less. This was a tactic used by many Castro loyalists to get information from young children to determine if a certain household was pro or against the regime. Adults would know how to respond to avoid any confrontation, but perhaps their young children would talk more about the politics of their home or what their parents were discussing amongst themselves.

We were careful enough to even question the trust level of our neighbors and, in some cases, family members. Now that Frank became Tio Frank after marrying Tia Vivina, he continued with his loyal support of the Castro movement, and my parents were extremely cautious of their conversations with him and even with Tia Vivina. Those family and friends who we could trust shared our concerns about the new Castro government and would huddle in quiet areas to share the latest news and compare options available, including emigration to another country. Our small group of trusted friends and relatives took good care of each other. It was a strategy that helped many Cubans survive. Relationships with some neighbors became cold with short comments when we crossed each other on the streets. *"Hola, buenos días."* (Hello, good morning.) *"Buenas tardes, señora."* (Good afternoon, Madam.) *"No hay mucho calor hoy."* (It isn't very hot today.) That was about the extent of our contacts. Short comments and no open-ended questions that would require a lengthy response. It was a tactic used by many to avoid long conversation or eliminate opportunities for responses that could implicate you.

Nobody was comfortable trusting just anyone with their political opinions. It was also common knowledge that many Castro loyalists were encouraged and, in some cases, required to report at least one anti-Castro supporter they knew, whether it was a family member, a neighbor, or a friend. The Castro regime wanted to know who was with them and who was against them. It was important for them to have a list of non-supporters. They rewarded these snitches with food and basic supplies that were usually difficult to obtain for identifying and reporting those who were not loyal to the regime. Obviously, Tio Frank was a serious concern to our family. Would he have the *"cojones"* (balls) to report us? Perhaps. Loyalty to Castro was Tio Frank's priority.

Some family and close friends would never comment about their opinions with my parents or anyone, but we always respected that choice and kept our distance. One morning, we woke up to find that a close friend of the family who kept his opinions to himself had left the country unannounced. He was gone overnight without a trace, leaving everything behind for the government to confiscate. My parents felt betrayed by their overnight exit but at the same time knew their friends had to keep their plans quiet to avoid any problems with their exodus.

I remember many afternoons playing with my friend Alberto on the sidewalk. He lived about a half a block away from us on the same side of the street and we usually met after school to play. One afternoon, I went to knock on his door because he was not in

Keep to Yourself - 1959

school that day. There was no answer. The entire family was gone in the middle of the night. I could not understand how that was possible. My parents assumed the entire family had the opportunity to leave the country together and took immediate advantage. Taking the time to say goodbye to family, friends, and neighbors could have jeopardized their exit. Surprising to me, that same experience occurred several times with other friends. Slowly, I was losing my social time after school.

Before departing for school, my mother would warn us to never comment in school about any political conversations we may have heard at home or anywhere. She feared that even a conversation between two first-grade students could get back to people who were loyal to the Castro regime and could perhaps cause harm to the family. It was difficult for anyone to trust their own close friends and neighbors. Everyone was cautious, discreet, and vigilant.

What made matters worse was the government establishing a neighborhood surveillance program by recruiting one homeowner in the neighborhood to observe the traffic patterns of their neighbors. They were called *Los Comités de Defensa de la Revolución (CDR)* (The Committees for the Defense of the Revolution), founded on September 28, 1960, with the primary purpose of performing routine vigilance against political interference and destabilization of the Castro government. Our neighborhood *Comité* was established across the street from us and two houses to the left. Mayra, an elderly woman with mousey white hair who never smiled and sat on her porch most of the day wearing the same housecoat while holding a pair of binoculars, was the only person living in that house now identified as *"El Comité."* My parents always warned us to never walk on the sidewalk in front of her porch and to use caution when crossing the street as we reached her house. We used to call her *"la bruja"* (the witch) because she did not like children and was always critical of kids playing on the sidewalk near her home.

Keep to Yourself - 1959

It was just like a cat and mouse game in our neighborhood between the Castro supporters and those who did not want to express any political views, which really meant they did not support Castro or his government. Initially, many families and friends that we trusted had a "wait and see" attitude and felt that the horrors of the Castro regime could not last long and, therefore, seeking asylum in another country would be economically disastrous for their family. My parents took the wait and see approach at first, but it was quickly changing into an "act now before it's too late" attitude. Unfortunately for many, when they decided they wanted to leave the country, it was too late.

After Fidel Castro took over from Batista, many dissident groups who were trying to remove Castro were responsible for several terrorist attacks, assassination attempts, and failed political coups. Military activity, gunfire, explosions, and the roar of military vehicles with heavily armed personnel became the norm everywhere in La Habana. A childhood friend of mine, Manuel, who lived across the street from us next to *"la bruja,"* was on his way to the grocery store when suddenly, army personnel raided a house that was on his route to the store and bullets began to spray between the house and the soldiers surrounding the house. Manuel was hit with a stray bullet in his left arm. A few days later, he was home from the hospital with a cast covering his entire left arm. Manuel was fortunate to be alive. It was no longer safe for parents to leave their kids on the streets without supervision. It was no longer a city where you could raise a family without fear. La Havana and perhaps most of Cuba turned into a war zone.

Keep to Yourself - 1959

CHAPTER 6

Touring La Habana 2018

We were riding in Ramon's Impala, exiting the deterioration of the Santo Suarez neighborhood, and struggling to get enough power for the vehicle to move when the lights turned green. With lots of dark smoke coming out of the exhaust pipe, we followed Avenida de Santa Catalina and turned right onto Avenida de la Independencia, where several stark monuments and government buildings were located. This was Ramon's suggestion as one of the tourist locations he liked to show his clients. At this point, after thinking about what my parents experienced because of a regime that took away basic human rights, their life savings, their home, and their possessions, I did not care to see any of the buildings or monuments praising a government responsible for the sufferings of many Cubans. I was more interested in interacting with the people.

The convertible provided us with a great view of the streets and the residents of La Habana, which was enough for me. Unfortunately, the warm Cuban sun was beginning to be a distraction, and my travel-mates wanted to see the monuments and government buildings. I was a good team player. I kept my mouth shut and played the tourist role for a while since the others in the car seemed to be enjoying the tour.

Up ahead was La Fuente Luminosa, a large fountain in need of repairs at the center of a major rotary. Built in the mid-1940s, the fountain was jokingly called "Paulina's Bidet" after the sister-in-law of then President Ramon Grau San Martin. President San Martin was a single man and his largely overweight sister-in-law Paulina Alsina had great influence over the President and Congress. She served as First Lady and managed the fountain's construction. I think Cubans have a way of expressing their unhappiness with the government in a comedic way. Many of my parents' friends referred to it as "Fidel's Bidet."

Immediately on the right was the Coliseo de la Ciudad Deportiva, Cuba's main colosseum for indoor sporting events, built in 1957 with a capacity of 15,000 spectators. I can still recall attending soccer games there with Tio Orlando, my father's youngest brother. Orlando and his wife Asuncion lived in a modest home with two daughters, Asuncion (who was one year older than Segundito) and Milagros (who was one year younger than Jorge). Orlando was an avid soccer fan and loved to take us all to soccer games whenever possible. There was one specific game when Orlando had access to the field after the game was over and photographed us on the field. It was an awesome experience back in those days for us to witness the size of the colosseum from the center of the field.

Adjacent to this colosseum, which also needed basic maintenance and repairs, were numerous baseball fields with bleachers and other sports-related structures. Not surprising, they were empty, a bit shabby, and worn.

Continuing on Avenida de la Independencia, we began to see hotels and government buildings built after the revolution, with architecture similar to what you would see in the old Soviet bloc countries: plain, simple, stark, basic, and – most of all – cheap and ugly. I suppose the best description to use would be "architecture lacking creativity". I like "cheap and ugly" better. Up ahead there was a fork in the road, and to the left was the Palacio de la Revolución that served as the House of the Cuban government. Next was the famous and impressive José Martí Memorial monument, completed during the end of the Batista regime in 1958. I could remember looking out from the back seat of my father's 1954 Buick, riding by this area in the early 1960s, and finding the street lined with military equipment including tanks protecting the Palacio de la Revolución from potential political threats and coups. Looking back on those days, I remember experiencing a feeling of apprehension in the air as we passed this unnecessary, enormous, and egotistical display of military strength.

We continued through the streets of La Habana, encountering several tree-lined boulevards with beautiful historic old Spanish-style buildings in desperate need of major restoration. I should emphasize "desperate need of major restoration" because many of these buildings needed more than just a good cleaning, brushing up, and some fresh paint. Most of these classical old Spanish architectural structures were simply collapsing on themselves and abandoned. The area reminded me of the decaying Roman Forum as it is today. I was frightened by the site of pedestrians walking by these buildings that could easily collapse on them if the winds shifted and became stronger. This old Spanish colonial, baroque and neoclassical styles of architecture arrived in Cuba in the mid-1700s to mid-1800s from Spain. Because of the rapid growth of the island's sugar industry, the wealthy residents and sugar merchants invested in construction of very grand urban buildings in and around the La Habana Vieja neighborhood.

Avenida Paseo used to be one of the classiest streets in La Habana, with large trees, wide promenades, and luxurious mansions on both sides. Today, it had no resemblance to what was there in the 1950s. Avenida de Los Presidentes, another great boulevard in La Habana, also had no resemblance to its earlier life. Now, it was home to distressed structures with an architectural identity that, in its day, would define La Habana. Buildings and boulevards that created a unique style to this city were now in need of serious preservation and restoration. Some may have simply been too far gone to be restored and saved. But they still stood there, sometimes serving as unofficial shelters for the homeless. A dangerous place to call home.

We drove by the major hotels, which used to be home to elegant casinos frequented by worldwide sophisticated and wealthy tourists prior to the Castro regime. Now, we moved through the Malecon, where we spent many hours as a family strolling by the stone-built embankment and esplanade facing the Caribbean. There, I saw the same view I remember back in the 1950s, people enjoying the Cuban breezes, walking hand in hand, sitting on the wall, and standing with friends sharing the news of the day. I also saw groups of tourists and residents taking pictures of each other. Further along, there were groups of people of all ages fishing under those clear Cuban skies and warm sun as we did back in those days. It was great to see the crashing of the waves on the stone wall. Finally, a view that was not much different than what I remembered.

We turned right onto Paseo del Prado (or as most Cubans call it, "El Prado") where many hotels, stores, and a canopy of trees lined the boulevard. Much of the tree canopy was missing today. Ramon acknowledged the sad condition of the boulevard and blamed the many hurricanes Cuba had experienced in the past 10 years. Again, we saw many beautiful buildings decorated in old Spanish architecture simply imploding on their own. There was little, if any, sign of construction or restoration work to save these historic structures.

A bit ahead was the famous "El Capitolio," which we could see as we sailed into the harbor earlier this morning. Built in 1929, it used to house the Congress prior to the Cuban Revolution in 1959, which abolished and disbanded all its members and reorganized with new members made up of Castro loyalists. Later, in the mid-

1960s, Congress was moved to the Palacio de la Revolución. El Capitolio had fallen into disrepair, but you can see some external restoration work currently being done. The design of this building was always compared to the United States Capital, but slightly higher, wider, and longer. It was a beautiful structure we could see from almost anywhere in La Habana because of its height at the entrance to the La Habana Vieja neighborhood.

****

As we got close to our agreed-upon end time with Ramon and his 1959 Impala, he seemed to be getting tired, so I asked him to drop us off at the Catedral de San Cristobal de La Habana. I'm sure by this time, he realized the four of us were not impressed by his public chauvinistic admiration of women. It is a different world on the streets of La Habana, and Ramon's behavior seemed to be an acceptable form of complimenting women. His demeanor towards women would get him arrested in the U.S. and charged with sexual harassment.

Once we reached the drop-off point, we could walk the streets of La Habana Vieja, visit Abuela Balbina's home, and stay close to our ship since we had to be back onboard by 4:00 p.m. Ramon parked his car around the corner from the main entrance of the church, we said our goodbyes, paid our fee, added a generous tip, and posed with him for a bunch of selfies in front of his treasured Impala. Ramon was an authentic Cuban personality right out of central casting. He was animated throughout the entire tour, and after we left him behind, we all agreed that he was the perfect driver and entertainer for us. I was grateful for him to knock on that door and get Consuela to invite us inside my old home. That alone deserved the generous tip he got from all of us. After Ramon drove away, I think he felt that he already did a day's work with the money we gave him and went home for his afternoon cerveza and siesta.

Now it was time to walk through a neighborhood I visited often, not just because Abuela Balbina, Tia Nena, and Esperansa lived there. I loved the narrow streets and sidewalks, the architecture, and the old Spanish balconies. I also loved the atmosphere the people gave the neighborhood. Everyone acted as if they knew each other. It was my second home in La Habana. Sadly, there were other moments when military vehicles surrounded specific homes and dragged people out into a truck to be taken away with other political prisoners. What would I find during my visit this time?

CHAPTER 7

La Habana Vieja
2018

Walking from our drop-off point, we turned the corner onto Calle Empedrado to approach La Plaza de la Catedral. The memories of the views I was seeing flashed through my mind when we arrived at this expansive public square. No military vehicles this time. All I could see now were tourists and local residents walking through the plaza, minding their own business. I didn't see people expecting to hide from potential gunfire. I could only see the military activity in my mind. That was in the past.

We approached the center and pivoted 360 degrees to see all the buildings facing the plaza. The Catedral de San Cristobal was the most impressive. Completed in 1777, Christopher Columbus' remains were kept there between 1796 and 1898 when they were taken to the Seville Cathedral in Spain. At the opposite end was the old corporate headquarters for Jose Arechabala where my father worked. I stood many times on that second-floor balcony on the right side of the main door looking out onto the plaza and the church. We walked inside the church and became speechless when we observed the preserved interior details. This was one of several churches my family would visit on Sunday mornings when fist fights in front of the altar were not the norm. To stand there now and see the interior of this magnificent structure was nothing less than an overwhelming experience. The expression on the faces of the other tourists next to us were the same as ours.

After leaving a small donation in a tin box by the front entrance of La Catedral, we headed outside and looked directly around the plaza again and to see that it was now surrounded by small restaurants, cafes, tourist shops, and art galleries featuring Cuban art. The sounds of musicians playing Cuban music seemed to be coming from every direction. Each restaurant and café had musicians and singers performing traditional Cuban music. As we got closer, we realized that the corporate offices of Jose Arechabala had been turned into a museum of colonial art open to the public, so we paid our entrance fee and slowly walked directly to the center courtyard. Unfortunately, that center fountain with tropical fish I used to enjoy feeding was removed at some point after I left Cuba and replaced by a contemporary sculpture. All the rooms were restored back to their original layout, so I could not recognize my father's office. Back in the 1950s, many of the larger rooms were partitioned to create working office environments. The restoration work done on this building was an improvement to the 1950s chopped-up office environment I remembered. I wished that many of the other structures we witnessed earlier today received the same restoration attention as this building enjoyed.

We walked from room to room and got to see the large reception hall on the second floor facing the plaza where Tia Vivina and Tio Frank had their wedding reception. There was also the large tasting room with a beautiful oak bar and walls covered in paneling. I could feel those Cuban breezes flow from the opened front windows to the center courtyard, just as they did back in the 1950s and early 1960s. The lush tropical plants in the courtyard were no longer there and were replaced by smaller plants which needed some tender loving care, including just plain water.

I started a conversation with one of the docents on the second floor facing the courtyard and told her how I used to visit this building in the 1950s when my father worked for Jose Arechabala. Her eyes opened and wanted to know more about my visits and my experiences there when I was a child. She asked me if I was carrying any photos taken during that time because their records were all destroyed, and they were trying to build an archive of photos and stories about the building and its previous occupants. She also wished we had been there the week prior, because she had met a man whose father also worked for Jose Arechabala and perhaps a connection could have been created that day.

I lingered around the perimeter of the courtyard on the second floor, absorbing the fresh air and the views. I remembered my times here, running up and down the stairs and around the balcony. Meanwhile, Arthur, Stephen, and Allen were patiently waiting for me at the front door and did not rush me as I took in everything around me and reconnected with this building. I am not sure if my father were still alive that he would be able to walk with me and follow my footsteps today. Perhaps his spirit was right behind me, guiding me around to the different rooms. Somehow, I felt him with me today. I could hear my mother yelling at me and telling me to stop running around the balcony.

My father spent 26 years of his life working here – his first and only job until he left Cuba. He began working at Jose Arechabala as an office boy during high school and later became the office manager. When Castro took over and nationalized the company, he remained for some time. Later, he was dismissed because the Cuban regime knew he was not a supporter. They knew my parents were planning to leave the country, so they concluded he was not one of them and therefore had to be dismissed to make room for

La Habana Vieja - 2018

someone who was supportive of their policies. He received no severance and had no options for future income support.

I walked down the stairs and across the courtyard to meet my husband and friends who were patiently waiting for me by the main entrance. I apologized for keeping them waiting, but they acknowledged the importance for me to be there and to absorb as much as possible. I was speechless as we exited the massive main doors of the building. I turned around before stepping down on the sidewalk and, for one final time, I looked to the center courtyard and all I could see was the fountain that was there when I was a child. The contemporary sculpture that replaced it was simply not registering in my mind.

****

We exited the main door of the museum and walked to the corner to take a left onto Calle San Ignacio where many shops, restaurants, and cafes continued to flow out into the street to entice the tourists. My next priority was to find my grandmother's home on Calle Amargura #308. After that, we had the rest of the afternoon to ourselves until we were due back on the ship. I knew from the wrinkled and torn street map I was carrying that Calle Amargura was off Calle San Ignacio, so we continued our walk and enjoyed all the trinket shops, art galleries, architecture, and the people that surrounded us. After a few blocks, we found Calle Amargura. We looked to the left and could see the top half of our ship in the port, so we took a right turn hoping that Abuela's house was in the opposite direction.

Many of the beautiful buildings with old Spanish colonial architecture around us were in desperate need of repair and basic maintenance. Walking by them gave us a better look at the insides since everyone kept their windows and doors open to feel those fresh Cuban breezes. I could see that the interiors of some of the homes and businesses had collapsed. It was sad to notice that people were still living inside these partially collapsed buildings. Some

La Habana Vieja - 2018

empty lots had piles of rubble from a toppled structure. Several buildings had imploded, leaving the façade standing. I could see that an attempt was made to create some minor reinforcements so the façade would not collapse onto the street. I began to panic that a chunk of a partially collapsed building would come crashing on our heads, so we leisurely moved our path towards the middle of the street to try to avoid any debris falling from above. The old Spanish sidewalks were barely wide enough for two people side by side.

There was a strange sadness in the air because, on this street, I could visualize the beauty it had back before I left. In those days, people gathered at the cafes, chatting with neighbors and smoking Cuban cigars. Kids with school uniforms headed home, maneuvering against the one-way traffic because the streets were only wide enough for one car. Residents chatted with each other from one balcony to the next on the other side of the street. That was their normal life. Today, it had much of the same activity, but the poverty level had increased significantly and the unsafe conditions they lived in were alarming.

I was getting closer to Amargura #308 and suddenly I saw the street number on a wall. The bottom half of the building's façade was still somewhat standing on its own with minimal support brackets behind the front wall. I could see sections of the floor of the spacious long balcony still there. Anything above that point was missing. The entrance to the building was there, but inside was an empty dirt lot. In the rear, there appeared to be a small shed. A man came out when he saw me enter the property. After a brief introduction, I told him my grandmother used to live here. He smiled and told me he wished we were here three years ago when the building was still standing and occupied. It collapsed because he was not able to repair water leaks from the roof, which rotted the main support beams holding up the second floor. He remained there, living in the shed, once the government removed all the debris. Nothing else was salvaged but the street-level façade and the street number next to the front entrance. A disappointing experience, but I was happy to be standing in that very same spot I was in many years ago.

We walked inside the property and around the abutting townhomes for several minutes. We continued to stare at the remains of the building while having conversations with the neighbors who told me about the day the building collapsed. I looked up and could see myself on that balcony, running up and down, in and out of the living room, driving my frail grandmother crazy. There were some good moments and some that were not as pleasant. I remembered being on the balcony many times and seeing military vehicles rolling both directions down the street, even though it was a one-way street. We all assumed they were searching for someone or a group of anti-Castro supporters. I remembered the looks on the people's faces when they saw a military truck approaching. Everyone scrambled to take cover inside a house or business in fear that they would be arrested or taken for questioning. It was a frightening experience for the residents. Nobody stood in the way of the soldiers.

Whenever Tia Nena would hear the roar of the vehicles coming, she would go out onto the balcony and, in seconds, drag me inside by my arm. Sometimes, Tia Nena and I would go on errands or even to the corner grocery store. When a military vehicle approached us, she would grab my hand, push me behind a door or column, and tell me not to make any eye contact with the people in the vehicle. If she had to, she would hold my face so tight to her hip that I could not see or breath and begin to choke. After the vehicle passed, she would always find a safe route back to the house. On several occasions we witnessed military personnel get out of their vehicles and enter a home. In less than a minute, they returned with at least one person handcuffed and shoved inside an enclosed truck that followed the caravan. I could understand why Tia Nena was always overly cautious on the streets during this time.

Looking at the partial shell of what was once a great old building, I remembered that famous day of Friday, March 4, 1960, a day off from school. My mother and I had gone shopping to El

Encanto department store earlier in the day, and we had just walked to Abuela Balbina's home and were sitting with her in the living room. We heard an enormous explosion outside at about 3:00 p.m. that rattled the entire house and knocked down all the figurines that were on a shelf on the back wall of the living room. It felt like a 10-second earthquake with a deafening blast. We were certain that the explosion was close to us towards the direction of the port – perhaps another terrorist attack. We ran to the balcony, as did all the other neighbors. Less than a minute after the explosion, there was debris from whatever exploded raining on our heads. About a half hour later, an even larger explosion coming from the same location shook the entire neighborhood once more.

It was obvious that a cargo ship or warehouse had exploded in the harbor and debris and oil was now showering the streets of La Habana Vieja. Within minutes, there were chaotic traffic jams of military vehicles trying to get to the port, and residents trying to leave the surrounding area. Tia Nena dragged me inside and closed the front doors to the balcony. It wasn't until much later that evening that my father felt comfortable driving us back home. It was still a frightening ride home, with army personnel on the streets and numerous checkpoints to search every car for weapons or bombs. We were part of those searches. As the military personnel approached our vehicle, my mother warned me to keep my mouth shut, not to say a word, and to make no eye contact with the military search crew.

The following day, we heard that the cause of the explosions was a terrorist act. The French freighter La Coubre had exploded in La Habana Harbor unloading her cargo of 76 tons of Belgian munitions and grenades that were transported from the port of Antwerp in Belgium to La Habana. Both explosions killed about 100 people and wounded another 300.

At the funeral for the victims, Fidel Castro accused The United States of the terrorist attack. The United States denied any involvement. Many said that the real reason for the explosion was the dock workers' lack of experience handling ammunition. Some said that a group of anti-Castro dock workers orchestrated the blasts. I don't believe we will ever know who was responsible for these explosions.

****

After staring at the façade of Abuela Balbina's home, entering the empty lot, and chatting with neighbors, there wasn't much more for us to do at Calle Amargura #308. This was the last address to visit on my list, the saddest of all the stops. I looked around and did not see any military vehicles racing up and down the streets. The people walking past us seemed to be more comfortable and less worried about military personnel abducting them or family members. Their housing conditions were far from satisfactory, but their facial expressions and their determination to survive was clearly visible and understood.

While walking through the streets of La Habana Vieja, I continued with my quest to photograph the people and create a small portfolio of the faces of Cuba. In most cases, if I was able to approach the person and politely ask permission to photograph them, they didn't reject my offer. In fact, many would signal to me and ask that I take their photograph as they attempted to pose like movie stars. No good deed goes without financial reward – their hands would quickly reach out asking for spare coins or dollars.

I gave Stephen a roll of U.S. dollar bills I brought with me for this purpose and a handful of coins from my pocket. He became the official financial administrator responsible for all the monetary transactions after a photo was taken. In some cases, my telephoto lens got some excellent personalities and expressions of residents from afar going about their daily routines without knowing they were the subject of my portfolio project. Those photographs were more casual and less staged. Looking at the collection today, I can truly see the mood of the people from their portraits.

Continuing with our casual walk around the narrow streets, I could see a corner cafe, crowded with residents and tourists bouncing in their seats to the music from the trio of musicians playing favorite classic Cuban tunes. At the next corner, a Spanish guitarist sat on a wooden box on the sidewalk and sung his heart out while strumming the strings of his instrument. Across the street, there was a small group of neighborhood friends smoking Cuban cigars and chatting, most likely about nothing important.

We walked to Plaza Vieja and sat in a small café on the corner of Calle Muralla and Calle Mercaderes. There, I could hear music coming from inside our café and from other musicians outside on the plaza. I saw kids playing in the center of the plaza and others with homemade bicycles pieced together with parts of many others. Now, it was time to order some lunch and cold cervezas, sit back, listen to the sounds of La Habana Vieja, and perhaps ask the musicians for a portrait shot before we leave.

****

After lunch was over, we realized there was not much time left before we had to board the ship, so we split up. Stephen and Allen went in one direction and Arthur and I in the opposite. We agreed to meet up at the martini bar on the ship before dinner to recap our day and chat about our walks after we split.

Arthur and I continued walking through the narrow streets and were able to enter some small churches and museums. Both of us were quiet as we tried to absorb and appreciate the remains of the wonderful architecture in this old Spanish neighborhood, the sadness of its condition, the generous residents, and the minimal, if any, effort that was being made to restore and maintain the neighborhood.

The coordinated effort required to restore this neighborhood is beyond what Cuba alone could accomplish. I can imagine an international group of contractors, architects, historians, and stonemasons working diligently for 10 years, 20 years, or more. The history of the neighborhood should be preserved. I don't believe this will ever happen unless there is an effort to attract

La Habana Vieja - 2018

international investments. That would mean a return to a capitalistic environment where the investors feel their capital is protected against another government nationalizing their investments. How do you guarantee investors that their investment is safe when the reputation of the country's leadership borders between lies and deception? More than likely leaning more towards deception. You change the leadership. The people should have the power to vote their leaders out of office or form another revolution. But perhaps, in this case, they don't have the will or the freedom to cast an honest vote.

CHAPTER 8

A Shopping Experience 1959

Walking the streets of La Habana Vieja in December 2018 made me think back to the typical shopping scene in the 1950s, which was comparable to attending an outdoor fashion show in Paris. Everyone was dressed in the styles of the times, and the department stores promoted all the international designers. The shops were always crowded, with a distinct atmosphere of class, luxury, and excitement. Downtown La Habana was a place to see and be seen by others.

The women at the cosmetic counters were constantly spraying perfume on other women who walked by their station. Everyone was carrying bags and boxes with their acquisitions of the season's fashions, making sure that the store's logo faced outwards for everyone to see.

In my mind, I could still see those afternoon shopping trips with my mother back in the late 1950s when La Habana Vieja was a safe place to shop. We would always take a taxi from home to our first stop, El Encanto, Cuba's landmark and most elegant department store. This was my favorite store because it had multiple shopping floors and, most importantly for me in those days, a significant toy department and the most popular and fashionable boys' clothing. El Encanto was the largest department store in La Habana, originally built in 1888, situated on the corner of Galiano and San Rafael in La Habana Vieja. At that famous intersection, there were huge department stores on all four corners: Flogar, Variedades Galiano, Fin de Siglo, and El Encanto.

El Encanto had been privately owned with almost 1,000 employees. But in 1959, the Castro government nationalized the building, the business, and all of its operations in La Habana and other cities where branch stores were located. At the beginning of the revolution, El Encanto always gave the impression that operations were normal. Over time, employees that supported the revolution began to show up for work wearing its signature guerrilla fatigues and berets. Committees were set up in the store to eliminate employees who were not in support of the revolution by harassing and intimidating them. Many were forced to resign and make room for supporters of Castro. It was all part of the master plan to eliminate those who did not support the regime.

On April 9, 1961, two days after my eighth birthday, a bomb exploded outside the front entrance, causing broken windows at El Encanto and many surrounding stores. This act of terrorism had an immediate effect on shoppers, and nobody felt safe on the streets of downtown La Habana. On the night of April 13, 1961, four days after that initial bomb exploded outside the main entrance, two incendiary devices exploded inside the store after its normal 6:00 p.m. closing, causing a huge fire that engulfed the entire structure. Unable to control the fire, the massive corner building collapsed before it could be saved.

A Shopping Experience - 1959

Later that evening, the government arrested an employee who was identified as the principal suspect who allegedly confessed to his actions and provided details about the devices used in the explosion. He also identified others who were involved, some of whom had connections with the CIA in Miami. The accused were later tried, sentenced to death, and executed by firing squad. Today, the site is just a small park that is poorly maintained.

We always would spend a significant amount of our shopping time at El Encanto. After we finished browsing through all the floors, my mother and I would walk to other stores in the neighborhood and perhaps stop at the crowded lunch counter in Woolworth's for a quick bite to eat. Everywhere we went, it was full of fashionably dressed shoppers wearing the latest styles, carrying their shopping bags, and enjoying the atmosphere. Until the day El Encanto was torched by an arsonist.

Life in downtown La Habana was never the same after the fire. My mother was afraid to go there for fear of more bombings and terrorist attacks. Three days after that destructive fire, Castro declared that his revolution was socialist. On April 17, 1961, four days after the fire, the ill-fated Bay of Pigs exile invasion began. A lot of major events for one week. Terrorist acts, bombings, looting, and gunfire throughout the city became a common occurrence. It was becoming clear that La Habana was not a safe city to raise a family.

****

Before the El Encanto fire, our shopping trips usually ended at Abuela Balbina's home on Calle Amargura in La Habana Vieja. There, we waited for my father to pick us up after work, giving us the chance to visit with Abuela Balbina, Esperansa, and Tia Nena. I enjoyed visiting Abuela Balbina's home because Tia Nena would always have a small present waiting for me. I did not like Esperansa hobbling towards me all the time trying to kiss me. It seemed like she always had some food in her mouth that would drool down to her blouse because of her facial disabilities, which always frightened me. My mother would look at me with that serious "Cuban mother look," which meant that I needed to kiss Esperansa back and give her a big hug. Oh my God, that was torturous.

One day, I was caught in Abuela's bathroom scrubbing my lips and cheeks after a kissing episode with Esperansa. I was not only denied the presents Tia Nena had reserved for me that day, but I also had to witness the serious Cuban mother look the rest of the day there, the ride back home, and all evening until bedtime.

Abuela Balbina's home was quite unique: a beautiful old Spanish colonial style two-story building with a classic balcony running the full length of the second floor. The ground floor was leased to a retail/warehouse operation. Abuela, Esperansa, and Tia Nena lived on the entire second floor, which included three bedrooms, a kitchen, a formal dining room, a center courtyard open to the sky, and a huge formal living room with four sets of double doors that opened to a beautifully ornate wrought iron and marble balcony. All the interior moldings were dark mahogany, and the opulent ceilings seemed to be at least 16 feet high. The interior doors between rooms were also dark mahogany with patterned glass inlay. The courtyard was surrounded by all the rooms with double doors to each room, providing great air ventilation.

Abuela's furniture fit the style of the home: dark, ornate, and heavy mahogany. The curtains hanging on the double doors were all lace fabrics and delicately hung on each panel. The floors were black and white checkerboard marble with a solid black marble border and numerous antique area rugs in high-traffic areas. Today, it reminds me of a set from an old 1920s Hollywood movie. It would have been the perfect setting for Gloria Swanson and Rudolf Valentino to tango. Or perhaps for Greta Garbo and John Barrymore to share a loving kiss as the sun shone through the French doors. It was a truly memorable home.

Sometimes, instead of going to Abuela Balbina's home after our shopping excursions, we would go directly to my father's office. There, my mother would wait in his office or in the reception area. I would either be assigned an empty desk and pretend I was a top executive of the company or go to the center courtyard of the building and sit on a bench by the beautiful old bubbling fountain in the center to feed the tropical fish inside. The courtyard was open-air, surrounded by lush exotic plants with that small fountain as a centerpiece.

Before Castro took over as dictator in 1959, the Jose Arechabala Company was a privately owned company and one of the largest Cuban conglomerates within the sugar and alcoholic beverage industries. It was particularly famous for the launch and production of La Habana Club Rum from 1934 to 1960. Unfortunately, the company became nationalized by the Castro regime, and the family that owned it lost its investment and emigrated to Spain.

As soon as my father's day at work was complete, the three of us walked together to his car and rode home for dinner. Our life during this time was very casual, safe and predictable. We never felt the need to look out for dangerous encounters.

****

We were walking towards the ship and, as we crossed the street and began to enter the terminal, I turned around for one last look. I could see Calle Amargura all the way to the end past Abuela Balbina's home. I never thought I would see this view again. Would I get the chance to return? Do I want to return? Why?

As soon as we got onboard the ship, we walked directly to our suite and onto the verandah with two glasses of Sauvignon Blanc to relax on the lounge chairs after an emotional day. We could see a lot of the activity at the dock as we slowly began to sail away. The sight of the skyline of La Habana over the old Spanish colonial rooftops drifted into our view. The beautiful sun-filled day we spent in the convertible and walking the streets was now changing, with heavier winds and storm clouds approaching from the west. The ship was now leaving the dock and navigating through the

A Shopping Experience - 1959

busy harbor where one freighter was coming in and another going out to sea.

The streets outside the terminal were also busy with commercial vehicles waiting to load and unload crates. Since we were the only cruise ship with tourists onboard and we were leaving the port, all the 1950s tourist taxis had disappeared. Perhaps they had moved to the hotels to take tourists out for nighttime tours. There were still a lot of locals walking the streets around the terminal, bicycles crisscrossing in between cars, and plenty of activity in and out of the old Spanish colonial buildings facing the warehouses and terminals. We were leaving La Habana, but the city continued with its own buzz, its own energy, waiting for the next cruise ship scheduled to arrive tomorrow morning. I now wished we were staying longer. Maybe next time.

Our next stop on this cruise was Santiago de Cuba, the second largest city of Cuba, with a population of just under 500,000 residents. It is located on the southeastern coast of the island at the far end of a large safe harbor. Before we got there, we had a chance to see the northern coast of the town Varadero from the ship's deck. I was fortunate to spend the summer of 1960 in a rented beach house just a few blocks from that beautiful long sandy beach. It was a great opportunity to get away from the political drama and uncertainty that was happening in La Habana. Varadero was the town that introduced me to my love of the ocean.

A Shopping Experience - 1959

CHAPTER 9

Summer at the Beach
1960

Terrorist attacks, assassination attempts, bombings, fires, demonstrations, and the roar of military vehicles racing on residential streets was beginning to become normal in Cuba after Castro declared himself Cuba's leader. There was an uneasy feeling in our household. We were always careful what we said, who we said it to, and where we went. We were rarely unaccompanied by either my father or mother. La Habana was turning into a combat zone.

During the summer of 1960, many Cubans were optimistic that another government coup would return the country to normalcy and restore the democratic constitution. Later that year, on November 8, 1960, a new United States President was elected, and on January 20, 1961, John F. Kennedy was inaugurated. Cubans who were concerned about the Castro regime were hopeful that the new President would overthrow the Castro dictatorship and help the island return to freedom and democracy. In the meantime, my parents' concern about our family's safety in a city that was experiencing turmoil increased significantly before the summer school break. They felt it would be safer if we spent the summer away from the city in Varadero, a two-hour drive away, in hopes that La Habana would be a safer place when we returned in September. Perhaps there would be another revolution during the summer. My father remained in the city during the week to continue with his job at Jose Arechabala. He would come to the beach every week to spend long weekends with us until we returned to school in September.

On the last day of school in June of 1960 and a couple of days after my first communion, we packed up the car and moved to Varadero. It was now almost 18 months since Fidel Castro and his army marched into La Habana. During those first 18 months, the Castro regime and opposition groups created a lot of uncertainty throughout the country. We were constantly hearing about failed political coups, terrorist plots, government investigations, confiscation of private property (including real estate), nationalization of many foreign and domestically owned companies, curfews, disagreements with the Catholic Church, and, most importantly, the elimination of any free press and suspension of what was left of The Constitution after Batista's departure. This was not what many Cubans had hoped for at the beginning of the revolution, including our family and friends. It was obvious why so many were now questioning the future of the country.

Our house in this quaint and small beach community was situated on a corner lot surrounded by lawns with many fruit trees that provided us with plenty of shade from the warm summer sun. It was a very safe town where we could keep our windows and doors wide open all day and let the cool ocean breezes flow in from the north side and out through the south side of the house. Just like

Summer at the Beach - 1960

those Cuban breezes, there was a constant flow of friends and new neighbors coming in and out of the house. Next door lived a young couple, Elena and her husband Mario. They had two sons about the same age as Segundito and me, plus one infant daughter less than a year old. The family was also in Varadero just for the summer and for the same reasons we were there.

Elena was a doctor at a local hospital in La Habana until she gave birth to her third child. Mario practiced law in La Habana and commuted back and forth to Varadero for long weekends like my father. Elena would visit our house often and always brought something good to eat for our mid-afternoon snack. They both had similar concerns about the future of Cuba and what to do if the political situation worsened. My parents spent many evenings on the porch with Elena and Mario discussing the future of the country and the options available to them. I know it was of great comfort for both couples to support each other, evaluate the possibilities for their families, and consider all the alternatives. They became trusted friends during the summer and helped each other plan for their future and safety.

Some of the other families in our neighborhood were also there just for the summer; others lived there year-round. Those that were there for the season like us also had similar concerns about spending the summer in La Habana with their children. Over time, my parents developed a trust with many more of the neighbors as they shared their political views and hoped for a quick end to the Castro regime. Our social life was much more laid back, and I felt that my mother was significantly more at ease in Varadero than she would have been if we had spent the summer in La Habana. Neighborhood moms were always stopping by to drop off freshly baked goodies they had just made or to just sit on the porch or under the guava tree to chat and perhaps share some juicy gossip. It was obviously important in those days to have family and friends that provided mutual support for each other.

As everyone became more trusting in expressing their political opinions, my parents continued to evaluate and reconsider their

Summer at the Beach - 1960

options for the future of our family if the Castro regime's oppression and injustice were not overturned by another coup. Everyone knew that Castro was not going to exit on his own or turn over the government peacefully. He was not going to restore the country to a democratic status on his own. So, the only option for a new democratic government was another military coup or an invasion from The United States.

All summer long, we would get our news about the Castro regime from Swan Radio or the nationalized radio stations. On August 5, 1960, the government passed a law to nationalize the rest of the U.S. businesses operating in Cuba, the Cuban electric company, the telephone company, petrol refineries, and 36 sugar refineries with an approximate value of close to $1 billion. Two days later, priests from Catholic churches in La Habana read on the pulpits in front of their constituents a letter from the country's bishops condemning the nationalization and other revolutionary measures as communist. Castro's relationship with the Catholic church was getting worse.

Spending the summer in Varadero was a great experience for me. I made new friends and learned to swim, ride a two-wheel bicycle, and ride horses. All three had challenges. I also got bit by crabs numerous times while playing with them on the beach. You would think that after the first few times, I would learn to stay away. But no, I was fascinated by these creatures and tried to grab them as they crawled sideways into the ocean.

Learning to ride a two-wheel bicycle was also a painful experience because all I could do every time I tried to get moving without help was to fall and scrape my knees on the pavement. One day, I finally got it, but at the expense of scraped knees and elbows covered with bandages. Add to those injuries the scabs on my hands from multiple crab bites. What a sorry sight!

There was an old horse stable two blocks from the house where we would rent horses and ride around town. Because of my age and height, I got the smallest horse every time. One afternoon, I felt overly confident and tried to act like the Lone Ranger on his horse.

Summer at the Beach - 1960

That display of stupidity got me a fall off the horse along with numerous bruises, scrapes, a few tears, and a deflated ego. Added to the existing crab bites on my hands and the scraped knees and elbows from learning to ride a bike, I probably looked like I had been abused!

There were plenty of activities to pass the time and avoid the political news. Somehow, I kept one ear on what was happening politically and followed my parents' concern about the future. We tried to fill our days with fun things to do, because we were in a safe town with basically no military commotion, government activity, or restrictions on where we could go and what we could do. There was no *Comité* established at this time in Varadero. There were no *brujas* wearing house coats with binoculars looking at all the movement in the neighborhood and making notes. Street traffic was minimal, so my mother allowed us to cross the streets and visit friends without her supervision. We always heard the same warning statement from her every day, several times a day, *"Siempre mira en las doz direcciones antes de cruzar."* (Always look in both directions before crossing.)

In Varadero, Segundito and I started our day after breakfast with a walk or bike ride to the beach. Jorge was still too young and stayed home with mom most of the time. Once we arrived at the beach, we would meet our neighborhood friends and sit around on the sand to chat and pretend we were all adults. It seemed like there was always a competition between us to see who had the best gossip of the neighborhood. I think there was a lot of exaggeration during these meetings. We would then jump in the ocean and enjoyed a lot of swimming and diving into the waves. This ended up becoming our morning pastime after the gossip got boring. We usually stayed at the beach until lunch time. I swallowed a lot of saltwater during that summer, but every time a large wave submerged me and tumbled my body back to shore, I got back on my feet and was determined to jump back in the water and into the oncoming waves. Perhaps that is where I learned to be strong-willed. Those waves

Summer at the Beach - 1960

were not going to kick my ass and keep me out of the water. After a while, I felt like I was diving into a brick wall.

Fighting the ocean always increased our appetite. So, after a delicious lunch back home of *"bocadillos con leche"* (sandwiches with milk), our afternoons included playing board games with friends at the house or perhaps a couple of hours riding our bikes through the neighborhood or riding horses through town. I was known to have a strange effect on any horse I would ride. Shortly after I mounted and got out on the street, my horse would always relieve him/herself on the pavement. In those days, horse manure was left there on the streets to be washed away by the afternoon rains or turned into "road pizza" by the occasional automobile tire – whichever came first. That was not a particularly great experience after lunch for me or anyone riding behind me. We were always expected to be home by 4:00 p.m. when it was time to sit back, rest, listen to the radio, and watch mom make supper. Life at the beach was simple and carefree. Sometimes I honestly felt our stay there would last forever.

＊＊＊＊＊＊＊＊＊＊＊＊

On the weekends in Varadero, *abuelas, tias, tios, primos*, and many others would come for a day of sun, surf, and sand. Somewhere in between the three, they enjoyed my mother's cooking followed by a short siesta on a lounge chair under the fruit trees with a Cuban cigar in one hand and a Cuban coffee in the other. At some point in the day, without fail, the adults would begin to chat about the most recent terrorist plots that were uncovered, changes in laws created by the Castro government, and rumors of another potential military coup. Everyone had their own story, and sometimes I wondered if some stories may have been exaggerated just to outdo another. At times, it felt like a competition for who had the best story or the best news of the weekend – somewhat like what we did with our neighborhood friends at the beach in the

Summer at the Beach - 1960

mornings. I was wondering when my parents were going to start to give awards for the most exaggerated story of the weekend.

That summer, there were continuous rumors about a Cuban exile group authorized by President Eisenhower training on the island of Useppa, just west of Fort Myers, Florida. Useppa did briefly serve as a CIA training base for the Cuban exile group preparing for the Bay of Pigs Invasion. Later that summer, the group was transferred to bases in Guatemala. Historical records indicate that at the same time the training was taking place, the CIA director briefed Senator John F. Kennedy, who was running for president, at his Hyannis Port home on Cape Cod. The meeting included a description of the training of Cuban exiles for operations against the Castro government. Kennedy was always skeptical about a potential CIA-sponsored exile invasion.

During the same time, Cuban militias captured members from numerous resistance groups in La Habana and other parts of the Island. It was obvious that there was a concentrated effort by the Castro regime to eliminate any contra forces currently on the island.

When rumors about things like this were discussed among family members, the surrounding mood became dark, angry, and gloomy. They were not angry at each other, but angry for what was obviously happening in our country. Angry because many other Cubans continued to support the Castro regime and therefore backed its efforts to destroy democracy in Cuba. It was troublesome for my parents to understand why anyone would want to support a leader who was lying to the public, openly corrupt, and a danger to the people he was supposed to protect. My father would say, *"Se tratan de tener poder."* (It's all about having power). Many followers get behind the powerful to reap benefits. They begin to lie to themselves and to others just to inherit power. They turn towards corruption and become a danger to themselves, their families, and their communities. These people usually don't care about morality. They look the other way when the mention of morality smacks them in the face.

Summer at the Beach - 1960

It was difficult for my parents to avoid these types of conversations, even though we were surrounded by the tranquil atmosphere of rest and relaxation at the beach. Family and friends needed a safe and supportive environment to release their frustrations about the government. Sometimes, the calming surroundings in Varadero allowed our weekend visitors to express themselves freely. Talks of having to emigrate to another country for a better life was discussed with our relatives but never while Tio Frank was around us. A very difficult choice for anyone to be forced to make. It was frightening to consider emigration, but many suspected that it may be our only option. Somehow, making lunch, entertaining, and keeping their eyes on three sons was not as relaxing as my parents expected. But I truly believe they were happy to provide a safe weekend environment for the entire family.

As we got closer to mid-August, it was time to start thinking of getting back to La Habana and getting ready to go back to school. My dream summer was soon ending. What awaited us in La Habana upon our return? I didn't believe it would be any better than it was before we left in June. The terrorist attacks, assassination attempts, bombings, fires, demonstrations, and the roar of military vehicles racing on residential streets continued all summer with no indication that September and the months to follow would be any different.

Summer at the Beach - 1960

CHAPTER 10

Leaving La Habana 2018

Our ship was now out of the harbor and sailing away from La Habana heading eastward. We left our cabin and walked up to the forward top deck to catch the views of the coast, but we could barely see the shoreline. The storm was just behind us to the west and approaching rapidly, trying to catch up with the ship. It was a beautiful sight to witness, we moved to the aft deck to watch the storm clouds get closer and closer to us. Unfortunately, it was just about time to meet Stephen and Allen at the martini bar. And, because of the weather and distance from the shore, I would not be able to see the shoreline of Varadero Beach. I did not mind, because there was so much more to think about and process from our tour of La Habana. That would require a martini at the bar and some fun socializing with our friends, including new friends we met on the cruise. Perhaps it would be a great opportunity to compare notes from our first stop in Cuba.

On our way to the bar, I continued to process many of my childhood memories based on what I experienced today. Every few minutes new recollections of my youth in Cuba would suddenly appear in my mind and I would stop to think and reconnect. We sat at the bar with Stephen, Allen, and a select group of new friends that seem to be on the same "bar schedule" as us. I caught myself at times staring into space, not participating in the conversation, and being a little anti-social. The bartender started to put on a show and began to demonstrate how he could make 10 martinis at the same time. After lining up all the glasses on the counter, he poured all 10 simultaneously from shakers stacked inside each other. A crowd gathered around the bar and erupted in applause – except for me. Although I watched him pour the martinis and appreciated his talent, the show really did not register in my mind. I was still thinking about what I saw today and remembering scenes in La Habana from my youth.

Suddenly, my lack of participation and social rudeness got me a kick under the barstool from Arthur, which made me wake up immediately and introduce a whole new conversation completely unrelated to what was currently being discussed. The following day would be a full day at sea before we reached Santiago de Cuba, so I had a lot of time ahead of me to download and work on my photographic portfolio, contemplating the scenes witnessed throughout our excursion with Ramon and on our own through the streets of La Habana Vieja.

****

I was up at dawn after an entertaining evening at the martini bar, a great meal with friends in the restaurant followed by an enjoyable Broadway review in the ship's theatre. Now it was time to visit the gym and work off the calories I consumed the previous night. Yes, that extra day at sea would prove to be extremely restful and mentally helpful. I continued to spend a lot of time selecting, adjusting, and going over the many photographs I took in La Habana, making the necessary cropping, light and color revisions photographers like to tinker with to improve their work. I was pleased with the number of great Cuban portraits I captured from everyday people on the street. Many of them were posed, and others taken from a distance with my telephoto lens were more candid and expressed a more somber attitude.

I had numerous photos taken at our old home at Calle J.H. Goss, so I emailed them to Segundito directly from the ship and got an immediate response of surprise and shock that I was not only able to find the house but also get inside and take pictures. Maybe it was because of what I learned on the beach in Varadero when the waves knocked me down, flipped me over, and dropped me on the shore – You get back up and try again. I really did not expect to find my old home let alone go inside and take pictures. I guess the saying is, *"No puedes ganar si no juegues."* (You cannot win unless you play.)

After a few hours working on photography, I went out to the pool deck and sat in a lounge chair by myself. Continuing to meditate about my childhood experiences here in Cuba, I thought about whether our brains in the first 10 years of our lives can be compared to a computer's hard drive, absorbing information and continuously uploading data that becomes part of our developmental future. Maybe that is the reason my childhood memories of Cuba are still so vivid.

****

I always liked to eavesdrop when my parents began a discussion about life, politics, family, and any other topic typical parents discuss when they are together and think their children are not listening. When they wanted to talk about a relative, neighbor or someone we would recognize, they switched their discussions to Cuban Code. But, as I mentioned before, by the time I was 6 or

7 years old, I broke the code and did not let on to them. I found it helpful to learn about any topic because their words and opinions influenced me directly. Obviously, their opinions were always "spot-on" to me not just because they were my parents but because their expressions, calming personalities, and rationalizations seemed to be normal, appropriate, and, not to mention, extremely convincing.

My father was a true gentleman. He never had anything mean or derogatory to say about anyone, even Tio Frank. He would always approach a problem with professionalism, logic, and rationale. If we acted in a manner that was not to his standard, he was there to correct us immediately with an adult attitude. How could we argue with his approach? He treated us like adults and, as a result, we wanted to behave and respond like adults.

My mother was strong-minded, tougher, and was not afraid to reprimand us using techniques passed on by many generations of Cuban mothers. She loved my father and my father loved her back even more. She was his wife, and she was going to support him 1,000 percent in whatever he decided was best for the family. We never saw them argue, and she never questioned his judgment. The love they had for each other was contagious and, as a result, I was extremely lucky to be part of such a loving family.

Being raised by them taught me many important lessons, but one that I will always remember is that love and hate are not born in us. We are taught at an early age the definitions of both. We are shown almost daily what love is and what hate causes. Those simple teachings can define us through the rest of our lives. The way we are taught these two words can have an impact on our future, the future of our families, our friends, and our communities. We must all be careful what we say and how we react in front of children – they listen and are more than capable of deciphering any code words you insert to keep your conversations private.

****

Ever since that summer on Varadero Beach, I have always seemed to gravitate towards the sun, the surf, and the sand. I have spent many of my adult days enjoying the ocean and the effects it has on me, whether during a short vacation or at a home we owned or rented. Whenever we lived more inland and away from the shore, vacations had to include a beach or ocean views.

During the mid-1980s when Arthur and I lived in Boston, we purchased a "handyman's special" (commonly referred to as a "money pit") beach house as a second home south of Boston in the quiet, small town of Hull. The house had spectacular ocean and bay views, but it was literally falling from years of neglect, abuse, and the spray of salt from the water. We hired a local carpenter, and our weekends and vacations for three years were spent working with him and renovating the house from top to bottom. It never really seemed like hard labor for us because we enjoyed the location so much and looked forward to weekends in Hull. When this second home was completed, we were offered better jobs in New York City and sold both the beach house and our Boston condo for a move to Sutton Place in New York City. That was a shocking change to our living environment. Boston and Hull had a significantly different personality than Sutton Place in New York City.

While living in New York City, we still managed to spend some weekends and vacation time in Provincetown, Massachusetts and Ogunquit, Maine during the summers. A later move to North Stamford, Connecticut in 1990 represented a step out of a hectic city to the quiet suburban New England countryside. Fortunately, Stamford's southern borders were on the shore of Long Island Sound which was a great location for boating. Yes, we bought a boat. And yes, it was a great day when we bought it and an even greater day when we sold it. The time in between could be another subject for a different book, perhaps. (Don't count on it.)

Not to jump too far ahead, but while we are on this subject, today we are both retired and live in Fort Lauderdale, Florida, where we can see the ocean from our condo balcony. We still spend a lot of summers in Provincetown to escape Florida's summer heat. There is something about the ocean that continues to attract Arthur and me to the shore. Perhaps it is the solitude and the meditational aspects of just looking at the vast open space and the horizon. Perhaps it is the continuous changes in color (never the same twice), the light or the smell of salty ocean breezes that has the power to energize anyone's spirit. Perhaps it is my recollection of my mornings in Varadero Beach. How happy and free I felt every day we went to the beach in Varadero. At one point, I used to wonder if I was a fish in a previous life. I can't be too far away from the ocean these days.

CHAPTER 11

Back to School
1960

When we lived in Cuba, we attended a private school called Valmaña on the corner of Calle Milagros and Calle D'Strampes, about a three-minute drive from our house. Shortly after Castro's government was installed, the government nationalized all private schools, including Vlamaña, and created new curriculums that included lectures about socialism, the benefits of Castro's revolution, and the pitfalls of democratic societies. All private schools were controlled by a government pushing communist and socialistic propaganda. The curriculum now included lectures on how the previous democratic governments in Cuba and other parts of the world including The United States were harmful to the people. The Castro regime was very smart to get the youth of Cuba indoctrinated early in life. Children will listen and support your agenda if they are taught to do so at a young age.

There wasn't much my parents could have done at this time. Keeping us out of school was not feasible. The *Comité* would see that we did not attend school and we would have been reported to the government. School was important at our age, and our parents could try and debrief us when we got home to explain the realities of the new government and the importance of free press and human rights.

Today, I think about my parents' efforts to keep us, at our age, thinking in the right political direction. I wonder if I were in their shoes, could I have been as determined? Would I have considered emigrating to another country because of the circumstances we were experiencing? Would I just give up and let the chips fall wherever they fall? It's time to look back now and see how their decisions were carefully planned and how all options were considered based on their personal experiences. It was not an easy decision to make.

****

The start of the 1960-61 school year was approaching, which meant saying goodbye to our friends at the beach and hoping we would see them again next summer, assuming we would return. At the end of August 1960, we returned to La Habana and began to get ready to start a new school year. This meant having to go shopping for new school uniforms and supplies. Yes, we all wore the same uniform in school. I did not mind because I did not have to be concerned about fashion styles or if my shirt matched my slacks. Those were important decisions for me at my age, and the uniforms eliminated that stress. All we had to do was to put on the uniform every morning and off we would go. My mother was not thrilled about going downtown to purchase new uniforms with three boys alone so, with help from Tia Nena, we were all marched inside El Encanto department store. There, we were fitted for dress shirts, khaki slacks, shorts, and ties with the school emblem. Everyone

Back to School - 1960

looked the same. This would be Jorge's first time in school, as Valmaña had special preschool and kindergarten classes. Everyone cries their first day in preschool, but Jorge was especially anxious to attend.

Segundito was much fussier than me about his uniform. He was older and felt he needed to look more like Elvis Presley or other contemporary music stars when he returned to school, so he wanted his slacks and shirts more tight-fitting. He was always very persistent about his opinion, and sometimes felt he could convince my mother. She was practical and always had the last word. She listened to his complaints, contemplated them for no more than 5 seconds, and simply responded with, *"No, y no me vuelvas a preguntar."* ("No, and don't ask me again.") She was the judge and the jury combined into one strong minded woman. Girls who attended Valmaña wore white skirts and white lacy blouses with the school emblem on the blouse, white ankle socks, and black shoes. A very feminine uniform.

Our first day of school finally arrived. The school bus stopped in front of our home. We ran out the front door anxious to get on the bus to see our friends and to talk about our summer experiences. As we climbed the steps and entered the bus, we were stunned. There were almost half as many kids on the bus as there were back in June. When we got to the schoolyard, there were many other school friends missing. My classmates were almost half of what I had before the summer vacation in June. My mother would tell us later that day that perhaps some of the families moved to another town or another school. The reality was that many of my school friends left the country and emigrated abroad to escape Castro's communist government policies.

It was tough to be missing neighborhood friends, and now school friends had gone without a trace. I was saddened. I would often ask my mother if we were going to move to The United States since so many of my friends had moved without saying goodbye. It was a heartbreaking and lonely beginning to what would most likely be an uncomfortable and difficult school year. It was not a

Back to School - 1960

time to get a decent education. The freedom for political expression everyone yearns to have was eliminated and now kids at a young age were taught to support the Castro regime. There were no other options if we continued to stay in Cuba.

Back to School - 1960

CHAPTER 12

Bay of Pigs
1961

What would you do if you lived next to an unfriendly neighbor? The new Communist government established by Castro was only 100 miles from The United States, which made U.S. government officials nervous and insistent on keeping a watchful eye on Castro's subsequent political activities. Even though Batista was a corrupt leader and a dictator, he was considered an ally to Americans and to American companies doing business in Cuba. The Americans owned a significant portion of the sugar plantations and other major industries on the island. Batista was also "anti-communist" and was very good about pleasing The United States leaders, whereas Castro did not like Americans incorporating their business in Cuba. He wanted to return Cuba to the Cubans. His major political catchphrases were "Cuba belongs to the Cuban people," "Return

Cuba to Cubans," "Cuba first," and "Cuba Si, Yanqui No." It was somewhat of a "Make Cuba Great Again" theme. Does this sound familiar to you? History seems to always repeat itself, the good, the bad, and the ugly. Mistakes are often repeated because we don't learn from the past, we try to ignore it, deny it ever happened, or simply restrict it from children's education.

Almost immediately after taking power, Castro began to nationalize American dominated industries. He did this with intimidation and bullying, and without any advance notice. In response to what was happening in Cuba, on March 17, 1960, President Dwight Eisenhower, at an Oval Office meeting with high-level national security officials and the Central Intelligence Agency, approved a CIA policy paper titled, "A Program of Covert Action Against the Castro Regime." The document outlined the establishment of an exile group to restore the revolution and help overturn Castro's rule. This would be achieved by building a radio station on the Western Caribbean island of Swan, less than 600 miles southwest of Cuba, to broadcast anti-Castro propaganda into Cuba. The plan would also gather intelligence from the exile opposition group to create covert events within Cuba. Most importantly, the document recommended that the CIA organize a military force outside of Cuba to be trained for an eventual deployment to overturn the Castro government. With this authorization, the CIA immediately recruited 1,400 Cuban exiles living in Miami and helped train them in Nicaragua and Guatemala to eventually invade Cuba and overthrow the Castro regime. The CIA and internal groups of dissidents were now responsible for many terrorist attacks around the country, including the bombing and burning of hundreds of acres of sugar cane, tobacco fields, and government buildings throughout the country.

The news from Cuban newspapers, radio, and television programs was not reliable and always supported the Castro regime. My parents were afraid that the continuous tensions between the U.S. and Cuba would result in an economic catastrophe for Cuba. They felt the propaganda the teachers taught their students in school

Bay of Pigs - 1961

about the daily news would affect our education. Fidel Castro blamed all the continued terrorist acts throughout the country on the CIA and the leaders of the U.S. It was also rumored that some of those terrorist acts were authorized by Castro's administration against dissident groups and carried out by his militia. He would then blame the U.S., especially the assassinations of some of his military leaders who he began to distrust.

Shortly after school began in September 1960 and seven months before the Bay of Pigs invasion, Fidel Castro addressed The United Nations General Assembly. He charged that the U.S. acquired Swan Island in the Western Caribbean and set up a powerful broadcasting station, which it placed at the disposal of war criminals. For several days after that famous speech, CIA sponsored flights from the U.S. dropped weapons and supplies to the Cuban resistance in Cuba. Some missed their targets and were acquired by Castro's army, while some reached their intended purpose. As early as October 1960, Cuban leaders warned of a U.S.-led invasion of Cuba based on intelligence information obtained by Cuba's security services. It was difficult to live an ordinary middle-class life in La Habana when you heard news of an imminent invasion and war.

In December 1960, unidentified planes, reportedly from the U.S., flew over several Cuban cities, dropping anti-Castro propaganda. Accusations between the two countries continued and became stronger than ever. It was obvious to Castro that an invasion was certain. Where, when, or how was the question, so Castro had to remain vigilant and keep his eyes open and his troops ready.

In January 1961, the U.S. government, now with a newly inaugurated President, John F. Kennedy, severed diplomatic relations with Cuba as Castro became a closer friend to the Soviet Union. Many U.S. politicians were not concerned about Castro's relationship with the Soviet bloc and felt that he did not pose any real threat to The United States. Just the opposite, President Kennedy felt that Castro's removal would show the Soviets and others that he was serious about winning the Cold War. The nationalization

Bay of Pigs - 1961

of many American companies and the confiscation of American assets was not something Kennedy was going to ignore.

It was Eisenhower's plan to train and arm Cuban exiles to overthrow Castro. When Kennedy inherited the plan, he expressed some doubts about its strategy, timing, and effectiveness. He was concerned that the Soviets and other countries who were friends of the U.S. would see this as an act of war. Kennedy did not want to be responsible, early in his administration, for disagreements with U.S. allies or for the start of World War III. With that in mind, the CIA offered to keep U.S. involvement a secret. If the plan was successful, the invasion would escalate and encourage the citizens of Cuba into an anti-Castro uprising on the island. As history has proven, keeping a secret in Washington, D.C. is almost impossible, and this secret was no different. Rumors about a possible invasion surfaced from the day the Eisenhower administration initiated the plan to the day the exile group landed on the beaches of Playa Giron in the Bay of Pigs.

The U.S. government knew that Castro had a small ineffective air force compared to The United States. The first step was for the Cuban exiles to destroy it and its runways a few days before arriving on Playa Giron. In early April, 1961, a squadron of American B-26 bombers that were used during World War II were painted to look like stolen Cuban planes and used to strike Cuban airfields. Unfortunately, Castro and his generals were tipped off and moved his planes to a different location before the air raid. Kennedy now suspected that the plan would be too small to succeed, and he became extremely concerned about getting the U.S. military involved. Unfortunately, it was too late to apply the brakes, since the Cuban exile brigade had already left Nicaragua and Guatemala, where they were training since Eisenhower authorized the plan. The brigade was on their way to the shores of Playa Giron on the southern shore of the island, only about 125 miles southeast of our home in La Habana.

In the early morning hours of Monday, April 17, 1961, less than a week after an arsonist leveled El Encanto, the invasion began. It

Bay of Pigs - 1961

was immediately a disaster, with multiple mistakes by the exile brigade. First, the plan for secrecy was impossible. There were so many rumors going around La Habana and other cities in Cuba of an invasion so Castro was alert and well prepared. Numerous acts of terrorism prior to the invasion escalated the warning signs for him and his generals. As soon as the invaders were spotted approaching Playa Giron, a radio station on the beach, which the reconnaissance team failed to spot, began to broadcast every detail of the operation to listeners across Cuba.

Everyone in our neighborhood hunkered down, shut the doors, windows, and lights, and gathered around the radio to listen to the news about the invasion in secrecy. Could this be the military coup everyone was waiting for? How long would it take for the Castro government to surrender or be overtaken by the exile brigade? Would Cuba return to a democratic country? All day long, military activity ran continuously up and down the streets of La Habana. The roar of speeding military vehicles could be heard inside our home. Nobody wanted to be seen outside in fear for their safety or of being accused as a traitor to the Castro government. The radio was our only immediate news on the invasion. But because all the stations were now controlled by the government except for Swan Radio, we were not certain of its honesty and accuracy. Even though the government-run stations began to claim victory shortly after the invasion began, many of us ignored them and did not want to believe their reporting.

The first night after the invasion, we tried to get Swan Radio (later named "Radio Americas" after the Bay of Pigs invasion) on our radio with our extended antenna. The Castro government tried to jam its signal numerous times, but many Cubans with better radios and sophisticated antennas could still hear their commentary and news programing.

The next several days were spent with the windows and doors closed, lights out, and Swan Radio on low volume to get the latest news. We did not want any Castro supporters from our neighborhood, including *El Comité*, to know that we were listening to an anti-Castro radio station for fear of retribution.

Bay of Pigs - 1961

Besides the fact that the air support they expected from the CIA was nowhere in sight once they landed on the beach, the exile brigade made two major mistakes. Coral reefs not far from the shore were not noted in the plan. Unfortunately, the reefs damaged some of the exiles' ships and sank as they attempted to reach the shore. Then, backup paratroopers who were going to assist in the invasion ended up landing in the wrong place where some were killed and others were captured as they landed. Castro immediately took control of the command post to fight this battle. Even though the exile brigade had some initial success, after three days of fighting, 1,100 of them were taken prisoner, 114 were killed in the battle, and some escaped by sea.

It was a frustrating day for many Cubans in Cuba and for those in Miami who were perhaps hoping to return to their homes. What was expected to be a liberation by the "Yanquis" became an embarrassment to those of us who were not supporters of Castro's tyranny. Others cheered in victory. The following day, military vehicles and personnel were again all over the streets in La Habana searching for anyone who may have been potentially involved with the invasion.

On April 20, 1961, shortly after the exile brigade surrendered, Castro appeared on television and delivered one of his famous four-hour speeches. He explained the reasons for the failure of the invasion:

> *Imperialism examines geography, analyzes the number of cannons, of planes, of tanks, the positions. The revolutionary examines the social composition of the population. The imperialists don't give a damn about how the population there thinks or feels.*

The following day, at a press conference, President Kennedy accepted responsibility for the failed invasion:

Bay of Pigs - 1961

There's an old saying that victory has 100
fathers and defeat is an orphan ... I've said
as much as I feel can be usefully said by me
in regard to the events of the past few days.
Further statements, detailed discussions, are
not to conceal responsibility, because I'm the
responsible officer of the government, but merely
because I, and that is quite obvious, but merely
because I do not believe that such a discussion
would benefit us during the present difficult
situation.

****

I was sitting in a ship's lounge chair by the pool, enjoying the breezes and the warm sun. I was on the starboard side of the ship watching, out in the distance, the southeastern shoreline of Cuba. I looked back at those days in April of 1961 and found it hard to believe that I was not frightened by all the activities surrounding the Bay of Pigs Invasion including the bombing and subsequent fire that destroyed El Encanto department store. A lot happened during that month. Maybe I was frightened; I don't remember. Perhaps it was my parents' protective actions that made us all feel safe at home. I know the fire at El Encanto was a heartbreaking moment to see on the television news the following day, the building collapsed in flames, all that remained was rubble. Mournful because I always had great memories of visiting the store with my mother, and now those special moments would never be repeated. Fortunately, the memories remained with me and they are still very vivid.

The invasion was a rare optimistic moment that perhaps the government would return to democracy and everything would go back to normal. I noticed that my parents, for a very short time at the beginning of the invasion, were no longer concerned about having to leave the country. It was almost certain that the exile brigade would succeed. That same thought brought some relief and happiness to everyone gathered around. Our radio received a stronger and clearer signal from Swan Radio than radios owned by some of our adjoining trusted neighbors. My parents invited some of them to our home to listen to the news on our radio. For three nights in a row after dinner and to avoid being seen by *la bruja* at *El Comité*, our neighbors, with the help of ladders and step stools, jumped over our courtyard wall to avoid being seen at the front door. We could have all been accused of congregating and perhaps charged with orchestrating a plan against the communist government during an important national emergency. It was a risky act, but we all felt the outcome of the invasion would be a positive ending to the Castro regime. Many of us wanted to be there listening to the events as they unfolded.

Our front door and windows were closed. Our curtains were drawn and most of the lights were turned off in the house. It was somewhat of an amusing sight to see our overweight neighbors trying to get over the concrete wall that separated our properties. What we had to do so we were not seen by *la bruja* was sometimes creative and sometimes just plain silly. People did not want to take any chances of being reported to the military. Crawling over a six-foot concrete wall was not silly, it was serious business to them.

****

Still sitting there on the lounge chair by the ship's pool, earphones in place with classical music coming from my iPhone, I realized how lucky I was today and how much technology has changed since 1961. I probably could have received a very clear signal from Swan Radio on my iPhone if the technology was available back in 1961. Maybe a crystal-clear video signal also.

****

Bay of Pigs - 1961

How quickly the mood in the room around the radio changed a day or two after the invasion started. The initial news from Swan Radio was encouraging, but soon the optimism on their programing changed for the worse. The news was not what we expected. The initial excitement on the day of the invasion withered away in seconds as soon as we heard the exiles were basically defeated by Castro's militia.

The exile brigade began to lose any of its original gains from the first day of the invasion. Now we knew the claims of victory by the government-controlled stations were very close to accurate. All the adults surrounding the radio were frightened and concerned. Their faces expressed their deep disappointment in the outcome. Concerned for their country, families, friends, and themselves. There was no question in anyone's mind that the Castro government was going to retaliate and punish anyone they thought was involved with this invasion or had one ounce of anti-Castro feeling in their soul. *El Comité* had the power and the list of anti-Castro neighbors to submit to the military who would then make visits for surprise searches and intimidation. Castro supporters were encouraged and rewarded to turn in their anti-Castro neighbors. Nobody was safe. Only a few were trusted, and even those who were trusted could have reported any relative or neighbor to the government if pressured.

****

Staring at the shoreline in the distance from the ship's deck, thinking about the sudden changes in attitude that evening by my parents and neighbors, sent chills down my back while sitting in the hot sun by the cruise ship's pool. We have all experienced the obvious satisfaction when we are confident about an event that is about to happen. And we've all experienced the shock and sadness when the outcome turns out to be the complete opposite, a massive disappointment, and a huge step backwards in our lives.

Bay of Pigs - 1961

The invasion had a finale that we could not believe or wanted to accept. Everyone was sure that Castro would be defeated. It is still hard for many Cubans to understand what went wrong. This was the worst possible situation, one that could endanger the lives of our families and friends. All the adults in that room looked like they had just seen a ghost. Pale faces, hands covering their mouths, tears running down their cheeks, and fingers running through their hair. They had nothing to say but the repetitive words, *"No puede ser. No puede ser."* (No, it cannot be.)

I was physically on the ship's deck but mentally back on Calle J.H. Goss, April of 1961 around a radio that just gave us shocking news. News that emotionally affected my parents and the other adults gathered around. They were all still sitting in the darkened living room whispering with doors and windows shut and curtains drawn. I then heard a waiter next to me asking if I needed another refreshment. Yes, I heard him, but I could not respond. He tried again and I did not move. Finally, he touched my shoulder. At least I thought he did, but it was my imagination of my mother touching my shoulder and asking us to go to our bedroom and get ready for bed. I sensed she did not want us to see the heartbroken looks on their faces and the faces of our neighbors. That's what a mother does, protect her children from the pain of sadness, disappointment, and hurt.

****

Just the opposite of what the CIA expected, the Cuban people did not revolt against the Castro regime during the invasion. The small CIA-trained army made numerous mistakes and did not receive assistance from the U.S. Air Force because that support was canceled the night before the invasion by Secretary of State Dean Rusk under President Kennedy's order. It was obvious that the Bay of Pigs Invasion was a political disaster for the Kennedy administration. It was also a personal disaster for the Cuban people who wanted the return of democracy to the island.

Bay of Pigs - 1961

There was no question that the fear of retaliation by the regime was on everyone's mind the moment Castro declared victory. It was time to maintain a low profile and go about your business unnoticed. It was time to blend in with the background and not attract any attention to ourselves. Lives depended on it.

CHAPTER 13

After the Invasion 1961

The day the exile brigade was declared defeated, the line of military vehicles ran up and down the main streets of La Habana in a celebratory mood to the delight of many supporters. Road blockades and vehicle searches were set up all over the city, and private homes were searched to identify and prevent any uprising by the opposition living in La Habana. That day, during the celebrations on the streets of La Habana, a very close friend of my parents was sitting on his balcony, watching the commotion created by the military and its supporters. Suddenly, a stray bullet from a moving truck loaded with military personnel struck him and killed him immediately.

During the early evening the same day, my parents felt obligated to pay their respects by visiting the widow at her home.

After the Invasion - 1961

They arranged for Abuela Teresa to stay with us while they went to visit with their friend who just lost her husband. Since Abuela did not own a car and did not know how to drive, that meant my father had to pick her up, bring her to our house, go out again with my mother to visit the widow, come back home to drop off my mother and pick up Abuela Teresa, drive her to her apartment, and then return home. That was a total of six times my father was stopped, interrogated, and vehicle-searched at various roadblocks that were set up throughout the city. He tried to avoid them by changing routes, but the multiple checkpoints were impossible to circumvent. I remember my father expressing concern about all the driving he did that night and the multiple one-on-one exchanges with the military personnel he could not bypass.

Abuela Teresa was now safely in her apartment and my parents were home with us. It was a lot of traveling back and forth, but it was important to visit a close friend who just lost her husband because of a senseless and irresponsible stray bullet from a military vehicle. My brothers and I were already in bed, but I was awake listening to my parents discuss the evening's events. My father continued to be concerned about all the activity in and out of our home, but he knew there was no way out of it – He felt compelled to visit their friend's widow. I heard him walk to the living room and tell my mother he wanted to look outside through the window. There was a military vehicle parked right outside our front door with several soldiers inside. After a few minutes, the truck pulled out and my father returned to the bedroom. Concerned about all that was going on outside on the streets of La Habana, I don't believe they slept much that evening.

The next morning, my parents acted as if it was normal day. We could not attend school yet until all the military activity returned to normal levels, whatever that meant. My father was dressed in his suit and tie, ready for work. He sat with us in the dining room for breakfast. After we were all done, he kissed us goodbye, not knowing the events that would take place the rest of the day.

It was bad enough that we were not able to attend school, but now we were not allowed to go outside to play with friends.

After the Invasion - 1961

There was not much for three boys to do inside one household. Our housekeeper, Georgina, was always disappointed when she came in and found all of us home from school. We used to tease her and annoy her during her daily chores around the house. So, this time when she entered and saw all three of us at home again, she made the sign of the cross, murmured something we could not understand, and continued to the kitchen. Georgina was an attractive and hardworking young woman in her late teens with beautiful dark creamy skin and long, shiny, black hair. She lived about two miles from our house and walked every day to help my mother with the chores of maintaining a household for my father and three boys. That day, we spent most of the morning in the courtyard playing or just being silly, trying to stay out of trouble.

Shortly before noon on the day after the failed invasion, I heard vehicle brakes squealing from several cars and trucks trying to park outside our home. I heard their doors slamming. From the side alley in the courtyard, I could see soldiers exiting a small truck and surrounding our house. I immediately panicked and ran inside the house with my brothers to tell my mother. Suddenly, we heard a strong and loud pounding on the door. She must have also heard the vehicles park right outside, because my mother was already on her way to the living room to open the front door. I stayed in the hallway behind a door looking directly at the men who banged on the door. *"Buenas tardes, señora ..."* (Good afternoon, ma'am ...) two men in dark suits and dark sunglasses presented her with some type of credentials, a badge or license, and said they were there to search the home. They told us to wait in the courtyard and stand against the concrete wall that separated the properties. No search warrant was required by the military.

The thugs entered our home with at least a dozen other soldiers in full combat gear, including rifles, handguns, and ammunition. In a matter of minutes, they turned the entire house upside down. Drawers were emptied and all their contents left on the floor. Mattresses were overturned to examine the space under the beds. Furniture was moved all around the house to look for hidden doors or compartments inside the walls. Kitchen cabinets were emptied

After the Invasion - 1961

and food left on the floor. Several soldiers climbed onto the roof to make sure nobody was hiding there.

At this point, my two brothers, my mother, Georgina, and I stood outside in the courtyard of our home leaning against the wall as we were told and held each other tight. We were all frightened but I tried not to show any emotion that might upset my family and Georgina, who had her hands around my shoulders. I could feel her shaking like she was at the epicenter of a powerful earthquake. She could not hold her nervousness any longer and urinated on the courtyard floor while standing there against the wall. My mother grabbed her and held onto her just as close and tight as her own sons. The soldiers noticed what was happening and as expected, did nothing to assure us we were safe.

This unpleasantness lasted only about 30 minutes, even though it seemed like hours. Luckily, we lived in a small house. When they were done turning the house upside down, one of the thugs with a dark suit and dark sunglasses (which he never took off during the raid) came to the courtyard and asked my mother where my father was. She knew he was expected home for lunch soon, but only told the thug that he was at work and she wasn't sure if he was coming home for lunch or staying to work in the office.

The raid produced nothing in our home that was considered anti-Castro. The soldiers left our house, got back inside their vehicles, and raced down the street. I remember my mother trying to compose herself after seeing our house in shambles. The invasion of our family's privacy must have angered her tremendously, although she showed no resentment in front of us. My mother gave Georgina a change of clothing from her closet. Georgina, still physically shaken, changed in the bathroom quickly, reached out for the mop in the kitchen, and, without saying a word or looking at any of us, mopped the courtyard. She returned from the courtyard and began the task of putting the house back together with us. My mother gave us orders to clean up our rooms while she worked with Georgina around the rest of the house.

After the Invasion - 1961

We all pitched in but before we could finish, my father walked in the house for lunch with a look of shock on his face at the turmoil around us. I think he knew exactly what had happened and was sorry he was not there to protect us. He rolled up his sleeves as well to help return the house to normal while my mother and Georgina finished making lunch. We all sat together at the table, Georgina included. There was no discussion of what just happened as we ate our lunch in almost complete silence. Today, I would love to know what was going through the minds of my parents. It was a painful day we never discussed openly.

It was not easy for my parents to hide their emotions that afternoon. My father still had a serious look of concern on his face after our lunch. We kissed him goodbye as he got in his car and returned to work. What he experienced when he reached his office that afternoon was something I am sure he never forgot.

****

Half of the house was still in shambles from the raid after my father returned to work. We continued with our chores of putting our clothes back in the closet and dressers and making our beds. There was a frightening feeling around the house after he left but there was no discussion, we just kept going with our cleaning and did not want to cause any trouble. My brothers and I knew that it was not a time to upset my mother or to annoy Georgina, so we were all on our best behavior while Segundito gave out orders to Jorge and me on what to clean up. We did not argue that day and did what we were told to do.

I think my mother knew in her heart that this day of surprises and drama was not over. Typical of my mother, she tried very hard not show her anger that afternoon or express her concerns in front of us or Georgina. She continued cleaning up the mess left for us by the thugs and their accomplices and tried to make conversation with Georgina about anything other than what just happened, including preparations for dinner that night.

After the Invasion - 1961

I was tidying our bedroom, organizing my clothes in my dresser, when I heard the phone ring. My mother answered the phone, *"Hola, digame."* There was silence for several minutes. *"Gracias por llamarme, Elena."* (Thank you for calling me, Elena.) My mother hung up. Discussions on the telephone were limited because everyone was afraid the government was listening to their calls. Elena was my father's assistant at Jose Arechabala, a very efficient, strong, and opinionated woman who was loyal and supported my father at work.

My mother picked up the phone again and called Abuela Teresa to tell her the brief details of her conversation with Elena. I was standing around the corner from where the phone was in the center hallway so my mother would not see I was listening to her conversation with Abuela. Evidently, from what I was able to hear and decipher from Cuban Code, the two thugs and soldiers showed up at Jose Arechabala after my father returned to work, arrested him, and pushed him inside a truck full of other men. Elena tried to ask the thugs where they were taking my father or why was he being arrested. She was told to mind her own business or she would join him. The truck left the Plaza de la Catedral and, just like that, my father disappeared from his work and, more importantly, from our lives.

****

News traveled fast in Cuba. It was less than 5 minutes after my mother's conversation with Abuela Teresa when the phone began to ring constantly all afternoon. I would peek around the corner and watch my mother on the phone. I think she was tired of telling the same story repeatedly to friends and relatives who called to express their concern. Everyone wanted to show support for my mother and us by coming over to the house to visit. She was afraid that there would be too many people visiting that afternoon and evening to check up on us and preferred not to have *El Comité*

After the Invasion - 1961

make any more notes about our activities or capture the license plate numbers of those visiting us.

Several days passed and there was still no news of my father and worst of all, there was nothing we could do. There were lots of rumors around town that hundreds of men in the city were taken prisoner. But there was too much inconsistency about how many, where they were being held, and when they were expected to be released, if at all. Nothing was certain and the rumors almost made the situation worse for us. We did not know his location, if he was safe, or even still alive.

My mother's strength kept our family together and focused on a positive outcome to this horrible act by the government. It was a way for Castro to retain control of the country and to scare anyone who would question his leadership and had any intention of organizing an uprising. She felt it was best if we continued our lives normally to avoid attracting attention. Schools opened, and we returned to our usual morning routine of washing up, brushing our teeth, getting dressed in our uniforms, eating breakfast, and having one last physical inspection by mom before we got on the school bus. I am sure it was difficult for her, waking up alone every morning during this period and getting the three of us ready for school by herself. She kept an optimistic outlook about the situation and prayed for a quick resolution and my father's return home – even though we still had not heard from him and did not know where he was sent. The government refused to release any information about the prisoners or to even acknowledge that they had arrested anyone.

Finally, 10 days after the raid, my father returned home unexpectedly. He returned in a cab which had to wait outside as my mother tried to simultaneously embrace my father and find money in her handbag to pay the driver. We got home from school shortly after he returned home. As the bus stopped by our front entrance, I stepped off and knew, from the bright look and smile on my mother's face, that my father was finally home and safe with us. She instructed us to be extremely quiet because he was very tired

After the Invasion - 1961

and sleeping in the bedroom. We were allowed a quick peek inside their bedroom so we could see him for a moment.

There was complete silence in the house until my father woke up later that afternoon. He came out to the courtyard where we were playing quietly and hugged us. He never spoke to us about his ordeal in jail. We did not ask, either. We were just happy he was back and happy to see a smile on my mother's face. When others asked him what happened or about the conditions in his cell, he preferred not to respond and would say, *"Eso fue todo en el pasado."* (That is all in the past.)

****

What was the purpose of putting my father in jail? Was it caused by all the activity in and out of the house the night their friend was killed by a stray bullet? Was it just a scare tactic to show the neighbors and family members what could happen if you are not a supporter of the government? Was it just a random pick from the list established by *la bruja*, the head of *El Comité*? Perhaps someone reported us as an anti-Castro household? Who reported us? Was it a neighbor? Maybe it was friend we thought was trusted? Could it have been a family member? How about Tio Frank? I am sure there were many questions like these in my parents' minds. At this point, the questions did not matter at all. The damage was done and there was no turning back the calendar.

It was not a time to look back, it was time to look ahead and keep our distance from those we did not know or trust. It was time to make some difficult decisions about the future of the family and evaluate if that future involved leaving the country and starting a new life in The United States or another country. It was an important decision, and one that my parents took seriously.

****

After the Invasion - 1961

There is no doubt in my mind that the events affecting our family shortly after the Bay of Pigs Invasion contributed to my parents' decision to leave Cuba as quickly as possible and before it was too late. It was now early May 1961, and the invasion had caused a closer relationship between Cuba and The Soviet Union. The relationship with The United States was obviously anything but friendly or cordial.

We knew that there would be more gunfire in the streets, assassinations, terrorist acts, and government coups. Hopes of returning Cuba to a safe democracy evaporated. We were still convinced that it was no longer a country in which to safely raise a family. It was no longer a country in which to invest the rest of your life and make an honest living. Shortly after my father's release from jail, a decision was made by my parents to start all required preparations to leave the country. It was time to go, no matter the costs.

There were rumors that Fidel Castro's government was planning to terminate parental rights and place minors in communist indoctrination centers in The Soviet Union. My parents believed this because they already knew what was being taught in schools during this time. It was a logical step for the government to escalate their indoctrination. How do you increase your followers? You begin with the children who are obviously impressionable and much easier to persuade. This was a government policy my parents would not tolerate. Therefore, after the Bay of Pigs Invasion, it became an easy decision for them to plan to exit the country.

****

Major significant events in our lives leave a certain mark on our souls. I believe these events are part of what shapes our character, defines our personality, and develops our disposition. In our youth, the lessons we learn and how we are taught to react to events like these by our parents or others always stay with us for the rest of our lives.

After the Invasion - 1961

The stoic stability that my mother displayed during the period when my father was missing will always be with me. The strength that both exhibited when they made the decision to leave the country, knowing that as a first step Segundito and I would be separated from them for an unknown amount of time, will always stay with me. Their attitude and example of courage and firmness is what made my brother and I survive when we were separated from them. They taught us an important lesson of endurance, willpower, and determination we could not have learned in any school.

Today, I look back on those days and can't help but feel the long-term affect my experiences as a boy had on my life as an adult. How they affected my personality and how I conduct myself. During our youth, we are all just sponges, constantly absorbing data that shapes our future. These experiences were major data uploads for me, and I am sure for my brother as well.

****

Now it was time to get up from this lounge chair, find my way back to the cabin for a nap, and then get ready to meet friends at the martini bar. That's what people are supposed to do when they are cruising.

After the Invasion - 1961

CHAPTER 14

It's Time to Leave
1961

Sometimes it takes a specific event to help us make a decision that has been lingering in our minds for a long time – an event that pushes us to either one side or the other side of the fence. We hope when that event occurs, it is not hurtful and it is not too late to implement our decision freely and safely.

Prior to the Bay of Pigs Invasion in April 1961, my parents waited for a sign that would help tilt their decision to leave the country or stay. There was always chatter that Castro's term was getting close to its end and, therefore, my parents did not want to overreact and make a wrong move. The invasion of our privacy and my father's incarceration for no reason was the tipping point for our family.

****

At the start of the 1960-61 school year, I found it difficult to focus on my schoolwork knowing that many friends had left the country. I was always wondering if we would end up staying or leaving the country as many of my classmates did. It was not the same school I attended the previous year. I was feeling uncomfortable, concerned about making new friends, and unhappy with the new teachers the government hired.

My schoolyard time with classmates was different this year than it was the previous school year. My mother would always say to us before we got on the bus, *"No hables con nadie de lo que decimos en casa."* (Don't talk to anyone about what we say at home.) I was now overly conscientious during recess of what I could say or not say in school. Many others in my class were very verbal during recess about expressing support for the Castro administration or uncomfortable about the current events taking place. It was obvious to me that my classmates were simply repeating what was being talked about in their homes. Anyone our age could not have developed an opinion on their own without parental input. I can hear my mother's warnings, so I kept my mouth shut when my classmates began to talk politics. I realized now how important it was for my parents to stress that we keep our mouths closed and not broadcast anything that was spoken at home when talk of politics came up in the schoolyard or in our neighborhood playground.

****

After returning to La Habana from Varadero, my parents noticed many empty shelves at the grocery stores. Some smaller neighborhood food stores were closing because they were not able to keep sufficient merchandise on their shelves. Our neighborhood butcher shop was about three blocks from our house where, on a normal day, my mother would phone in an order and Segundito and I would go there to pay the bill and pick up our order. One day, the phone kept ringing and there was no answer from the butcher. My mother sent me there with a list to give to him. When I got there, the doors were locked. The butcher saw me standing by the door, approached the door, and opened it only halfway. He told me to tell my mother that they were closing and would only open when they received more inventory. He also warned me that what they were expecting to receive would only be a small fraction of what they used to carry, and once that was sold, they would close the store again until the next delivery.

Food shortages create desperate consumers willing to do anything to bypass the system and feed their families, it's an instinct. Lines began to form outside the store the moment rumors spread that a delivery truck was seen outside the butcher shop dropping off inventory. To spread out the small amount of merchandise they received, shop owners would display the following notice, *"Solo uno por hogar."* (Only one per household.) This was a common sign in every grocery store and butcher shop throughout the city. Availability became controlled by the government because people would start fist fights in the streets if they saw someone from a different neighborhood in line at their local store. People were creative and thought they could send one child to stand in line at the butcher down the street while they stood in line at another butcher five or six blocks away.

When chaos erupted at the food lines, that's when the government took control, and the country was forced to adopt a socialist food production and distribution system that ensured a survival level of heavily subsidized food for everyone. Every Cuban family had to register for a *libreta* (ration book) they could use at their local grocery store. The basic *libreta* products were guaranteed to last for one month, but they were never enough. Where to find eggs was and still is a common subject of discussion in many households. The rations of rice and sugar were adequate, but other products lasted only five or six days, so you had to be creative and assertive to find where and how to buy extras on the black market. The shortages on the grocery shelves were caused primarily by the embargo and the difficult relationship between Cuba and The United States after Cuba nationalized all the U.S. companies and assets doing business in Cuba.

We managed with what we could obtain. We had to stay well connected to know when to stand in line and to bring the *libreta* with us. My mother was always an excellent cook and knew how to stretch ingredients to make a healthy meal for the entire family and Georgina. We all had to economize and be as creative as possible, so we started to raise chickens in our courtyard, which we bought as baby chicks. At any one time, we would have four or five chicks running around the courtyard. When they got older and turned big and fat, Georgina knew how to break their neck, pluck all the feathers, clean them, and chop them up. I started to get personally attached to the chickens – I gave them each a name and helped with the feeding, so watching them get their neck broken was difficult to view. Every square inch of the chicken was used in our meals (except the feathers). It was impossible to enjoy our meals, because now it was Georgina's turn to tease us. When she brought dinner out to the table, she would say, *"arroz con Octavia,"* instead of *"arroz con pollo."* (chicken with rice.) The following night, our menu was *"caldo de Sofia"* instead of *"caldo de pollo"* (chicken soup). Somehow, adults always get the last laugh.

Cuban Christmas Eve dinners typically include a *"lechon asado"* (roast pig.) My parents were determined that this year was not going to be different. We were able to find and purchase a small live baby pig a few months before Christmas with some help from family members of Georgina who lived in the countryside. Yes, we kept the pig at home, but he stayed inside the outdoor bathroom adjacent to our courtyard. What a mess! We spent three months constantly feeding the pig with scraps to fatten him up. Every day, Georgina had to take the pig out of the bathroom and hose him and the entire room down because of the mess he created. It seemed like he never stopped eating all day. Between the pig and a few chickens around the courtyard, it was a full-time job feeding the animals and making sure they got big and fat. Like the chickens, we got attached to the pig, so we named him Pedrito.

On December 23, 1960, the day before Christmas Eve, it was time to say goodbye to Pedrito. Georgina's father came to the house with his collection of sharp knives. He set up his table in the middle of the courtyard and greeted Pedrito with a deceiving smile. My mother dragged us inside the house and closed all the doors leading to the courtyard. Thanks to her, we did not witness the slaughtering of Pedrito, but we were sorry to hear him squeal and to see the sprays of blood on the windowpanes from our hallway.

Pedrito got quite fat at our home. There was enough of him for us and several other family members that Christmas Eve. Dinner was not as enjoyable as other years. *Pedrito asado con arroz, frijoles negros, and yuca* (roast pig with black beans, rice and yuca) comprised our main entrée on December 24, 1960.

****

Everything changed at our home after the Bay of Pigs Invasion. Now it was time to get organized and follow the ever-changing regulations if we wanted to leave the country. During that time, we had to go on with our lives and maintain a low profile until the entire family was safe in The United States.

My parents decided to begin the process by sending Segundito and me alone to The United States as part of the Operation Pedro Pan exodus organized by the Catholic Charities in Miami. There was no U.S. embassy in Cuba after the Castro revolution, so the State Department partnered with the Catholic Church to grant special visa waivers for children to emigrate safely to The United Sates and eventually reunite with their parents and other family members. We were told it would take several months to get the visa – the wait was worth it.

My parents completed and submitted all the paperwork; it was now a waiting game. Hundreds of children had already left the country and many more hundreds had submitted their paperwork after the Bay of Pigs Invasion. The wait-list was far from short. Between 1960 and 1962, there was a mass exodus of more than 14,000 unaccompanied Cuban minors ages 6 to 18 to The United States. It was the largest mass exodus of children caused by a political suppression in the Western Hemisphere.

The plan was for Segundito and I to reach Miami and claim asylum when we arrived. At that time, The United States government would request of the Cuban government that our parents and immediate family members still in Cuba be allowed to leave the country and join their children as a humanitarian gesture. This was known to be the fastest way to leave Cuba during this period. Many of the children had family members in The United States with whom they could stay until their parents arrived, which could take anywhere from 6 to 18 months. Some, like us, did not have family stateside, so we would initially stay in a former military housing camp in Florida City, Florida, coordinated by the Catholic Charities and the State Department. The camp was about an hour drive southwest from Miami.

All we could do at this point was sit back and wait until we received authorization to leave the country. We were on the waiting list and hoped that the program would not cease before we were able to leave safely. Authorization could arrive in a month or two or even in a year. We just didn't know when to expect it. There was nothing else we could do but remain calm and continue to go about our daily activities without raising any suspicion from *El Comité* across the street.

****

School curriculum expanded after the Bay of Pigs Invasion to include more socialist-related history and pro-Castro civics lessons. Very often, school friends would just disappear and not return to school. Some emigrated to The United States, Spain, or Venezuela. Others were simply removed from the school by their parents because of the indoctrination. There were political consequences

It's Time to Leave - 1961

if you prevented your children from attending school and denied them the new communist curriculum. Many parents hid their kids inside their home until they were given authorization to leave the country.

I remember hearing my parents talk about rumors that the government was taking children that were not attending school from the cities and sending them to the farms to cut sugar cane. The farms had little if any working equipment and insufficient labor to keep up with the supply of sugar cane needed for the export market. Bringing city kids to the country to cut sugar cane was an opportunity to increase the labor force at the farms and maintain the minimum exporting quota that was needed. The local *Comité* would notice your children were not in school and immediately report it to the government. Rumors of new regulations giving the government authority to send children of a certain age to The Soviet Union for months of education and indoctrination continued to surface in the neighborhood. It became very difficult to decide to keep a child away from school. The alternatives could be worse.

Finally, the end of the school year arrived in June 1961. Unfortunately, my parents decided not to go to Varadero this summer in hopes that we might receive notice about our visas and flight to The United States soon. It was not an easy summer for three boys to be kept inside the house and play only in the courtyard with the chickens. Many of my neighborhood friends had already left the country, some were in the process of waiting for their visas, and others were not going anywhere because their parents were either confident that Castro would be removed from power or they were supporting his government and felt that *"todo esta maravilloso"* (everything is wonderful.) I could hear my parents angrily saying to each other that anyone who still supported Castro was living in an unrealistic world of lies and were unable to see or understand what was happening to their country.

July and August dragged on much too long since there was nothing to do but wait. Most of my neighborhood friends were gone and the new families that occupied their homes were not to be trusted. September was now here, and I thought that perhaps returning to school for the 1961-62 school year would occupy my time and I would not think too much about when we would be allowed to leave the country.

The student population of Valmaña in September 1961 had changed significantly from previous years. Homes that were confiscated by the government from families who left the country were now occupied by other families that supported the Castro regime. Their children were now attending Valmaña because it was no longer a private school – it was a government-run school with a specific government-designed curriculum. The socialist teachings and indoctrination continued to expand. Many teachers who taught at the school for years left the country and those who remained were now being replaced with a much younger group of teachers loyal to the Castro regime. The new teachers dressed in revolutionary army green outfits, including berets seemed barely old enough to drive a car. Still, there was nothing we could do but wait for our visa waivers.

****

The 1961 Christmas school recess was approaching. There was still no word about our visas or flight to The United States. It was now almost 7 months since all the paperwork was submitted, and we still had not received a response back from the Catholic Charities. Communist indoctrinations at Valmaña were increasing, so my parents decided not to send us back to school after the holiday recess. To avoid being noticed by *El Comité*, Segundito would stay home and my father would bring me to Tia Nena's house in La Habana Vieja on his way to work in the mornings where I would stay until he left work in the late afternoon. La Habana Vieja was a more congested neighborhood, and it was easier for me to blend in and not be noticed that I was not attending school.

I had a lot of chores when I spent my days with Tia Nena, since Abuela Balbina was ailing and required a lot of help. I would be

Abuela's messenger and assistant, getting her anything she wanted. At times, I thought she was abusing my help. All I heard was, "Get me my Bible," "It's too warm in here, get the fan," "Don't forget my rosary," "Change the radio station," "Get me a glass of water," "Adjust my pillow," "The breeze from the fan is hitting my face," and "I need a blanket." That was just in the first hour. I didn't mind. She kept me busy and perhaps she was so demanding just to entertain me and keep me out of trouble.

Sometimes, afternoons after lunch were dedicated to playing cards with Abuela Balbina. It was frustrating at times because she would just fall asleep holding her cards. That's when I would peek at her hand and then wake her up to keep playing. Tia Nena would laugh every time she saw me cheating, but she never told Abuela Balbina. Finally, one day I was caught by Esperansa, the snitch. She started to howl when she realized I was cheating, which woke up Abuela Balbina as I was spying on her cards. Abuela threw her cards at me, and in her Galician accent, called me a *"tramposo!"* (Cheater!) and laughed along with Esperansa and Tia Nena.

Errands meant having to go out and walk the streets of the neighborhood. I always loved to walk in La Habana Vieja and admire the old Spanish colonial architecture, so Tia Nena would drag me along like a puppy. I believe she enjoyed taking me for long walks in the neighborhood and introducing me to all her friends she would meet on the streets. Tia Nena was a very social woman and was liked by many people in the neighborhood. Her popularity was obvious to me by the number of people who would reach out to her as she walked the streets of La Habana Vieja just to acknowledge her and say, *"Hola Nena. ¿Como estas?"* (Hi Nena. How are you?) She always walked the streets waving to her friends like a famous movie star greeting her fans.

****

During the first week of February 1962, we received the notice we were expecting. Our visa waiver was approved. The notice

It's Time to Leave - 1961

also instructed us to immediately arrange for flights to Miami on February 17. A new wave of excitement in our household began as preparations for our departure commenced. I believe that my parents were physically ready to send us to Miami on a moment's notice, but no parent could be mentally prepared for what was about to happen. It was now time to implement "Phase 1" of their plan to leave Cuba. There were no "how to" books on how to handle the next couple of weeks. There was no turning back at this point.

CHAPTER 15

Santiago de Cuba 2018

Out in the distance, I could see the lush tropical mountains that form the background of the southwestern coast of Cuba. Looking out the window from the ship's gym, we were getting closer to the coast and the sights became clearer as a slight early morning fog withered away, and sunlight began to cast an unusual light on the mountain tops. Sailing into the Bay of Santiago de Cuba was one of the most beautiful natural sights I have seen from a cruise ship. We approached the shore and, as we got closer, we could see the mouth of a very long and narrow channel with various turns surrounded by the lush Caribbean greenery. As the ship entered, those mountains were now all around us. We left the gym and watched from the pool deck the local maritime pilot boat pulling up to our ship. The pilot jumped onboard to assist the captain in maneuvering the ship through the harbor. It took about 20 minutes for the captain and pilot to sail the ship around the tight and curvy channel before we entered the huge Bay of Santiago de Cuba.

We could see the city at the end of this magnificent underutilized safe harbor. Thick, lush, dark green vegetation continued to wrap the mountains. The city seemed to be strategically placed at the far end with the continuous mountain range encircling it. We were reaching the docks now, and the linesmen on the docks were ready for the ship's crew to throw the mooring lines so they could secure the ship on the bollards. A perfect coordinated effort which always goes unnoticed by the passengers.

As soon as we could disembark, we headed to the gangplank and walked the streets of the city to experience the colorful architecture and people. Everywhere we walked, the residents were sitting on their front porches or standing on street corners socializing with their neighbors and greeting the tourists walking the streets. We approached Parque Céspedes on the corner of Mercado La Plaza and Santo Tomàs where there was a group of about 100 of mostly . women, and children doing their early morning aerobics exercises in the open air. There were three energetic aerobics instructors on a makeshift stage playing very loud and lively Cuban music on a set of outdoor speakers. Their energy level was infectious to one another and to the tourists watching. Everyone had huge smiles on their faces as they followed the instructors and danced to the rising heavy beat of the Cuban music. It was a great photographic scene for my portfolio.

Parque Céspedes was across the street from their local cathedral, Santa Basilica Metropolitana Iglesia Catedral. In both, the park and on the steps of the cathedral, locals congregated to chat, smoke their Cuban cigars, or pose for pictures taken by tourists. The Cathedral was built on the top of a hill overlooking the city. You could see the two neoclassic towers located on either side of the façade. In between, there was a magnificent archangel with fully open wings, which could be seen from the port. The location, the people, and the overall scene provided a colorful, and artistic welcoming backdrop to the city. It was a great and friendly introduction to Santiago de Cuba. We stopped and talked to many of the locals in Spanish and in English. All were more than happy to pose for pictures, chat, and ask questions about famous Hollywood, music, and sports stars in The United States.

We continued our walk around the streets and kept being approached by people wanting to pose for pictures. I suppose my Nikon camera and the attached zoom lens made me look like a professional photographer. At the corner near the steps of the Cathedral were several elderly women with extra-long lit cigars between their fingers chatting with each other at a high rate of speed and expressing themselves with lively and rapid hand movements. At the end of the street south of the Cathedral, children were playing baseball in an empty lot dressed in clothes that had not seen detergent in a while. Next to them were men selling anything they could sell while riding on top of their carts full of used household merchandise dragged by donkeys. Everywhere we looked, there were old automobiles from the 1940s or 1950s acting as a taxis for tourists. It was a truly impressive assortment of photographic material to capture in one day. The views brought me back to another time in the history of Cuba. The scene was more reminiscent of a Hollywood set.

Walking the streets, I glanced through the windows at some of the butcher shops and food stores in the neighborhood. I noticed that many were closed and those that were open did not have a lot to offer. We continued our walk, and while admiring the architecture of the city, I started to wonder if the residents were still standing in line for one chicken breast per household per week? Were they raising their own chickens in their backyards? Were they still required to register for a *libreta* to be used at their local grocery store? It didn't seem like they had any more options than we did back in the early 1960s. The store shelves told me a lot about the quality of their lives. It was sad to see so many of them empty.

Fifty-eight years have passed, and it looked like not much had changed, perhaps the shortages are more common today than

Santiago de Cuba - 2018

they were in the 1960's. I spoke with several of the residents I was photographing about the lack of basic groceries in Cuba. All of them agreed: the rationing of chicken, eggs, rice, beans, soap, and other basic products were expected to be implemented in order to deal with the decline of staple foods. The government was blaming the recent hardening of the U.S. trade embargo and a steep decline in aid from Venezuela because of the collapse of their state-run oil company.

I saw a woman standing on her front porch with a little girl cradled on her left hip. Beneath the girl was a boy about 9- or 10-years old staring directly at me while hugging his mother's left thigh. I asked if I could take their photograph. The mother looked directly at me and responded, *"Sí, pero necesito dinero para alimentar a mis hijos."* (Yes, but I need money to feed my children.) Even if she had the money, did she have access to milk or basic nutrition for her children? I did not see a lot of options through the grocery store windows we passed. I suspected that whatever was not available in the stores they may be able to find in the black market, at a much higher price.

There must have been news about a cruise ship with American tourists in the harbor. It seemed like the entire town decided to go outside to greet the tourist and hope to earn a few bucks. Their business strategy was simple; go out and pose for pictures, offer walking tours of the city, or provide transportation in a classic automobile. The young boy hugging his mother's leg never took his eyes away from me, even though his sister was constantly pulling on his hair. After taking a few pictures of the family, I reached over and gave a couple of bills to mom on the porch, the boy finally smiled, and I shot one more photo.

As we were leaving, I said to Arthur, "That boy could have been me, or my son, or my grandchild." As we reached the corner, I began to imagine a scenario where my parents decided not to leave the country. Perhaps I would be on the streets of La Habana, driving a cab or trying to do anything to earn a living from the minimal number of tourists who visit. Would I have had the education I

Santiago de Cuba - 2018

received in The United States? Would I have had the opportunity for job advancement? Would I have had the resources to support a family?

We kept walking until we stopped at a small café on Calle Aguilera near the Plaza de Marte and ordered beers for all of us. It was just past noon and the café was full of locals; we were the only tourists. Uneven tables with small, mismatched chairs lined up on the sidewalk very close together. I could not help hearing the conversations at the four surrounding tables.

In front of us there were two women having lunch, being very animated and overly dramatic while talking about their cheating husbands. Both were talking at the same time at a high rate of speed using their hands to better express themselves. It was difficult for me to listen and understand their grievances at their verbal rate of speed, but I got about half of their conversation. I wondered if they could hear each other. I am sure after lunch was over, they both went home to make love to their husbands. All would be forgiven and forgotten as soon as they opened their front door.

To my right, there was a young couple with one small child in a baby carriage that looked like it was passed down by three or four generations. Most of their limited conversation revolved around their in-laws and the gifts they received from them for the child. They were very quiet and perhaps also listening to the two women in front of me chatting about their cheating husbands. Watching them together as a family gave me a visual image of the future of Cuba.

Behind me were two men drinking Cuban coffee and smoking cigars. The cigar smoke was so strong and thick, I had difficulties drinking my beer. Their conversations revolved around the prettiest girls that walked across the park. They were not polite or politically appropriate. In fact, if they were in the U.S. and someone heard their conversation, they would have been arrested and charged with sexual harassment.

And finally, on my left, a lonely man sat reading the American classic "The Catcher in the Rye" by J.D. Salinger with his second cup of Cuban coffee and a big Cuban cigar. How did he get this book? It was not translated in Spanish, so he obviously knew the English language. Perhaps he was just showing off and was only holding the book and pretending to be reading? I didn't think that was the case. I was impressed. I should have introduced myself and shared a conversation with him. A lost opportunity for me.

This was a locals' hangout. I was certain that the people around us were regular customers who visited the café quite often. They all seemed to know the waiters and just about everyone who worked at the café. Our waiter was enjoying the conversation between the two women in front of me. I wondered if any of them tried to listen to our conversation.

It was a great location to just sit back and watch the people of Santiago de Cuba go about their daily business. Some stopped for a mid-day café, others walked by doing their daily errands, kids played in the park, seniors just sat on the park benches with sad faces and not engaging with each other as the world unfolded in front of them.

I could understand the language, so I decided it would be more fun to eavesdrop on my neighbors and perhaps learn something about their lives in Cuba. What I heard was perhaps not much different from what I would have heard in The United States, with a sprinkling of Cuban dramatics and some distinct hand movements for emphasis on key words and phrases.

There was still a sense of sadness deep in their faces I could not ignore. Sitting under partial shade from a huge banyan tree and watching the people of Santiago de Cuba stroll by was absorbing and cultural. The December afternoon warmth was filtering through the leaves while we all enjoyed our beers, the scenery and for me, the conversations. I stayed focused on the chatter of patrons sitting around our neighboring tables and kept eavesdropping as new customers replaced the others. I could stay here all afternoon and entertain myself, learning more about life in Cuba today than if I read any guidebooks. I convinced myself that I needed to practice more dramatic Cuban hand movements in my own conversations when I got back on the ship!

Santiago de Cuba - 2018

CHAPTER 16

Dress Rehearsal
1962

A successful opening of a show usually comes after a carefully planned dress rehearsal. The show could be a stage presentation or just another day in our lives. If you can practice a routine before a performance, why not take the time to prepare yourself, physically and mentally? What harm could it cause?

The week before we received our official notice from Father Bryan O. Walsh, director of the Catholic Welfare Bureau, with our visa waiver and flight instructions, our neighborhood friends received a similar notice. Miguel and Angel were about the same age as Segundito and me. They lived with their parents Josefina and Miguel, Sr., and their maternal grandmother, Mariana. The rear of our properties touched and were only separated by a common six-foot concrete wall.

I remember the huge guava tree in the middle of their backyard, closer to our property line than their home. Some of the branches reached over our side of the wall, so during the guava season, we had plenty of fruit for us and Georgina. Their backyard included a small concrete shed with a flat roof in the corner against the dividing wall. Miguel and Angel would climb onto the roof of the shed and jump over the wall into our property when they wanted to come over and visit with us. Sometimes, we would do the same but only when Georgina and my mother were not watching. It was easier for us to climb on the roof of the shed than walk around the block to visit.

On the day of Miguel's and Angel's flight, my parents thought it would be a friendly and neighborly gesture for our family to go to the airport and wish them a safe journey. My parents obviously had an additional agenda for that day: they wanted to see and experience the process their family had to go through in the terminal so they would be better prepared when it was our turn to do the same in a few days. We were happy to be able to see them and wish them well prior to their seclusion in the glass enclosed room which many Cubans nicknamed *"la pecera"* (the fishbowl).

Inside the fishbowl, there was an insufficient number of folding chairs lined up right next to each other. In the front by the entrance, there were several long tables set up for check-in and baggage examination. Miguel and Angel kissed their parents and grandmother goodbye, entered the fishbowl, waited in line to be checked in, and handed their luggage to a guard. Once everything seemed to be in order, we could see through the glass wall that they were sent to a corner with other children who were traveling alone until they were called back to examine their luggage with the guard.

I watched Miguel's and Angel's parents and grandmother holding back tears as they stood on the outside of the fishbowl looking inside at their sons sitting on the floor with frightened looks on their faces. There weren't enough chairs inside the fishbowl, and as more people entered, all they could do was just remain standing and wait patiently or sit on the floor. Both took turns

Dress Rehearsal - 1962

sitting on the floor until they boarded the plane. Josefina, Miguel, Sr., and Mariana would not take their eyes away from the two boys. Mariana had her right arm around her daughter's shoulder while Josefina stood in front of the glass wall with her left hand covering her mouth and her right hand holding her husband's hand. Miguel, Sr. appeared tired, defeated, and helpless, with bloodshot eyes. I am sure they wondered if this was going to be the last time they would see their only sons. I looked around the outside of the fishbowl and saw many others like Josefina, Miguel, Sr., and Mariana holding back tears and trying not to express emotions that would upset their departing loved ones.

Today, when I remind myself of this scene, I am amazed at the personal strength the families demonstrated that morning. *"No les dejes saber que estamos tristes."* (Don't let them know we are sad.) I kept hearing that phrase circulate among everyone standing there. Families who did not know each other suddenly were holding each other's hands to provide and receive comfort. I saw my father put his hands around my mother's shoulders to let her know she was not alone. I stayed close by with my parents. I felt my mother's hand holding mine and then squeezing it very tight. She was not going to let it go. I am certain both were focused on what they would do in a few days. Did they doubt their personal strength to see the same exercise carried out next week with their two eldest sons inside the fishbowl? Perhaps they needed to experience this moment with our friends so they could get through the day that would soon come.

It seemed like hours before the plane was ready for boarding. Finally, those of us who came to say goodbye to Miguel and Angel, including their parents, grandmother, and other relatives, got the clearing to walk up the stairs to the open-air observation deck on the roof of the terminal to see them board the plane. There, we could see the plane directly in front of us, a Pan American propeller plane, as all the passengers slowly filtered out of the fishbowl onto the tarmac and walked to the rolling stairs to board the plane. Some of the passengers stopped to turn around with tears running down

Dress Rehearsal - 1962

their cheeks, trying to find their family on the observation deck to wave to them one last time. Others tried to turn around, but it looked like the pain of seeing their family one last time or having their family see them crying was far too much to bear.

Finally, we saw Miguel and Angel as their family began to shout and wave their white handkerchiefs. The noise was deafening. The emotional outburst from their family as soon as they came out onto the tarmac was heartbreaking. Miguel and Angel found their parents in the crowd and waved back with big smiles on their faces. Josefina and Miguel, Sr. waved with pretend smiles on their faces. The tears that were running down their cheeks were now wiped by the same white handkerchiefs they used to wave goodbye. Mariana could not stand there any longer, so she walked over to the back of the observation deck and sat down on the floor against the wall to cry privately.

Everyone was pushing and shoving to be out in front to see, for one final time, their families or friends board the plane. There was a small sense of happiness in the crowd for those who were leaving the country for a better and safer life, but the sadness of the separation overpowered any feeling of joy. I stepped back because I was getting crushed by adults much taller than me. They were all screaming the names of their family or friends walking towards the plane to get their attention. As I stepped further away from the railing, I could now see behind me several people up against the back wall of the observation deck sobbing uncontrollably. There was no place to sit. All the benches and chairs were removed to prevent anyone from lingering around the observation deck too long. Some people were so emotional seeing their families board the plane that they simply collapsed on the floor of the observation deck as others tried to comfort them and lift them up.

I saw Mariana still sitting on the floor crying. I approached her and held her hand until her daughter saw us and ran over to be with her mother. I envisioned myself in a few days walking towards those same rolling stairs to board the plane and looking back to find my parents waving to me. Would I be able to find them

Dress Rehearsal - 1962

in this crowd? Would they be sad and crying as much as Josefina, Mariana, and the other family members I watched now? Would there be someone there to comfort my family?

The rolling stairs were removed, and the plane's door shut. The screaming and waving from the crowd on the observation deck continued as loud as before. We could see passengers sitting in window seats waving back. As soon as the plane began to taxi to the end of the runway, there was a prompt and sudden silence throughout the crowd. It felt like the calm before the storm. Everyone stared at the end of the runway to watch the plane make a U-turn. In less than a minute, the plane began to rev its engines and move faster and faster. As it approached the direct view from the observation deck, the crowd again began to scream the names of their family or friends inside the plane while waving their white handkerchiefs. For a short second, as the plane passed by us, we could barely see the passengers sitting in widow seats waving back. Shortly thereafter, we could see the plane lift off right in front of us. Everyone around me was still waving their white handkerchiefs until the plane finally tilted upwards and vanished into the clouds. It was now time to leave the airport.

The crowd became instantly silent for what seemed to be only 10 to 15 seconds after the plane disappeared from our view. Suddenly, people began to feel the gravity of the plane's departure. Many of them began to cry again. Some were inconsolable. It was contagious. There was no place to sit down to collect yourself or to be comforted. I saw Josefina sitting on the floor with her mother Mariana crying uncontrollably and Miguel, Sr. rubbing her back as he held his white handkerchief to his eyes.

The same scene was repeated many times over before we were able to reach the exit. The sobbing and crying seemed to escalate. No words were spoken, there was only the sound of emotions throughout the crowd. People were trying to comfort others who they had never met before. This was the first time in my life when I personally witnessed humanity consoling those in need. Many of them needed reassuring words that everything would be alright in the future, a hug, or just someone to be there to hold their hand.

Dress Rehearsal - 1962

I don't believe what we saw that day was an experience my mother wanted us to see. There was an older woman sitting on the floor by herself about the same age as Abuela Balbina or Abuela Teresa, unable to control her grief. I wanted to go to her and give her some comfort, perhaps just a hug. I did not know her, but she seemed like she needed someone to just hold her and assure her that all would be fine. That act of kindness was dismissed by a soldier behind us pushing everyone away and down the exit stairway to the parking lot. My mother grabbed my hand and my father grabbed Jorge and Segundito and rushed us down to our car to avoid any issues with the soldiers.

No words were spoken in the car on the ride back home. That scene I had just experienced left a mark on my soul, never to be forgotten. Even though we didn't discuss what we saw that day as a family, I know it left a similar mark on everyone's soul. I feared that next week we would have to experience it again personally. Segundito and I inside the fishbowl while they were looking at us from the outside. That thought left me feeling uncomfortable during the ride back home. I could not imagine my parents crying in public view the way I saw many people do that day.

I am not sure this "dress rehearsal" was such a good idea. Sometimes, knowing what is to come can be much more damaging than what you expected. I was able to see what my family would experience the following week if everything went as planned and we left Cuba on February 17, 1962. Perhaps it would have been better for Segundito and me if we were not there.

Dress Rehearsal - 1962

CHAPTER 17

February 17, 1962

Sometimes, the past come to your mind at the least expected times. What triggers the memory? A comment from someone? Perhaps someone familiar walking by? Maybe a specific scene that is captured by eyes? The connection could have been made an hour ago or in the last second. I don't fight it. I go with it.

Halfway through our cold cervezas at the café in Santiago de Cuba, we decided to stay and order sandwiches. We were all enjoying the views from our table, and my mind wandered back to the morning I left Cuba alone with Segundito. Father Walsh's authorization letter asked us to make arrangements with Pan American Airlines, so my parents scheduled the first flight on February 17, 1962 from La Habana to Miami departing mid-day. It was required by the Cuban government for us to be at the airport very early in the morning for check-in and baggage inspections.

February 17 - 1962

On February 7, the day after receiving Father Walsh's notice, President Kennedy announced a more encompassing embargo on trade between The United States and Cuba in response to actions taken by the Cuban government. Fidel Castro immediately retaliated with new regulations and restrictions. One of them was limiting the amount of clothing we were allowed to take with us to Miami. In addition, we were not allowed to travel with any money or jewelry on us. My parents were concerned that the flight would eventually be canceled if political disagreements between the two countries continued at this fast pace.

Lunch arrived at the table. At the same time, those memories of the morning of February 17, 1962 continued in my mind. It was a clear and sunny winter morning, not unlike today in Santiago de Cuba. The flight was on schedule. We left the house with our minimal belongings and got inside my father's car for the drive to the airport. I sat with Segundito in the back seat of the Buick. Jorge and my mother were in front, my father was driving. Segundito and I were dressed in matching suits and ties with a white handkerchief inside our front jacket pocket. The suits were created by a tailor friend of my parents who wanted us to look like two Cuban Wall Street executives who never grew up.

Abuela Balbina did not come to the airport but gave us each a wallet with a small photograph of our family on the inside left and a religious medal sewn on the inside right. She told us the medal would protect us anywhere we went. We could not take any money with us, so the only other item inside the wallet was some minimal identification. My mother expressed a concern over the medal being considered "jewelry" by the inspectors that could cause us some delay or other serious problems at the airport.

From the back seat of the car, I looked outside through the window before we drove away and realized I was never going to see my house again. It was the first time I truly felt frightened since the decision for us to leave alone without our parents was explained to us. It was a very quiet ride to the airport. No one made any conversation. Perhaps we were all thinking the same thoughts.

February 17 - 1962

Maybe we were all frightened of what was about to occur at the airport. What could be going on inside the minds of a mother and father who were sending their eldest sons to a foreign country with no guarantees that they would be reunited soon.

Halfway to the airport, the fear of permanently losing my family and all my familiar surroundings became crystal clear to me. I wanted to ask my father to turn the car around and go back home where I thought I would feel safe and secure with the people I knew and loved. I soon realized that saying anything to my parents about not wanting to go to The United States at this point would be devastating to them, so I kept my mouth closed and did as I was told.

We arrived at the airport early in the morning as the government requested. It seemed like complete chaos, not unlike a scene from a Three Stooges movie. It was a duplication from last week when we were here to say goodbye to Miguel and Angel. People were rushing in every direction, women were crying, there was screaming as people were saying goodbye to family members. At the entrance to the terminal, there was an angry group demonstrating and yelling about the government's injustice and the way families were being torn apart. I knew this was going to be unpleasant for my family and a repeat of our experience last week. This time, my brother and I would be on the other side of the glass wall, inside the fishbowl.

My parents protected us and rushed us inside the airport terminal with our luggage in tow that now, because of the new restrictions, was small enough for my brother and me to carry without any help. Before we were ushered into the secluded glass enclosed waiting room, we saw many friends and relatives who came to the terminal to say goodbye. There was another kissing scene by the aunts, and my mother wiped red lipstick from our faces before she would allow us to enter the fishbowl, knowing it would be the last time she would see us until they were able to leave Cuba. And not knowing when that date would come, if ever.

Both my father and mother were very brave and strong. Their last words to us were, *"Asegúrense de cuidar el uno del otro.*

February 17 - 1962

Comportanse bien." (Be sure to take care of each other. Behave yourselves.) I did not cry. My brother displayed tremendous strength that day and held my hand as we both entered the fishbowl with our luggage. We got our papers and passports checked in and approved before we were escorted to a section with about 10 to 12 other children who were traveling alone to The United States. Some of us had to sit on the floor because, again, there was limited seating available. I could see my parents on the other side of the fishbowl waving to us and watching every move we made. I was beginning to feel like a mannequin at the old El Encanto department store. Their eyes were fixed directly at us and they would not leave for the observation deck until we were ready to board the plane.

After what seemed to be hours and hours of nothing to do but stare at each other in the fishbowl, our luggage was checked to make sure we only had the minimal clothing allowed and no jewelry or money. Anyone who tried to bring more was taken aside where the guards decided what was going to be returned to the luggage and what would be thrown into a pile on the floor (which most likely became available for the guards' personal use after we all left).

We stood there in front of our luggage as a soldier opened it and emptied the contents on the table to count the number of pieces we were carrying. We passed inspection and everything was dumped back inside our small bags. I could see my parents in the distance on the other side of the glass wall noticing that we passed inspection. My mother waved to us and signaled that they were going up to the observation deck to see us board the plane.

Soon after the luggage was examined, the doors to the tarmac opened and everyone was slowly escorted one by one from inside the terminal out onto the tarmac to a rolling cart-mounted staircase that led to the airplane's passenger door. My heart began to beat faster and faster. I felt that this was the end of my life in Cuba, and soon we would be up in the air on our way to a new life. I remember passing through the open doors of the fishbowl, walking halfway to the plane, and turning around to see the outdoor observation deck

February 17 - 1962

on the second floor of the terminal in front of the Pan American propeller plane. Just as we saw it last week. But this time, the view was from down below on the tarmac.

The observation deck was full of people trying to get the attention of their family members and friends as they walked from the fishbowl to the plane. I remembered the same scene from the week before. That time, I was watching closely the expressions on the faces of families and friends upstairs on the observation deck. This time, I was too far away to identify any faces. As I approached the rolling staircase with Segundito, the roar from the people up above was significantly louder than I remembered from last week. It was like I was a performer entering the stage at a rock concert.

I could not hear my parents call to us. I stopped and looked back to see if I could find them up above. Everyone seemed so small. I still could not identify any faces in the crowd. People were waving white handkerchiefs at us. Some were yelling the name of their family member or friend walking towards the plane. I still could not find my parents. I stopped and stood there one more time, shielding my eyes from the sun to see if I could find them the way Miguel and Angel found their parents the other day. Nothing. I knew they were there. But I could not find them in the crowd.

Suddenly, we were told by one of the soldiers guiding the passengers into the plane to keep moving or else we would be detained and not let out of the country. We did as we were told. All those emotions that I was hiding now surfaced. My heartbeat raced rapidly, but I did not cry, but I was scared.

I was halfway up the stairs to enter the plane. I turned around one last time and I still couldn't find my parents and Jorge. I remembered the scene on the observation deck last week and wondered if my parents were there trying to get our attention or perhaps crying against the back wall on the floor of the observation deck. Were any of our relatives or friends next to them providing comfort? I could not see them, but I felt them up there waving at us, saying goodbye.

February 17 - 1962

Inside the plane, we were able to sit together with the other children traveling alone. It was a very emotional time as we waited for everyone to enter and for the flight attendants to close the door. Some of the younger kids started to cry as adult passengers tried to console them. Many adults were also sobbing as they entered the plane and walked down the aisle to their seat. Just like the prior week, the urge to cry was contagious. Whenever I saw someone break down, I wanted to do the same. I wondered if my parents were up there on the observation deck still waving to us and crying. I kept wondering if someone would hold their hands and give them comfort?

Finally, the plane's door closed and the cart-mounted stairs were rolled away manually. Just like last week, the plane began to taxi away from the terminal and, at the end, turned around and began to speed up rather quickly. As it raced by the terminal, I could still see the crowd of people on the observation deck waving goodbye with their white handkerchiefs. Everyone on that side of the plane began to wave back. As soon as the wheels were off the tarmac, a huge applause erupted in the cabin, which muffled the sounds of the sobbing passengers.

I knew that shortly after takeoff, the crowd on the observation deck would begin to weep again while the soldiers pushed them along to clear the area. A memorable day, I thought. Was someone on the observation deck looking after my parents and Jorge? What is the rest of the day going to be like for us? What is the rest of the day going to be like for them? I still did not cry, but I was frightened.

February 17 - 1962

PART TWO

The brave man is not he who does not feel afraid, but he who conquers that fear.

- NELSON MANDELA

CHAPTER 18

It's the People
2018

Spending time in Cuba during our cruise made me realize how lucky my brother and I were that our parents arranged for us to leave the country back in 1962. In La Habana and Santiago de Cuba, we spent limited time with the residents, photographing them and engaging in short but friendly conversations. We saw their living conditions and how they dressed. We visited their stores and witnessed the empty shelves. We looked into their eyes and felt their desperate need for aid. There was a sadness deep inside their souls that could not have been covered up by those friendly photo-op smiles when tourists arrived in town.

My parents' fears of the economic consequences of Castro's policies were on target. Many expected Castro wouldn't last long after the revolution. *"Es imposible que este idiota puede mantener el control de Cuba.* " ("It is impossible that this idiot can maintain control of Cuba."). I remember those words spoken by family members and many of my parents' friends. Those who bet on an early collapse of his administration and stayed behind paid dearly. Those who emigrated paid a different price – They left all their possessions to start a new life, including leaving behind many family members. There were significant consequences for either choice.

Today, I wonder if a lack of political interest by a majority in Cuba was the cause of Castro's leadership longevity. He was very smart to open the exit doors in his early dictator years, allowing political dissidents or anyone who opposed his policies to leave the country. He treated Cuba like a pressure cooker – When it was ready to explode from the pressure, he released some of the steam but kept the heat going. His policy was to eliminate anyone who disagreed with him, discredit and disqualify the free press and keep his loyal subjects by his side (who were mostly unqualified and would never question his actions). Today, we still experience similar policies with dictators and dictator wannabes who call themselves "leaders." History does dangerously continue to repeat itself because people tend to forget or ignore the past.

****

We finished our lunch at the café by the Plaza de Marte in Santiago de Cuba and began a leisurely walk back to the ship. The afternoon was young and people were still mingling at the cafés, street corners, front porches, and steps of the *Catedral*. I still heard Cuban music all around. I wondered if the music would still play later when the ship sailed away from the dock? Would vendors still sell their wares? Or will they go home and wait for the next cruise ship to arrive?

My Nikon camera was hanging from my neck around my shoulder as we got closer to Parque Céspedes where the aerobics dancing class was held earlier in the day. An elderly woman with a leathery face covered in a road map of wrinkles stopped me. She was smoking a lit foot-long Cuban cigar and wore soiled clothing that released a sickening, musty tobacco odor. She approached me with a big smile and reminded me that earlier in the day I was taking pictures of the aerobic dancers in the middle of the park. She told me that now it was her turn to pose for me. She looked right at me with those Norma Desmond eyes and heavily painted eyebrows, struck a pose like a true Hollywood movie starlet, and waited for me to take several shots as she attempted multiple poses after each click of the camera, just like a fashion model. I had to follow her poses, photograph her, and give her a couple of U.S. dollars, which likely provided her with a few days of nourishment and another cigar. In return, she gave me an even bigger smile while holding that massive cigar in her dark yellow stained teeth. She was a character who earned her tip, and I got my money's worth, too!

On our way back to the ship, I thought about the level of excitement that tourism in Cuba could bring to a city like Santiago de Cuba. For just a few hours, the residents came out to greet us, offer taxis and guided tours, and posed for pictures to make money. A welcoming act for the tourists with financial rewards for the residents.

I looked around again and realized how political events can have such a significant impact on people's lives. Sometimes politicians don't seriously consider the impact of their decisions on the lives of the people they serve. If their policies cause hardship, they deny it. If they are the sole beneficiaries of new regulations, they wrongfully claim they are "good for the people," If someone points out an error of judgment, that person will face retaliation. That is not how to serve the people you govern.

Some of the residents accepted Castro and adapted to his rule because they had no other alternative. Others in better financial positions were able to pick up their lives and leave. Neither option was easy to accept. I suspect that many of the people I saw in Santiago de Cuba were there today because in the 1960s their parents and grandparents had no other choice but to adapt. Or perhaps they tried to leave but were unsuccessful.

As we approached the docks, I saw tour buses and taxis dropping off the ship's passengers that ventured out during the day to see the city and surroundings. I wondered if they experienced the same observations of Santiago de Cuba we encountered. Were their views censored by the local tour guides? The ship's crew and port staff were funneling the passengers towards the only security desk at the entrance of the fenced-in area surrounding the dock. They were all working diligently to get the passengers back on the ship – a job the locals cherish whenever a cruise ship comes to town.

The people of Santiago de Cuba can reap such economic benefit from cruise ship tourism. After the ship sails, how many more residents would have the financial resources to put food on the table for their family, pay their rent, or add small amounts to their savings because of tourists? What are they doing today in 2021, since tourism from the U.S. was eliminated shortly after our cruise? Are the streets of Santiago de Cuba as lively today as they were when we were there?

I thought back to Ramon, our taxi driver in La Habana. He was probably in his early 30s and spoke three languages, Russian, English, and Spanish. He picks up tourists at the cruise docks every morning, takes them around the city, and earns some money to survive and maintain his car.

If my parents did not send me out of the country, how would I have survived after coming out as a gay man? Maybe I would have stayed in the closet in fear of retribution. Perhaps I would have been forced to marry a woman and had children. One of them could be Ramon's age. They would most likely be driving tourists around town so their family would have a roof over their heads and some food on the table. Maybe I would have been a cab driver myself, using my father's 1954 Buick as a way to make money and support my family. More than likely, I would've had to be creative and hold multiple jobs to survive. I suspect many of the residents need to manage more than one job, assuming they can find them, because one may not be enough to support a family. And holding only one job may be too risky if circumstances change and opportunities are gone.

****

The ship began to coordinate preparations for its departure from the port. We were in the lounge on the top deck facing the bow, examining all the activities down below on the docks. We saw the last tour bus approaching the ship to drop off a group of tired-looking passengers. Linesmen were in position to do their job. The ship's staff greeted the last group to return to the ship and packed up all the tents, tables, ramps, and railings that were set up earlier. It was an amazing orchestration of teamwork. Within a few minutes, the ship was ready to leave and began to move away from the docks. The captain blew the ship's horn as a maritime signal to announce we were sailing away from the port.

We were headed back out to the Caribbean Sea towards Cienfuegos and Trinidad. But first, we had to go through the beautiful narrow channel at the mouth of Santiago de Cuba Harbor. This time, it was sunset. The colors of the sky and water were simply magical. The sun was beginning its descent behind the mountain range as we passed, once again, through the narrow channel. The sunlight provided a beautiful display everywhere we looked. The foliage across the mountains were deep dark green covered by a creamy late afternoon fog. The sky and the bay were almost the same bright blue, difficult to distinguish between the two. The pilot boat was in front of us again to guide us through the bay and the narrow channel. As soon as we were out at sea, it picked up the pilot that helped guide our captain out of the harbor and returned to the port.

Out to sea, we headed west. We were still sitting in the extremely comfortable chairs in the lounge facing the windows towards the ship's bow as the sun sank into the western Caribbean

Sea. That one final striking multi-color display in the sky, when the sun dropped into the sea, was unforgettably beautiful yet only lasted a minute or two. It was a truly memorable visit to Santiago de Cuba and an impressive departure as we watched nature perform in front of us.

CHAPTER 19

Welcome to Miami 1962

Shortly after the plane lifted from Cuban soil, I heard the wheels fold into its belly. I looked around at all the people sitting in the cabin with us and asked myself if this was really happening. I couldn't ignore the loud sounds of the passengers behind me sobbing. I wasn't sure I could hold back my own tears much longer. I decided if I had to release the floodgates, I should do it while looking out of the window so nobody could see my face. I held it back. I knew my parents would be upset if someone told them I cried on my way to Miami. It was a stressful day, and at this point the day was far from over. It was just the beginning, the beginning of a new life for me.

We were on that plane to Miami because of policies created by a government and the reactions to those policies by my parents.

Welcome to Miami - 1962

We knew that decisions affecting our lives from the time the plane lifted from Cuban soil would now have to be made without our parents' guidance. It was time to remember what they taught us, because we were going to need those lessons to steer us in our new life.

****

I sat in a window seat during my flight to Miami. Most of the time, I stared out the window with amazement at the view and the experience of being above the clouds. This was my very first airplane ride. It was a strange sensation when the inside of my ears popped shortly after the plane took off. Within minutes, the plane reached a steady altitude, and the flight attendant passed chewing gum around the cabin. I did not know the purpose of the chewing gum during the flight. The lady sitting behind me must have heard me complain about my ears and suggested I put a stick of gum in my mouth and begin to chew. Feeling better, I went back to the window and looked down to see the blue-green waters of the Caribbean in between the white puffy clouds with soft spots of grey. I only wished I could have shared my first airplane ride with my entire family and not just Segundito.

My eyes were still fixated on the colors of the water, clouds, and sky. I realized that now, at the age of 8, I had to act more like an adult, take care of myself, and assume responsibility for my actions. Yes, my brother was 11, and I am sure he felt the need to protect his younger brother. I am sure he was under more pressure being the eldest, so I had to be there when he needed me and not make his job more difficult.

My parents were no longer around to answer questions, respond with help, settle a dispute, or protect us from making mistakes. We hoped to be reunited soon, but the timing was not certain or even guaranteed. Cuban regulations on exiting the country changed almost daily, and the relationship between the U.S. and Cuba was changing just as often. It was impossible to determine how long we

Welcome to Miami - 1962

would be apart from each other. In the meantime, we had to remain strong.

As we approached Miami, I saw cars, roads, and houses from the window. I saw the shore of Miami Beach and remembered our summer stay in Varadero, hoping that someday, I could visit the beaches below. It felt like we were approaching the airport because everything was getting bigger and closer to us. Before I realized what was happening, we reached the beginning of the runway as the plane's wheels hit the pavement for a smooth landing. All the passengers onboard erupted in applause. Finally, we had arrived in a democratic and free country. It was a slow taxi to the terminal as the airport personnel drove a rolling cart-staircase to the door for the passengers to disembark.

The doors opened and everyone jumped to exit at the same time, so the flight attendant needed to make an announcement to prevent a stampede in the aisles. I was half the height of most of the passengers on this plane, so I could have been crushed in the aisle before I got to breath American air.

As we got outside and began our walk down the stairs, I saw several passengers kneel on the tarmac to kiss the ground. I found it strange back then but today I understand the significance of their actions. We entered the terminal, stood in line inside the very modern interior, and were checked in by the extremely friendly immigration staff. The words, "Welcome to The United States," were repeated by everyone. It was a significant difference than the way we were treated by the Cuban military when we left. After getting our papers checked and our passports stamped, we were escorted to baggage claim to pick up our bags. All the Pedro Pan kids stayed together at the baggage claim section and then were taken to another location in the terminal where we had to wait for a bus to take us to Florida City, our new home. There, the Catholic Charities, with the help of the State Department, obtained a former army housing campus to be used for the Pedro Pan children until they could be relocated to foster homes or orphanages run by Catholic organizations around the country.

Welcome to Miami - 1962

While sitting in the corner of an air-conditioned room designated for the Pedro Pan children only, I heard a woman from a distance yell my name and Segundito's name. It was Susana, her husband Freddie, and their daughter Susie. Susana was a close friend of Tia Nena and had lived in Miami since the early 1950s. Tia Nena had notified her that we were arriving on the morning flight on February 17, and Susana wanted to come to the airport and see us before we were transferred to Florida City, our destination of the day. The chaperone supervising us told Susana that the room was restricted to the Pedro Pan children only. Somehow, Susana convinced the woman to let her and her family take us to lunch across the hall. She promised to return us within half an hour.

We crossed a busy hallway outside the waiting room and entered a beautiful restaurant located less than 50 feet from where we were seated with the other Pedro Pan kids. The restaurant was extremely busy, but we managed to get a table for the five of us after a few minutes. A busy restaurant usually comes with delays in service. Finally, lunch arrived for everyone. My huge club sandwich was placed in front of me with a mound of delicious fries. I was not going to leave anything on the plate. Just as we were finishing and Freddie paid the waiter, Susana mentioned that we were there for longer than a half hour, but she was certain that the bus would not leave us behind. *"No se preocupen, el autobús no puede irse sin ustedes."* (Don't worry, the bus can't leave without you.) Famous last words.

We walked back to the waiting room only to find everyone gone. All the luggage, including ours, was gone. There was nobody around to ask where the Pedro Pan children were sent. I panicked. After several minutes, Susana was able to find someone who informed us that the Pedro Pan children left on the bus as scheduled. They tried to find us but could not wait any longer. They suggested that we sit there until the afternoon plane arrived, which would have another group of Pedro Pan children. We could ride the bus to Florida City with them.

This is not what I was expecting during my first couple of hours in The United States. Susana, Freddie, and Susie told us not

Welcome to Miami - 1962

to worry, to wait in the room, and we would be taken to Florida City on the next bus. Susana also confirmed that our luggage was in the first bus that already departed the airport terminal. She and her family left, and all we could do was sit in this lonely room by ourselves wondering if we would ever get to our destination and find our luggage. We were alone, in a strange room, with only the clothes on our backs and our passports in our pockets. This time, I could not hold back. I was terrified. I cried.

I know my brother was with me all this time and he played a very important role from the time we entered the fishbowl, but I still felt alone and sad. A lot of emotions flowed through me from the time I woke up early in the morning. I could not keep them in any longer, I had to release them. Crying was a natural response, but I am certain that I upset my brother terribly. I hoped he would not feel guilty and blame himself for not doing his job of protecting me. My parents' last words to us as we were escorted into the fishbowl were, *"Asegúrense de cuidar el uno del otro."* (Be sure to take care of each other.)

He played the grownup role, hugged me, and tried to assure me that all would be fine and we would have a home and a bed to sleep in by nighttime. A flight attendant was walking by us and noticed I was crying while my brother was holding me. She stopped and hugged us both. She talked to us for a few minutes and tried to assure us that everything would turn out fine. All I could envision was being told to leave the airport at night and having to walk down the road by ourselves to find someone to take us inside their home for an overnight stay. I guess that was the Cuban drama finally coming out of me that day.

While waiting for the late afternoon flight to arrive, all we could do was sit there quietly and stare at the walls. Yes, we were comfortable – airport personnel kept entering the room, checking up on us and giving us candy, peanuts, sodas, and anything that would keep us happy and occupied. Some would even stop and chat with us in Spanish. It was a comforting feeling to know that the staff at the terminal cared about us and did not want to see us upset.

Welcome to Miami - 1962

Later in the afternoon, we began to see more activity around us as we were informed by the terminal staff that the afternoon flight from Cuba had just arrived. Within minutes, people were approaching the baggage claim area, collecting their minimal luggage, and exiting the restricted area to meet families and friends cheering on the other side. The scene saddened me. I felt alone and wondered what would happen the rest of the day. I knew my family was not going to be there at our journey's end. There was an empty feeling in my stomach that I tried to ignore. I kept quiet, sat in the room with my brother, and waited for the next set of instructions.

After a few minutes, a group of young kids were ushered into our room. It was the afternoon Operation Pedro Pan arrivals. The same chaperone that escorted us in the morning was escorting the new group. She saw us sitting there alone and wondered why we did not get on the early bus. As we tried to explain what had happened, she somewhat dismissed our explanation and warned us not to leave this time. The new kids that arrived looked as scared and frightened as the group we were with earlier in the day. We waited inside the terminal, as instructed, for the transportation to arrive outside and take us to Florida City. After a few minutes, we were escorted through the terminal's door and we all squeezed inside two vans designated for us and our luggage.

The ride to Florida City was quiet, there were hardly any words spoken. I could see that everyone in the van was frightened. Who wouldn't be? I looked out the window and saw that the sun was beginning to set on the western horizon. It was already late in the afternoon. The early winter sunset made it difficult to see anything outside on our way to Florida City.

There was a young man who lived on campus sitting in the front seat with the driver. He tried to make us feel relaxed and comfortable, and started to talk to us about the campus, the rules, and how the property was organized. Older children who were with us were sent to a separate camp just a few miles away, so when we made a first stop, some of them were separated from their younger siblings. It was an emotional moment to see two brothers

Welcome to Miami - 1962

being separated only because of age. It was unfortunate that this had to be explained to them while they were riding in the van. I was relieved my brother was not old enough for us to be separated.

We finally reached the camp. It was surrounded by a chain-link fence with a large wide gate at the entrance which needed to be unlocked and opened by a guard. Inside, I could see there were many one- and two-story homes lined up like the board of a Monopoly game on either side of the main drive. In the rear, there was an open field and a large circus-sized tent. We were told the tent had multiple purposes and used as a school, dining room, exercise room, evening cinema, and for Sunday church services.

The vans turned into the driveway of one of the homes that seemed to function as a welcome/administrative center. We gathered for a quick check-in, a light meal, and brief introductions. Everyone was still nervous and frightened. It was an uncomfortable feeling with new faces and unfamiliar surroundings. We finally connected with our luggage, which had arrived earlier in the day with the first wave of Pedro Pan kids. I sat next to Segundito on one of the bunk beds in the living room to listen to the administrator give out instructions, go over our schedule for tomorrow, and answer any questions. I could tell he was trying very hard to make us feel relaxed and comfortable in our new country – a difficult job after an overwhelmingly emotional day for a group of kids.

It was already late. We were told we would stay in the administrative center overnight. The girls traveling with us were placed in a house next to the administrative center. Tomorrow after breakfast in the tent, we would all return here to be assigned a home on the campus. Now it was time to find a bed somewhere in either the living room or the dining room, change into our sleeping clothes, get in line with about a dozen kids to use the only bathroom available, and go to sleep. When the lights were out, the administrator in charge left for his own private bedroom down the hall.

This long and difficult day was finally coming to an end. The only consolation was that we were not alone; everyone in this room

Welcome to Miami - 1962

was experiencing the same. We were all strangers united by the same experience we witnessed today. We knew the pain each other faced today. I was sure it would get easier beginning tomorrow morning – it could not be worse.

I was emotionally tired and mentally stressed by the time I got under the covers. There were not enough single bunk beds between the living room and the dining room for all the boys. Segundito and I slept in the same lower bunk bed squeezed into the corner of the living room. It wasn't five minutes after the lights went out that I began to hear some of the kids sniffling and crying very softly in the dark room. It was difficult to hold back my tears again, so I buried my face in my pillow and cried myself to sleep. Tomorrow would be a new day.

Welcome to Miami - 1962

CHAPTER 20

A New Home
1962

I heard someone whispering in the other room. I opened my eyes and looked up and found myself in an unfamiliar location. I suddenly became aware of my surroundings while the entire previous day flashed through my mind in seconds. Segundito woke up and asked if I slept OK. My pillow was damp, and I wondered if the cause was my tears or nervous sweat while I slept.

Within a few minutes, I saw other kids waking up and sitting on their beds waiting for the next set of instructions. It was an awkward moment, trying not make eye contact with each other to hide our emotions. The administrator who welcomed us last night walked in the room and announced for everyone to rise and shine, line up for the bathroom to clean up, brush our teeth, make our beds, get dressed, and prepare for breakfast inside the tent. Since today was Sunday, we had to attend church services later in the morning after breakfast, which would be in the tent as well.

While waiting for my turn to use the bathroom, I walked over to the window to look outside. There was a slight chill inside the house, but it was a beautiful winter day outside in Florida City. The house was surrounded by overgrown tropical foliage covering most of my view, but I could see an empty street, a sidewalk, and other homes also surrounded by similar foliage. I was now eager to go outside and investigate my new neighborhood.

Next in line for the bathroom, I found my toothbrush inside my luggage and the small Dopp kit the supervisor handed each of us the night before, including a tube of toothpaste, a small bar of soap, a toothbrush, and a comb.

Beds were made, teeth brushed, faces washed, hair combed, and dirty laundry set aside. I had on a fresh outfit, and I was ready for breakfast. Usually at this point, my mother would stand by the door and inspect our appearance, using her veto power to make revisions or give her approval. Now, I realized that would not happen. Instead, I turned to Segundito to get his approval. To make sure I knew who was in charge, he grabbed his comb, added a little water, and re-combed my hair. I looked in the mirror and did not notice any difference. So be it.

We waited outside for everyone in our group, and we all walked together to the tent for breakfast. On our way there, we introduced ourselves. I kept looking around the campus to get acclimated to my new surroundings. I saw kids coming out of every house heading over to the tent for breakfast. We entered the tent where the staff had set up picnic-style tables in one corner where we could all sit and enjoy our meals. Breakfast for today included an individual box of cereal, a small container of milk, and a small container of orange juice. I looked for a bowl for my cereal and milk, but I saw how the other kids managed and realized I had to cut the box open in the front, tear through the inside lining, pour the milk inside the box, and just enjoy it. The box was my bowl – clever.

It was extremely crowded in the dining area of the tent, so we were not allowed to stay too long and mingle with each other. We were asked to give up our seats as soon as we finished with our cereal to make room for other kids coming inside for breakfast. The dining room seating was not sufficient to accommodate all the kids living on the campus at one sitting. I realized that between last night's sleeping arrangements and this morning's breakfast seating, the facility was overwhelmed, especially as new kids arrived daily. I wondered if an equal number were sent away.

Segundito and I stepped outside and socialized with some of the other kids we had met yesterday on our morning flight. They thought we had been kidnapped because we did not return to the waiting room from our lunch when it was time to leave for Florida City. They were glad to know we were safe.

We walked around the campus and saw a playground at the end next to a baseball field and a volleyball court. A lot more kids were walking around the street on their way to breakfast or coming out of the tent as we walked back to the house where we slept last night. We were told we would attend mass in the tent later in the morning. After the service, we were expected to return to the house to get our assignments for our new home and meet our new house supervisors before returning to the tent for lunch.

It had been a while since I attended church services. I didn't expect to experience any fist fights, arguments, or demonstrations here like we had experienced in La Habana. The inside of the tent was rearranged after breakfast to accommodate the mass. It was very crowded. There were not enough seats, so many of us had to stand on the sides and in the back of the tent or sit on the floor. During the service, I looked around at all the kids. Every so often, I saw someone wiping tears from their eyes. The priest's sermon was encouraging and helped me accept this new life in the U.S. I was sure it helped many others also. I tried to understand and appreciate how lucky we were to have left Cuba. He was very comforting and urged everyone to pray for our families back home, for their safety, and for a speedy reunion. Personal strength was important to survive this difficult time we had just begun to experience. Everyone around us experienced the same; we were all equal. The priest's words of wisdom, understanding,

A New Home - 1962

and compassion during his sermon were very helpful. He made us feel good about ourselves and gave us hope for a happier future. Perhaps I might enjoy church services here more than I did in La Habana. I needed to hear someone of authority, besides my brother, assure me that all would be fine in the future.

The service ended with a final hymn accompanied by an upright piano that needed some serious tuning. Everyone began to exit and enjoy the rest of the day. Since it was Sunday, there was no school scheduled until the next morning. Everyone had the day off to enjoy. It was also a day for visitors to come to the campus or take the kids out for the day. We were not expecting any visitors.

We returned to the administrative house to be introduced to our new house supervisors who escorted Segundito and me and another set of brothers, Manolo and Manuel, to our new home. It was a small and narrow two-story townhouse on the other side of the main street. The first floor was lined with bunk beds in two separate rooms plus two more in the kitchen. Several small dressers were positioned between the beds to store clothes. A small closet in each room was also available to hang clothes. There was not much room in the closet, so it was best to squeeze all our belongings in our assigned drawers. Laundry bags were passed out for our dirty laundry, and we were instructed to write our names on labels that hung from the pull-strings used to close the bags.

Our house supervisors were a young Cuban couple, Jose and Lolita, with a teenage son, Johnny, who lived on the second floor of the townhouse. They had their own private living arrangements upstairs and spent a lot of time this morning making sure the four of us were comfortable, acclimated, and introduced to our roommates. We shared the first floor (and its single bathroom) with about 20 other boys. In the galley kitchen on the first floor, there was one small refrigerator for any food we wished to keep and one small stove to heat up any leftovers we saved from dinners at the tent.

Johnny, our house supervisors' son, was very hospitable and helped us unpack. He gave us instructions on how the laundry was collected and delivered. He told us about the schedules for meals

A New Home - 1962

in the tent, school, recess, and other activities that were organized throughout the campus for entertainment. Jose and Lolita explained the house rules, curfew times, and noise restrictions. All seemed reasonable since the rooms were so crowded. We were instructed to stay within the fenced-in area of the campus unless we were accompanied by a house supervisor or received written permission from the administrative office.

Once we all got settled, Manolo and Manuel decided to walk with us to the tent for lunch, rearranged again to provide seating for a meal which included sandwiches and soups placed on a long table where everyone stood in line to help themselves. I could get used to this routine. We sat with Manolo and Manuel and learned about their life in Cuba. They were approximately the same age as Segundito and me. They told us about their experience at the airport leaving La Habana, which was like ours except they tried to bring extra clothing that the guards rejected. They were curious about how long they would be allowed to stay on the campus and concerned, as we were, about the overcrowding of our house and the facilities.

Another kid, Luis, sitting alone next to Segundito, joined in on the conversation and informed us that the objective was to place us in foster homes or in orphanages around the country run by the Catholic Church. This provided the Pedro Pan kids an opportunity for a better education until their parents were able to join them and made room for the new kids arriving daily in Florida City. I wasn't sure I wanted to believe Luis. I had just arrived and was still trying to get comfortable and accustomed to my new surroundings. I was not interested in making another move too quickly to somewhere unknown and further away from our parents.

After lunch, we toured the campus with Manolo and Manuel, and sat on a bench to chat more and get to know each other. We moved over by the volleyball courts and watched as several kids began to play. The priest who gave the sermon earlier in the day came over to the baseball field next to where we were seated with gloves, bats, and baseballs, and started to organize two teams to play. He was the self-designated pitcher for both teams and tried to

A New Home - 1962

recruit us to join, but we told him we had just arrived yesterday and preferred to watch the game from the sidelines.

There was a lot to absorb on our first day, we were truly emotionally exhausted. I could see outside visitors coming onto the campus. Some of the kids spent time with their guests touring the facilities while others were taken outside for a Sunday drive. We did not know anyone in Miami except for Susana, Freddie, and Susie who we just met for lunch yesterday. It was simply a day for us to experience our new surroundings and unwind after an overly stressful day yesterday.

I wondered what the rules were to make a phone call to Cuba. There was no phone service in our new house, but there was a phone in the administrative house where we slept last night. I thought it would be a good idea to call home and let our parents know that we arrived safely in Miami. We were informed that the office notified our parents already and assured them that we arrived safely.

We spent the rest of the day walking around the campus, chatting with Manolo and Manuel, and sometimes just sitting on the grass and staring at nothing. I was grateful for what was in front of us and happy to just sit around the campus relaxing.

****

This was the first day in a long time that I did not hear any news about what was happening in Cuba, including political coups, bombings, demonstrations, or assassinations. It was a great feeling to be away in a safe environment and not worry about anything outside this fenced-in property. I wondered what our parents were doing during the past 24 hours and sad to not hear their voices. Were they thinking of us as we were thinking of them? Did they receive any political news that may affect their future departure from Cuba?

Years later, I read that around the same time we left Cuba and arrived in Florida City, a major U.S. secret operation known as Operation Mongoose was being developed. Authorized by

President Kennedy, it was implemented to train for terrorist attacks and covert operations coordinated by the C.I.A. at strategic sites in Cuba. The operation was headquartered in a building at a former Naval Air Station about 12 miles south of the main campus of the University of Miami, very close to the Operation Pedro Pan campus in Florida City.

The focus of the operation was to undermine and remove the Communists from power. It aimed to help Cubans overthrow the Communist regime, including Fidel Castro, and encouraged a citizens' revolt in Cuba by October 1962. Policymakers in the U.S. wanted to see a new and stable government in Cuba with which the U.S. and the people of Cuba could live in peace.

Some of the C.I.A.'s goals included intelligence gathering to create and support a popular Cuban movement by developing an underground network in various Cuban cities. They also enlisted the assistance of the Catholic Church to bring the women of Cuba into specific events that would undermine the Communist system. All this was being organized just a few miles east of our new campus. Obviously, while we were living in Florida City, we were not aware of Operation Mongoose and its activities.

In March 1962, less than a month after we arrived in Florida City, a classified C.I.A. memorandum sought to obtain proof of events which the high-ranking U.S. military personnel would consider justification for an American military intervention in Cuba. The formally classified document also explained the way in which the C.I.A. and Joint Chiefs of Staff sought a purpose to invade the island in a manner acceptable to the American people and American allies. The intention was to find a good cause for invasion that would receive general support from the U.S. voters and our international allies, and to carry out the military actions with the internal support of the Cuban people and exiles living in the U.S.

The document suggested military intervention in Cuba should not involve The Soviet Union, since Cuba was not part of the Warsaw Pact, and the U.S. had not seen any significant evidence of a connection between Cuba and The Soviet Union at this time. That changed several months later as soon as Castro became aware of a potential U.S. invasion.

There were 32 specific plans that were considered under Operation Mongoose. Some were already being implemented, and all varied in many directions, but the primary purpose was to effectively disrupt the Cuban government and economy, including destruction of Cuban sugar crops and mining of harbors.

On February 20, 1962, three days after we arrived in Miami, a schedule of events was presented by U.S. Brigadier General Edward Landsdale and overseen by Attorney General Robert Kennedy. His brother, President Kennedy, was briefed on the guidelines a month later. The outline included a program of political, psychological, military, sabotage, and intelligence operations, including assassination attempts on key political leaders through October 1962.

Every month, a different event was to be implemented to destabilize the regime and slowly defeat Castro. Some of the details included the publication of anti-Castro political propaganda, armaments for militant opposition groups, the establishment of guerrilla bases throughout the country, and preparations for an October 1962 military intervention. Many plans were designed by the C.I.A. to assassinate Castro, but none were successful. It seemed that Castro was always tipped off and evaded any assassination attempts.

Learning about Operation Mongoose years after it was officially authorized by President Kennedy confirmed the rumors we were all hearing in Cuba shortly before and after we left in February 1962. If we had heard these rumors throughout the community and on Swan Radio, I am certain the Castro regime was more familiar with the details than the C.I.A. may have expected. Perhaps this is the reason why Castro's assassination was never successful. Many believed that he might have outsmarted the C.I.A.

If we were able to confirm all this information while we were living on the Florida City campus, our lives there would have been more difficult, especially being away from our parents. Knowing that serious military actions were being planned by the U.S.

towards Cuba would have been difficult to ignore. I am sure the staff at Operation Pedro Pan would have had difficulties consoling the hundreds of kids on the crowed campus who still had families back in Cuba.

****

After a leisurely day of enjoying our new surroundings and meeting new friends, it was now time for our first dinner, so we walked to the tent, again, with Manolo and Manuel. There, we met other boys at our table and talked about our lives in Cuba and about our families we left behind. It seemed that most of the kids we met were new to the campus. Nobody seemed to have been there for more than one or two months. Everyone at our table was helpful in updating us on the rules and regulations and school activities that would begin for us tomorrow.

As with any introductory conversation between kids our age, some of them warned us about associating with a group of kids that were always getting into trouble. One of them pointed in the direction of a table and advised us to never sit with that group. Having this many kids in an overcrowded and confined location is bound to generate some trouble. I had no reason to get involved. My brother and I were smart enough to stay away from trouble and mind our own business.

After dinner on Sundays was usually time for movie night. A small screen and projector were brought into the tent for the kids to sit around anywhere we could find and watch a Hollywood flick. On this night, we sat on the ground near the screen. I was tired and did not understand most of the movie since it was all in English (without subtitles). I slept through the boring parts, which was most of the movie.

Now it was time to walk back to our house and get ready for bed and our first day tomorrow in a U.S. classroom. It was a peaceful and calming experience today compared to the stressful day Segundito and I, and others, experienced yesterday.

A New Home - 1962

CHAPTER 21

Reflecting at Sea
2018

Nothing can be more relaxing than sailing on a beautiful sunny day, sitting in a lounge chair, adult beverage in hand, looking out at the sea with a mountainous coast on the horizon. Thoughts tend to move through your head at record speeds. There's lots of chatter from others surrounding you, but you don't hear a word. It's hypnotizing, reflecting at sea.

We were on the ship for another day at sea before we reach Cienfuegos and Trinidad on Christmas Eve for a two-day visit. Being at sea for the day gave the four of us an opportunity to relax by the pool, enjoy the views of the Southern Cuban coast, and recall and share our impressions of what each of us had experienced so far in Cuba. We had conversations about our individual knowledge of Castro's Cuban revolution, what we learned in school, and our own personal recollections of the events that changed everyone's lives in Cuba. I obviously had more personal experience, but I was curious about the knowledge others had about what was happening in my home country on that famous New Year's Day in 1959 and during the years that followed.

We were all disheartened by the deterioration of the classical Spanish architecture and the level of poverty everywhere we visited. Castro had always blamed the U.S. embargo for the economic conditions, but his actions of nationalizing foreign property shortly after he took control of the country was not considered a positive diplomatic act. What did he expect the U.S. government would do? Tie a bow around every company and asset he confiscated from the U.S. and hand them over to him with a smile? Ironically (but mostly sadly), many of the foreign businesses he nationalized collapsed within a few years.

His desire to protect himself and the country by courting a relationship with the Soviet bloc proved to be a strategic mistake. The Soviet Union ended up having serious economic and political issues of their own. That, combined with a complete collapse of faith from their citizenry, led them to dissolve in the mid-1980s. When that happened, the badly needed economic support of the Soviets ceased and Cuba's economy went into a tailspin. The same experience repeated itself following Cuba's relationship with Venezuela, which had also provided the country with financial support until the collapse of the Venezuelan oil market.

The past 50-60 years of Cuban history prove that Fidel Castro made many huge political and economic miscalculations to which he would never admit – always blaming someone else for the deterioration and economic collapse of Cuba. It is worth repeating that history has demonstrated that it is not unusual for egotistical political or business leaders with a domineering personality and overpowering aggressiveness to ignore advice from experts nor learn from their own mistakes. Castro and many other failed leaders like him take great pride in letting people know they are smarter than anyone else that surrounds them. They never trust anyone and probably sleep with one eye open.

Reflecting at Sea - 2018

In retrospect, Fidel Castro's strength was mostly in his ability to convince his followers of his lies and protecting his own skin from assassination attempts. Yes, there was a lot of corruption during Batista's reign and those of his predecessors, but Castro's turning Cuba into a complete socialist/communist state plus biting the (U.S.) hand that fed the country was the nail in the coffin and the noose for Cuba and its people.

The four of us reached a consensus on the international political and economic effects of Castro's policies. We also agreed how he could have handled the events during the first 3-4 years of his administration to achieve a much better relationship with the U.S. and the rest of the world. As long as Cuba is not free and democratic, we couldn't see life improving on the island.

The people of Cuba would like nothing more than to live a normal life and be given the opportunity to become economically secure. That is not too much to ask – It is what all of us want in our lives. The conservative political stance from the original Cuban exile group living mostly in and around Miami has steadfastly been against lifting trade embargoes or establishing any normal relationship whatsoever with Cuba. Many politicians cater to this powerful voting group and, therefore, the embargoes continue. The four of us agreed that this is the primary cause for Cuba's poverty and poor economic conditions. Choking the people of Cuba will not return the country to a democratic state. It hasn't worked for more than 50 years, and it will not work for the next 50. These policies are only hurting the Cuban people, not the leadership.

A younger generation of Cuban Americans is developing more open, more democratic opinions for future U.S./Cuba relations. We need to admit that the U.S. policies have done nothing to improve relations or restore the country to democracy. You can't help but conclude that these policies only created a greater distance between the two countries and, more importantly, increased suffering for the Cuban people. Unfortunately, the actions of the Cuban government towards their own people and within the international community over the past decades makes them untrustworthy.

Reflecting at Sea - 2018

How does a government change its image? Perhaps for Cuba the only way is to change the government, change its leadership. That requires the people living in Cuba to demand and force change. Based on past abuses by the government towards people who wish for a better life, it is difficult to imagine and highly unlikely that there will be another successful internal revolution in Cuba anytime soon. I hope I am wrong but that is the only way Cuba will return to economic strength in the Americas.

****

The sun was now setting in the western Caribbean, dipping into the sea again. It was time for our regular early evening visit with friends at the martini bar, followed by a relaxed dinner in the main dining room. Tonight, the four of us would end the evening with a show in the ship's main theatre. I was hoping it would be a lively production that wouldn't put me to sleep, I was wrong.

I love days at sea because they give us the time to relax, enjoy the services the ship provides, and recharge our mental and physical batteries. It also gives me the opportunity to go through my photographs, select the best, adjust them, and set aside some for potential future art exhibits or books.

****

Arthur and I were up early the next morning after a long night of drinks, food, and entertainment. It was time to visit the gym again to work off some of the extra calories we consumed since we began our cruise. I was on a cross-trainer machine staring directly towards the bow of the ship, facing west. I began to see the dull light from the sun rise in the eastern sky. We approached another narrow inlet to the Bahia de Cienfuegos. We could see the pilot boat approaching the ship to drop off the harbor pilot and guide us through the channel and over to the dock.

At the mouth of the inlet, there was the small, quaint fishing village of Jagua on the port side of the ship, which looked more like a Hollywood set than an actual village. There was an impressive castle situated on a small hill at the entrance by the water which I am sure was used at one point to protect the city from pirate invasions. We passed the narrow channel and, once again, like in Santiago de Cuba, there was a huge bay surrounded by lush, deep green tropical foliage. At the northeastern end of the bay, in the distance, we could see the city of Cienfuegos. It was another dramatic harbor entrance.

We were scheduled to be in the port of Cienfuegos for two days. Today, the four of us would board a tour bus for an hour and a half ride to visit the city of Trinidad. I am not a fan of crowded tour buses, so I would probably choose to close my eyes and sleep the entire way to Trinidad. I considered hiring a private cab to take me there instead of riding on a bus full of tourists. I am capable of trying anything to avoid a crowded bus.

CHAPTER 22

A New Life
1962

I woke up several times in the middle of my second night in the U.S. feeling lost, not knowing where I was, and wondered if my new life in a new country would be permanent or temporary. What would happen to us if our parents were not allowed to leave Cuba? Would this new life get better over time? Would I get stronger as time passes? I thought about how I would feel in a year.

It was peculiar to be in unfamiliar surroundings without the reassurance that my parents were in the room next to ours. I was 8 years old and telling myself, while lying in bed, that I needed to be more independent, confident, and self-assured to survive. I was no longer a child, and I was only going to make it through if I learned to act and respond more like an adult. I left my childhood behind when we left La Habana two days ago. It was important for me to understand this change in my life and accept it. Fighting it would only make matters worse.

It was time to get out of bed and get ready for our first day of school in the U.S. It was odd not hearing directives from my mother as it would be on a normal school morning. Today was different; we had to follow our own instincts without supervision. We just had to concentrate and make sure we did everything we were supposed to do before walking out the front door. It was time to act and respond like an adult.

We were on our way out for a short walk to the tent for breakfast followed by school in the same location. Suddenly, I realized that unlike in La Habana, I didn't need any warnings from anyone about discussing politics with schoolmates. I should not be expecting a socialist/communist curriculum in school. There would be no teachers dressed in revolutionary army green outfits and matching berets. I wouldn't get interrogated when I returned home about any new socialist/communist lessons introduced during class today. Our first day would be like a return to our normal school days before the revolution.

Classes started in the tent after a quick breakfast but because it was our first school day in Florida City, we had to wait to register and get assigned to a class by a woman who was pretending to be too important for her job. It was obvious she was not happy with her assignment. She was extremely disorganized and frustrated by the number of children who needed directions to a class. *"No es mi culpa;"* (Not my fault,) I wanted to say to her.

Designating the students to a class should have been simple – It was only based on age and which class could squeeze in more students. Unfortunately, all the teachers were complaining they had too many students in their class and tried to reject new additions. There was nothing they could do; space was limited and no one should be left out. No matter how crowded the space may have appeared, there was always room for one more. I was disappointed to see so many angry adults arguing with each other instead of trying to find a solution that worked for them and, more importantly, for the students.

A New Life - 1962

There must have been at least eight to ten separate classes spread around the perimeter of the tent, each with about 20 to 30 kids. There were no walls in between, which created a constant noise level and made it impossible to hear anything clearly. Every class had a designated instructor, a blackboard on wheels, and only about half the number of chairs needed for everyone to have their own place to sit. The rest of us sat on the floor. After a few days we realized it would be wise for us to arrive early and get a place to sit near the front of the class so we could hear the instructor.

On our first day, we were given a booklet with blank pages to take notes, and a small plastic container with a couple of pencils, a small pencil sharpener, and an eraser. School books were nowhere in sight but I did get some loose sheets of paper with math equations printed on them and another set with basic English phrases and translations in Spanish. I wasn't concerned. It didn't matter. I was still better off with what was in front of me than with what I was getting in Cuba just before we left.

I felt sorry for the instructor assigned to my class, Señora Ana, who was obviously frustrated by the size of her class, the lack of seating, and the minimal learning tools that were available. She was determined to provide us with an education no matter what it took. Every day, new students arrived to class. Every day, some left the campus because their parents or other family members arrived from Cuba or they were relocated to foster homes or orphanages around the country. It was almost impossible for the teacher to follow a specific teaching program when her students came in and out of the classrooms like a revolving door. Perhaps the primary objective here was just to keep the kids busy by feeding them as much information as they could absorb. At the very least, the classes provided us with basic mathematics lessons, an introduction to the English language, and some fundamental knowledge about U.S. history and the government's structure. There wasn't much more we could expect at this time.

When you have an overly populated student campus, it is expected that some unpleasant incidents will occur by a select group of troublemakers. One of the kids from the group that was pointed out to us on Sunday began a fight with another kid sitting on the floor in the class next to ours. At first, it was just the two of them. While the instructors were trying to separate them, others joined the rebellion. What was most likely a minor disagreement turned into a free-for-all where friends from both sides joined in until more teachers got involved and separated everyone. A few bloody lips and some black eyes resulted from the rumble. The group of fighters got removed from the tent, and we returned to normal as if nothing had happened. I remember asking one of my classmates, as the kids were being escorted outside, if the campus had jail cells. He did not know. I don't believe they were sent back to Cuba as punishment.

****

News of anything that was happening in Cuba while we were living in Florida City was mostly minimal and usually came from rumors or discussions kids would have with their house supervisors. Later in life, I found out that around this time, U.S. government officials were still continuing to secretly review Operation Mongoose and believed that time was running out to pull off the secret operation. They concluded that the Cuban people were beginning to feel helpless and losing hope very fast. Cubans were searching for optimistic information with more reports of internal and external resistance and a sign that these endeavors were beginning to work towards overthrowing the Castro regime. Ramped-up efforts were requested from all agencies and departments that were assigned to Operation Mongoose.

A classified intelligence report by the C.I.A., which became public information years after we arrived in Florida City, showed that although roughly only a quarter of the Cuban population stood behind the Castro regime, the rest of the population was both disaffected and passive. Those that were passive had given up and accepted the present regime as the government in power. This is what always happens when a significant portion of any country's population is not involved or not interested in the political process or in electing its leadership. *"Deja que alguien más se preocupe por eso ..."* (Let somebody else worry about it ...) was their attitude until decisions began to affect their personal daily lives. Then they asked themselves, *"¿Cómo pudo pasar esto a nosotros?"* (How could this happen to us?)

The report also indicated that an internal revolt within Cuba was highly unlikely on its own. Some of the U.S. government officials criticized the handling of Operation Mongoose and believed that U.S. national policy was too cautious. During the review, a suggestion was made for the U.S. military to train more guerrillas for another eventual invasion. Late in March 1962, a large-scale amphibious landing military exercise was conducted off the coast of North Carolina.

A group of C.I.A. and U.S. military leaders provided more specific plans in early March 1962 for the first phase of Operation Mongoose. The primary objective of this phase was to gather hard intelligence and participate in or support political, economic, and covert actions that would set the stage for another revolution in Cuba. They would be prepared to pull away with minimal loss of assets and U.S. prestige and continue planning for a decisive U.S. intervention in October 1962, approximately seven months from then.

We obviously did not have any idea that all this planning was being done just a few miles from our campus. Rumors throughout the campus continued daily about a potential U.S. military intervention, but these rumors were all unsubstantiated and we felt that some were perhaps overly exaggerated. Today, I feel that the leadership at the campus in Florida City was trying to keep the kids away from political news concerning Cuba and rumors about what was happening. They wanted to create a positive and healthy atmosphere and avoid the obvious chaos that could occur with concerned children whose parents and other family members were still in Cuba. My brother and I agreed that there was no reason for

A New Life - 1962

us to get agitated and worried about the rumors that were being spread around the campus. Rumors can only cause more heartache, and most of them were undocumented and not believable. We just needed to be patient and calm, mind our own business, and ignore many of those claims.

****

After our first day of school ended, we were asked to go to the administrative building to fill out some required paperwork. Many of the kids who had arrived on Saturday and Sunday were there in line for the same reason. We finally got to sit with Maria, one of the administrators who asked us some basic questions about ourselves, our family and our health. They also needed information about our parents and Jorge so their departure from Cuba could be expedited. During the interview, the administrator advised us that the Florida City campus was just a temporary home and, due to the increasing population of kids leaving Cuba and the crowded conditions of the campus, we were being considered for relocation to another facility in the U.S. that was run by the Catholic Church and would provide a better educational environment. She showed us pictures of potential facilities and we agreed to consider our options if a good opportunity became available. The educational benefit alone would be great to us since all the facilities were run by the Catholic Church and none of the schools were considered facilities for delinquent kids.

We left the administration center with a feeling of discomfort at the thought of having to move again so soon. Though, it could be an easy move since we had no personal ties to anyone in Miami. The only people we knew who lived in the area were Susana, Freddy, and their daughter who we had just met for the first time Saturday morning. My concern centered around being placed in a remote location and attending a new school where nobody could speak Spanish to us while we tried to learn English. Segundito and

I decided to consider an offer when it was presented to us, but to avoid worrying about deciding to relocate at this time.

While living in Florida City, we became friendly with several kids in the campus. Almost daily, one of our new friends would tell us that they were given notice to relocate to another facility. I began to feel the same way I did in La Habana when my school and neighborhood friends disappeared overnight. We also learned from many of them that the relocation was not necessarily an option. The administrators were very convincing that the move would be in their best interest and promised them a better education until they were able to reunite with their parents. I began to realize that once they found us a facility that would take the two of us, we basically had very little input, if any, and we would have to go. The thought of moving further away from our parents to a strictly English-speaking school frightened me and lingered in my mind. It was only fear of the unknown.

The following Sunday, Freddy and Susana came to the campus to visit us, take us out for a ride, and treat us to lunch. I was sure to warn them several times that we had to be back to the campus by 4:00 p.m. Because of our experience at the airport when we arrived, I wasn't sure they would let us back inside if we were late. Perhaps I was being overly cautious and a bit dramatic. During the car ride, they told us they had spoken on the phone with our parents and assured them that we were happy in our new surroundings. They also suggested that the following week they would take us to their home during visitors' day where we could call them directly and spend time talking to them. I could not wait until the week passed.

Still thinking about our discussion with Maria the administrator earlier in the week, we asked Susana and Freddy their opinion about the relocation opportunities being suggested. Without any hesitation, both seemed to agree with the recommendations and were confident that if the school was run by the Catholic Church, it would be a great educational opportunity for both of us and perhaps a better living environment. I still had some concerns – perhaps it was just the fear of another move. It was difficult to consider only

A New Life - 1962

the educational benefits and not give some thought to the living arrangements and the lack of Spanish-speaking friends.

****

Freddy and Susana returned to the campus the following week, picked us up early in the morning, and drove us to their home in Miami for lunch and, eventually, a phone call to our parents in Cuba. Shortly after we arrived at their home, Susana made arrangements with an international operator for a direct call to Cuba. A few minutes later the house phone rang – it was the first time since we left Cuba that we heard our parents' voices. It was great to speak with them. An emotional moment, but I forced myself to hold back any tears throughout the entire conversation and tried to give them assurance that we were both happy and we were looking forward to being reunited soon. We were able to chat with them for almost a half hour and updated them about a potential move to a better facility run by the Catholic Church at another location in the U.S. Susana got on the phone with them to reassure them it would be a positive opportunity for us – they concurred. After saying goodbye on the phone and promising to call back when we had more information on a move to another school, I placed the receiver down and hung up.

There was an eerie silence in the house after the phone call ended. Nobody knew what to say. We were all feeling the same sadness and awkwardness of not knowing what to do or say. I was already missing their voices.

A New Life - 1962

CHAPTER 23

Moving Again
1962

Simple and predictable. That's how I would describe our first couple of weeks in Florida City. It was somewhat comforting to know that all the kids there had the same experience leaving Cuba. Everyone was missing their parents. We were not alone, and that was reassuring.

Mondays through Fridays we were in school until mid-afternoon. After school and before dinner, we enjoyed spending time with new friends. We always tried to find a spot somewhere on the campus to sit and chat. One of the kids in our house owned a small transistor radio that was given to him as a gift by a friend of his family who visited him. If he joined us, we would listen to music or the latest news in Spanish transmitted from a Miami-based radio station.

All the houses on the campus were crowded with bunk beds, and ours was no exception. There was little if any room inside for couches or chairs. If we stayed inside, the only place to sit was on our beds. Outside of our front door, there was a small patio with several outdoor tables and chairs that were always occupied whenever the hot Florida sun was not beating down on that side of the house.

After classes were over for the day, the campus staff would set up a couple of ping-pong tables inside the tent, and kids would gather around to organize tournaments before dinner. The volleyball court was always busy after school, and baseball teams would coordinate their time on the baseball field. There was also a small basketball court near the entrance to the campus that always had a group of kids playing during our free time. There were plenty of extracurricular activities to participate in after school. Anyone could be part of them, sit and watch, or walk freely around the campus and socialize with friends. It was important to encourage the kids to go outside of their dorms since the interiors were very congested.

While some of the kids played baseball, volleyball, and other sports, we enjoyed just sitting on the sidelines like spectators and fans. Or we would sit somewhere around the campus to relax with new friends. Sometimes, we would find a picnic table next to the administration center and take turns playing games, including checkers and tic-tac-toe. From that same table, we were able to periodically see the transportation vans pulling into the driveway filled with new Pedro Pan kids as they were escorted into the building and given house assignments. The frightened looks on their faces as they exited the vans were the same as ours when we arrived a couple of weeks ago. There was nothing we could say to make them more comfortable besides a friendly greeting of, *"Bienvenidos amigos a los Estados Unidos"* (Welcome my friends to The United States.) We had firsthand knowledge of how they were feeling, and we wanted to say something that would make them feel welcome. It would have been difficult to try to explain

Moving Again - 1962

to them that time will help heal their wounds – You just have to experience that yourself.

The population at the Florida City campus was growing every week. Just over 14,000 Operation Pedro Pan kids left Cuban soil between January 1960 and October 1962 (the end of the program). Those who could not join relatives in Miami were placed in one of these campuses. All the Pedro Pan housing facilities in the Miami area were run by the Catholic Church and supported by corporate and individual donations. There was little, if any, federal funding used for Operation Pedro Pan. The U.S. government allowed the Catholic Church to use the Florida City campus for the program, which was empty military housing at the time. The number of kids arriving in Miami from Cuba averaged approximately 100 per week. During the beginning of the operation, the average was much smaller. As the popularity of the program increased in Cuba and more families became aware of it, the numbers grew, especially during the final 10 months of the program.

It was difficult to live in these crowded conditions but we knew the alternative could have been worse. We had to adapt and make the best of the situation. My brother and I will always remember the heroic efforts of the Catholic Church and the staff at the campus to provide a clean home with supervision, food, recreational activities, and some schooling. Children leaving Cuba without their parents needed comforting and assurance that the decision to leave was in their best interest and that they would soon be reunited with their parents. The administrators, staff, and house supervisors at the campus did everything in their power to provide the best possible living conditions under the circumstances. We were grateful. I'm sure many of the other Pedro Pan kids felt the same as we did.

****

Almost daily, someone we knew was given notice to transfer to another school or a foster home. Within a few days, they were on a plane and off to a new location. We lost track of many kids we

Moving Again - 1962

met at the Florida City campus because none of us had a permanent mailing address, so it would have been impossible to remain friends and communicate by mail. We never heard from any of these kids once they left, and always wondered what their experiences were like. Today, social media has helped united some of us, but after 60 years, since the beginning of the exodus, it is difficult to remember names and faces.

Someone on campus once joked that the transfer to another facility or foster home was only a smokescreen. They suggested that the kids who left were sent back to Cuba to do hard labor on the farms! That was not an appropriate joke to tell kids who were worried about moving again. Unfortunately, sometimes I was a bit gullible and wondered if it was true or partially true. The joke remained in my mind longer than it should have. There is always a prankster in every group.

You could feel the campus getting crowded. The need to send more kids to other facilities was obvious as the incoming flow of children increased dramatically over the short time we were there. Each house had reached maximum capacity or was very close to it. You could not bring another bunk bed into our dorm, so the only way to make room for the incoming kids was to transfer more kids to other locations. In some homes, siblings were asked to share a twin bed. Even the facilities for education and recreation were insufficient and strained for the number of Pedro Pan residents. We knew our time here in Florida City was going to be limited. We saw the writing on the walls.

****

About three weeks after arriving at the campus, we found a note on Segundito's bed asking us to stop by the administration office. I strongly suspected that the purpose of the meeting would most likely be to encourage us to leave for another facility somewhere in the U.S. The following day, after school, we both walked into the office and were greeted by Maria, the same lady we had met when

Moving Again - 1962

we initially registered. She told us she had "great" news because she was able to get us and two other brothers into an excellent facility just outside New York City. We could stay there, attend school, learn English, and as soon as our parents arrived, we would be reunited with them quickly. Later in the day, we found that the two brothers were Manolo and Manuel who we knew from the first day we arrived.

Maria proceeded to show us pictures of St. Agnes Home and School for Boys and assured us we would be more comfortable there and would most likely have the opportunity to visit New York City during field trips the school would organize. I looked directly at her and said: *¿No hace frío en Nueva York ahora?* (Isn't it cold in New York now?) She acknowledged it was cold but she promised to provide us with winter coats and sweaters before we departed. *"Ah, te acostumbrarás. Todos lo hacen eventualmente."* (Ah, you will get used to it. Everyone does eventually.)

St. Agnes Home and School for Boys was founded and operated by the Dominican Sisters in Sparkill, NY around 1884. It was located just north of New York City, about a half hour drive from Times Square, assuming there was no traffic. The pictures Maria showed us were not very inviting. The campus consisted of several old Victorian/Gothic-styled buildings, including a gloomy looking dormitory with a huge dining room in the basement. There were also some separate buildings. One housed classrooms for all the children, a large chapel, a small hospital/medical center, and a gymnasium. Another building was used as a residence for the nuns. In the middle, between all these buildings, there was a huge open field used for recreational purposes. The buildings and the setting looked like scenes from a Vincent Price horror movie. Maria sensed my disappointment and concern, so she immediately put me in my place. *¿Qué esperabas, vacaciones en un club privado?* (What were you expecting, a vacation at a private club?) Why not?

Perhaps I was being too critical. Segundito was sold on the idea of going to a different school that had more space with better learning opportunities and more comfortable housing. Being close

Moving Again - 1962

to New York City did not seem to be a perk to me but my brother thought the opposite. Before we left the administration office, I was beginning to accept the idea of moving up north. I'm not sure I had much of a choice. There was almost no downside to the decision. We had nothing to lose. If we did not like it or if we were unhappy, we would try to figure out what to do at that point. Meanwhile, we were almost certain that our parents would be allowed to leave soon and therefore we would not be there for a long period of time. I liked the possibility of having Manolo and Manuel join us at the school. At least we would know someone there and could communicate in Spanish. My brother warned me that it was important for us to learn to speak English quickly and moving away from the Florida City campus would help us accelerate that goal.

We only had two days before we boarded another plane. This time, we would go much further north to New York. During those two days we were each given some winter wear such as a heavy coat (mine was missing two buttons) and a couple of sweaters. We made arrangements at the administration office to call our parents in Cuba and also notified Susana and Freddy. Our parents were happy for us after Maria spoke with them on the phone to assure them that the new school would be safe and ideal for our education. Today, I can't imagine my parents' reaction just over 100 miles away from us when we told them we were moving much further north near New York City. They were not able to be with us, and I am sure they were concerned about the decision even though they did not express any negative reactions over the phone. I suppose that is what parents do.

Susana and Freddy were kind and generous when they heard we were relocating. They came to the campus before we left to bring us more clothes. Some were their son Herald's clothes he had outgrown. Other items, like underwear, were just purchased for us. All our new friends at the Florida City campus were excited for us. We were more comfortable about the move after friends encouraged us. Since we knew that our friends Manolo and Manuel would be joining us, we felt the four of us could stick together and protect each other.

Moving Again - 1962

****

The Miami airport was about an hour drive from the Florida City campus. The night before we left, Maria told us the driver insisted on getting an early start to Miami for our morning flight to La Guardia Airport in New York to avoid getting stuck in Miami's rush hour traffic. On the morning of our flight, while everyone else in our room was sleeping, we got out of bed, washed up, and dressed in our custom-made suits so we would again look like those two Wall Street executives who left Cuba and never grew up. Our bags were packed the night before.

As we were heading out the door with Manolo and Manuel to meet the van outside the administration office, our house supervisor Lolita came downstairs to say goodbye. She brought us four small bags with sandwiches and cookies she baked the night before so we would have a snack on the plane. She warned us that she always cried every time she said goodbye to the kids as they left the house for a (hopefully) better life. That morning was no exception. Tears were running down her cheeks as she told us the same lines my mother said when we left Cuba: *"Segúrense de cuidar el uno del otro. Comportanse bien."* (Be sure to take care of each other. Behave yourselves.)

We all boarded the van to the airport with the driver and Maria sitting in the front seat. Our ride there seemed endless as I sat looking out the window and remembering the drive to the airport the morning we left Cuba. Again, I asked myself if this was the right choice for us. Why did I always have second thoughts when it was too late to do anything about it? I was expecting this move to be much smoother than leaving Cuba. I wondered how this day would end. Our flight schedule would allow us to reach St. Agnes before sunset but we had one layover in Washington, D.C. and did not have to change planes.

At the Miami airport, the van parked in an adjacent lot and Maria took us inside the terminal to our designated gate. She introduced us to a flight attendant who took our tickets and pinned an ugly

Moving Again - 1962

ribbon on our lapels with the label, "Child Traveling Alone," which felt like an advertisement to be kidnapped. The flight attendant was responsible for us getting on the plane and provide help, if needed, during the flight to New York. Once we reached La Guardia, she would turn us over to a representative of St. Agnes who would drive us to the school. We were warned not to take the ribbons off our lapels and to be sure they were seen when we arrived in New York. The orchestration sounded more like an exchange of hostages. I was terrified I would get lost in New York and never found again. I did not want a repeat of our experience at the Miami airport when we arrived from Cuba. The "Child Traveling Alone" ribbon was not going to help me if I got lost.

We were finally escorted onto the plane and sat in our designated seats in the first two rows. Segundito and I sat in the front row, and I convinced him to let me sit by the window. Manuel and Manolo sat immediately behind us. I stared outside through the window until the plane lifted off the ground and leveled off above the clouds. I was still frightened about the move but anxious to see our new home. I continued to wonder what the rest of the day would be like.

Moving Again - 1962

CHAPTER 24

Christmas Eve
2018

It was the day before Christmas, December 24, 2018. After a quick breakfast in the ship's main dining room, the four of us went back to our cabins to get ready for what I had convinced myself would be an uneventful ride with a busload of tourists to Trinidad, about an hour and a half drive east of Cienfuegos. I could see from our cabin's verandah the buses beginning to line up and the tour guides and drivers running around getting lists from the ship's staff of passengers going on their separate tours. It seems like complete chaos but by the time we disembark, it is always flawlessly coordinated as long as you pay attention. Unfortunately, there is always be a group getting on the wrong bus because they did not listen. They are usually the passengers who complain the most about the smallest issues.

I began to feel claustrophobic just watching the activity of the buses outside. I am not a good traveler when there is a bus full of tourists involved. That, many of my friends would say, is an understatement. I always find these buses incredibly uncomfortable, with seats designed for children under 10 years old, sound systems that never work, windows that do not open, and air conditioning that blows hot air. The minute I enter this type of setting (especially with a group of nagging tourists), my claustrophobia kicks in and I must close my eyes, pretend I am asleep, and pray that the tour ends soon before I snap at someone. In my effort to understand my claustrophobic condition, I performed a quick search on Google and found the following definition:

> *... a situational phobia triggered by an irrational and intense fear of tight or crowded spaces. It can be triggered by things like being locked in a windowless room, being stuck in a crowded elevator, or driving on a congested highway.*

"Intense fear." Yes, I understand that experience – I will agree. "Irrational," no. There is nothing irrational about my reaction to the bus situation I just described. Perhaps the definition should be revised to read:

> *... the rational condition most likely triggered by a crowded tour bus designed for children 10 years of age, and occupied by cranky, finicky adults acting like unruly 10-year-old kids.*

As we started to disembark and proceed to one of those dreaded buses, I considered backing out of the tour and instead just walking around the town of Cienfuegos by myself. I also considered hiring my own private taxi to take me to Trinidad. Sensing I was having

Christmas Eve - 2018

second thoughts, Arthur looked at me and told me to "get inside the fricking bus and go to sleep." He was way too familiar with my "rational" reaction to tour buses.

Once I climbed inside the bus, my experience was almost the opposite of what I just described above. Roomy seats, a strong air conditioning system, and an excellent sound system. This bus even had its own "head" (nautical term for bathroom). Unfortunately, the tourists were dreadful. I can't blame the bus for the quality of the other passengers. I was impressed by these Cuban (made in North Korea) tour buses.

On our way to Trinidad, we passed by many non-working farms and a few sugar cane and tobacco fields. I did not see anyone working the land or any type of farm equipment anywhere. The tour guide could not provide me with a satisfactory answer as to why there was no activity on these hundreds of acres of farmland. I am still perplexed by this scene. Perhaps a strict socialist/communist environment is not the answer for economic success? It was difficult to understand why the land was not being cultivated and was currently overgrown by weeds. It was sad to see these farms going to waste when there are hungry people living in the cities that surround them. I don't get it.

The scenery from the bus was spectacular. Acres of farmland overgrown with grass and a backdrop of the lush Escambray mountain range that runs through the Gran Parque Natural Topes de Collantes, a national park. The Escambray mountains were used by anti-Batista rebels to hide during the revolution. After Batista fled and Castro took control of Cuba, CIA-sponsored anti-Castro rebels (*bandidos*) hid in the same mountains. Only an hour west of Cienfuegos is Playa Giron, where the exile group who trained in Central America to overthrow the Castro regime landed on April 17, 1961 and were defeated within a few days. Some of them hid in the Escambray mountains for days before they were eventually captured. This area is full of Cuban history.

The town of Trinidad, a four-hour drive from La Habana but only about one and a half hours from where our ship was docked, is a UNESCO World Heritage site since 1988 with a small population of just under 75,000 residents. Its main industry is tobacco processing but the town is well known for its 16th Century colonial architecture and cobblestone streets. The bus stopped around the corner from Plaza Mayor, a neo-baroque main square which is surrounded by grand colonial buildings that have been excellently restored. Next to Plaza Mayor there are a couple of museums and a beautiful 19th Century cathedral, Iglesia de la Santisima, with massive, vaulted ceilings.

I was impressed with the view of the 1500s architecture and 1950s cars trying to get through the uneven cobblestone streets. I could see there was an obvious coordinated restoration effort of buildings that had given the town a distinct colonial personality we didn't see anywhere else in Cuba. Like La Habana Vieja and Santiago de Cuba, there were people mingling around Plaza Mayor, nearby restaurants, and street corners. Again, we could hear traditional Cuban music playing inside the cafés, from the center of Plaza Mayor, and on the steps of the cathedral. It must be enjoyable just to sit in one of these cafés, absorb what is in front of you, and relish the sounds of Cuban music echoing from every corner.

After some obligatory visits to landmark sites with our designated guide, we spent the balance of our time in Trinidad on our own, walking the streets of the old town. Some of my best portrait-style photography was shot in this neighborhood. In the distance, I saw a gentleman with a perfectly manicured beard wearing a straw fedora. He was elegantly dressed in a navy-blue sport jacket, white shirt, tie, dark green slacks, and shiny shoes to match. He was pinned with a large gold brooch on the lapel of his sport jacket and sat by himself on a bench against a bright orange wall. He created a classic scene for a perfect photograph. He looked directly at my camera, no smiles, just a simple pose holding his Cuban cigar. Click. It seemed like everywhere I turned, there was someone ready to pose for pictures (and willing to accept a small monetary compensation). Another resident sat by the entrance to a warehouse with a perfectly ironed blue shirt, sleeves

Christmas Eve - 2018

rolled up to his elbows, a classic straw fedora hat, a cigar in his mouth, and his eyes directed at my camera. Click. Next to him, another gentleman was similarly dressed, resting his elbow on a small birdcage housing a couple of finches. Click. A lady with a pair of sad looking eyes sat behind a railing waiting for her picture to be taken and a dollar bill. Click. This continued for most of our free time in Trinidad.

We walked inside a tourist shop a few blocks from the center of town. Towards the back of the store, there was a door leading to a large outdoor terrace where several Cuban artists were displaying their two- and three-dimensional art works for sale. Further in back of the terrace, between an old shed and an orange tree, I saw a young boy manually turning a homemade spit pierced with a *cochinito* (baby pig). That scene reminded me of Pedrito, the pig we raised in La Habana that was slaughtered by Georgina's father. The young boy was probably the same age I was when Pedrito went to his reward. Suddenly, I realized the importance of the pig on the spit. Today was December 24. It was Christmas Eve and *lechon asado* (roast pig) was the traditional Cuban meal on this day.

The young boy was given the responsibility of manually turning the homemade spit for hours until the pig was golden brown. I photographed him with the pig and spoke with him for a while. He shared some of his family's cooking secrets, providing me with details on how they seasoned the pig, the timing on the spit, the level of heat, the distance of the fire from the pig, etc. I was impressed not only by his culinary knowledge and detailed explanation of the preparation process but also by how he constructed the spit only using tree branches from the tree next to his fire pit. A future Cuban celebrity chef.

To my surprise, he told me his name was Antonio. *"Yo también. Mi nombre es Antonio."* (Me too. My name is Antonio.) I told him that I was born in La Habana but currently lived in The United States and was traveling throughout Cuba for the past several days. I also shared my story of raising a pig in La Habana one year and having it slaughtered for the family to feast on Christmas Eve. His

Christmas Eve - 2018

eyes opened and he told me that he had been feeding this pig for the past 3 months in the shed that was next to the spit. He admitted he was sad to see the pig slaughtered but knew it was important for his family to have a traditional Christmas Eve dinner. The sad look in his eyes told me that he was still regretting the demise of his pet pig. I personally knew the feeling of turning a spit with my pet friend rotating over hot coals. We both stood there and stared at the pig. I needed to get back to the ship soon, so he looked directly at me, shook my hand like an adult, and thanked me for sharing my story with him. I responded graciously, *"Gracias por compartir la historia de tu cochinito también."* (Thank you for sharing the story of your pig also.)

Antonio seemed like a special young man – very confident about himself, friendly to strangers, and a hard worker. I would have loved to stay there for dinner that night and would even pay the family for the entire cost of the pig and whatever else was on the menu. That was not realistic, just a dream. I gave Antonio a $5 bill and wished him *"Feliz Navidad"* (Merry Christmas). He took the bill, did not look to see the denomination, shoved it in his pocket, and said, *"Gracias amigo."* (Thank you, my friend.)

We continued with our walk back to the center of town where the bus would meet us and take us back to the ship. The skies were getting darker, and the wind was picking up and blowing through the wet and slippery cobblestone streets. There were less people out; it looked like most of the tourists had left the town and the remaining residents had retreated to their homes. There was a mysterious feeling walking through the lonely streets. The streetlamps were beginning to light and cast shadows on the street. A passing shower created a glossy surface on the ground. People walked in the street between the cars and mule cart traffic because the sidewalks were only wide enough for anyone to fit single file. The lights inside the homes were beginning to reflect on the wet sidewalks and cobblestone streets. I looked inside the homes and saw many of them with minimal if any Christmas decorations and simple furnishings. Some had televisions, others had radios turned on high volume. All were preparing for their Christmas Eve dinner.

Christmas Eve - 2018

We reached Plaza Mayor in the center of town and found our bus. As we boarded, I took one last look at the Plaza and surrounding structures. I was pleasantly surprised by the ongoing restoration efforts and the personal charm of this historic town. Inside the bus, I took a quick look at my camera screen to see the photographs I shot today. I noticed the fashion of the residents matched the style of the town: Simple but elegant and neat. You could tell the residents were proud of their hometown.

The bus was finally departing after a quick headcount to make sure nobody was left behind. There is always that last tourist still in a trinket shop trying to decide what to buy. We were heading back to Cienfuegos. The farms we saw on the way to Trinidad were now shaded by the mountain range and more difficult to view because the late afternoon sunlight between the clouds created a silhouette of the Escambray mountains. It was a beautiful, picturesque scene to remember. A memorable and pleasant day in Trinidad.

Christmas Eve - 2018

CHAPTER 25

Welcome to New York
1962

It was an unusual feeling that came over me when I got on the plane in Miami not knowing much about our final destination. I felt I was walking into a dark room unable to see what was in front of me. I had no ability to turn around. It was a fear of the unknown. In time, I was certain that the lights would be turned on for all of us to see.

The flight to New York was obviously going to take much longer than the flight from La Habana to Miami. In addition to the distance, we were scheduled to make a one-hour stop in Washington, D.C., which would get us to La Guardia airport sometime late in the afternoon. Sitting in my window seat, I tried to talk myself out of the worries of moving to a new location and a climate I had never experienced. We were given proper winter clothing before we left Florida City but somehow, I still felt unprepared. How long would we have to live there before our parents were able to leave Cuba? Nobody could give us that answer.

The view from the airplane's window was just white puffy clouds below the plane. There was not much we could do to entertain ourselves and make the time pass. There was an elegantly dressed lady with a beautiful smile and a Jackie Kennedy pillbox hat sitting next to Segundito on the aisle seat. She spoke very little Spanish, and Segundito spoke very little English. Somehow, they managed to communicate, so I turned on my eavesdropping skills during their awkward conversations. She said her name was Isabelle and asked us where we were going and why we were traveling alone. The flight attendant stepped in and explained to her that we were part of Operation Pedro Pan, our parents were still in Cuba, and we were being relocated to an orphanage just north of New York City until our parents were able to leave the country and join us. Isabelle told us she had a winter home in Miami Beach but lived the rest of the time in New Jersey, close to New York City. She showed us pictures of her two sons and a daughter, all three grown up and living on their own.

Between a mixture of English, Spanish, and an occasional use of sign language (a.k.a. Spanglish), we managed to somehow converse with Isabelle. She expressed interest in our well-being and urged us to call on her at her home if we needed anything or had any problems at the orphanage. She also wanted to visit us there once we got settled into school, so she gave us a note card with her full name and telephone number. I was touched by her kindness and generosity and would have felt comfortable calling her after we got settled into our new home. Her sincere interest in us and desire to make sure we were comfortable when we arrived was heartwarming and made me feel better about this move. Sometimes, that is all it takes to release your worries, the kindness of a stranger and sincere concern for one another.

Lunch was now being served on the plane – macaroni and cheese, a typical American meal, but foreign to me at the time.

Welcome to New York - 1962

Where was the *"pollo con arroz y frijoles"* (chicken with rice and beans)? As I was trying to finish up my lunch, the plane was beginning to hit air pockets, which made me spill some of that macaroni and cheese on my new suit. Segundito, who felt the need to act like a parent, insisted on cleaning the mess on my pants with his napkin dipped in his glass of water. That's what older brothers do for their younger siblings.

I finished my lunch just as the turbulence increased and the plane began to shake uncontrollably. Flight attendants removed all the trays, and I suddenly began to feel sick to my stomach, a sensation I could not avoid. Segundito said my face had turned pale and I could hear my stomach making noises I had never heard before. Isabelle rushed to get an air sickness bag from the pocket in front of her and gave it to me. I did not know what she wanted me to do with the bag, so she demonstrated in a quick version of sign language, and I followed her instructions. I grabbed the bag, brought it close to my mouth, and proceeded to vomit in the bag. The food combined with the shaking plane was enough to make me lose my lunch. My ego was deflated. It was not a pleasant feeling considering I was sitting on a plane dressed in a suit trying to act like an adult. I was just happy I did not get any more food on my suit. It was time to rest. The flight attendant came to pick up the bag and brought me a glass of club soda to settle my stomach. I closed my eyes and pretended to sleep but continued to listen to Segundito's conversation with Isabelle and continued to imagine what we would experience once we arrived at our new home.

Getting ready for landing in Washington, D.C., I looked out of my window again and, as we broke through those puffy clouds, I began to see a large city with houses, roads, and cars. It was now a dark and gray sky above us, and the view below was equally dark and gray. Some of the grassy areas were lightly covered with snow. In the distance, I could see the Capitol building similar in size and style to El Capitolio in La Habana. There were lots of green parks surrounding beautiful buildings that I suspected must have been used for official government business.

Welcome to New York - 1962

The plane made a U-turn and, within a couple of minutes, I could hear the wheels being lowered from the belly. Before I realized what was going to happen, the plane landed on the tarmac.

We were now in Washington, D.C. The flight attendant told us not to leave the plane, this was not our final destination. She kept looking at us to make sure we did not leave our seats. Did she really think we would try to escape? Where would we go? It would have been fun to do a day tour of the city – perhaps another time. Isabelle remained in her seat also since she was traveling all the way to New York City like us. She was relentless trying to learn more about us and kept asking about our family back home. Did we miss them? Did they know we were relocating to New York? When did we expect them to join us? It was a bit awkward trying to have a conversation with Isabelle because of the language constraints but Segundito and I enjoyed trying to communicate with her, and her interest in us made us more comfortable and secure.

****

We were back up in the air. Just as I heard the wheels fold into the belly of the plane, I could again see the U.S. Capital building and various monuments scattered through a large park in the distance. Some areas were green, others were dusted with light snow. The skies were still dark and gray, and now rain was hitting my window. In just a few minutes, the plane climbed over the clouds and the sky turned bright and clear again. As soon as we were allowed to remove our seatbelt, I got up and turned around to check on Manuel and Manolo who were both very quiet and sitting directly behind us. I think they were equally frightened about the move to St. Agnes. Isabelle introduced herself but it was not easy to have a conversation with the boys seated behind us. Soon enough, we would be landing at La Guardia. I hoped someone would meet us at the airport and take us to St. Agnes. I was afraid we would be stranded at the airport in New York.

Welcome to New York - 1962

****

We were preparing for landing and were instructed to buckle up again. I could see in the distance the skyline of New York City. What an impressive view from the plane. Shortly thereafter, the wheels hit the tarmac again. This time, everything around us was either wet or covered with snow or ice. It was sleeting (a mixture of ice and snow), which I had never seen before. The airport personnel, dressed in bright yellow raincoats, were directing the plane towards the terminal. Some of the vehicles on the tarmac were covered with ice and snow, and the airport personnel were scraping the windshields of their vehicles. The doors opened, and the flight attendant asked us to wait until all the passengers left the plane. At this point, we said goodbye to Isabelle, and she reminded us to make sure we called her at home when we got settled at the school. The plane was now empty. With several umbrellas, we were escorted down the stairs and into the building. As soon as I got outside of the plane, I felt my lungs fill with that cold and damp Northeast winter air. It was a shock to my Cuban lungs. My face was cold, and my ears began to sting. Welcome to New York!

Once inside the terminal, we walked with the flight attendant to a designated section to pick up our luggage. As we waited to retrieve our bags, an older gentleman with a young man in his early teens approached the flight attendant. They spoke to her and each exchanged envelopes with some type of paperwork they examined and folded back inside. The flight attendant turned to us and told us the gentlemen would take us to St. Agnes. She said goodbye and wished us well. Her mission: accomplished. The exchange of the hostages was complete. The young man with the driver spoke Spanish, so we were able to communicate more with him than with the driver. We gathered our luggage and quickly walked outside to a parking lot where their vehicle was parked. Once again, my lungs filled with this uncomfortably cold and damp air. It was still raining very hard, and I could feel snow and sleet landing on my head and shoulders. Once we got inside the large station wagon,

Welcome to New York - 1962

the car heater was turned on and in a few minutes the air felt warm enough that I could remove my coat with the two missing buttons.

The car ride to St Agnes was relatively quiet. The driver and the young man, who introduced himself as Marco, sat in the front seat with Manolo. Segundito, Manuel, and I sat in the back seat. Our luggage was in the rear of the station wagon. The view outside could not have been gloomier. The traffic, in typical New York fashion, was gridlocked – barely moving. The only enjoyable moment was the experience of crossing the George Washington Bridge. We were on the upper deck, and the view of the city behind us with a light fog hovering over the tops of the buildings was a truly amazing site for me to see. I had never visited a city this large – I was overwhelmed. The buildings were all extremely close to each other and very tall.

Marco told us more about St. Agnes and assured us we would love living there. He explained that the living accommodations in the dormitory were segregated by age group. I stopped him immediately and asked if Segundito and I would be separated. Because we were three years apart, we would not be in the same building. The same applied to Manolo and Manuel. That was not what I wanted to hear. We asked how many others spoke Spanish at the school. He warned us that only one or two nuns spoke some Spanish and that there were two other Pedro Pan kids that arrived a month or two ago. Besides that, he was not certain if anyone else spoke Spanish. I was looking out the window at this point and saw cold, dark gray skies and wetness all around. I asked myself, "How do I get out of this situation?"

The rain and sleet was still coming down hard. The pavement was wet, and snow accumulated on top of the cars and lightly over grassy sections. As we got closer to the town of Sparkill, our new hometown, there was more snow on the ground. It was getting darker outside and the traffic was not getting any better. Segundito noticed that I was feeling distressed and said to me, *"No te preocupes, todo saldrá bien."* (Don't worry, everything will turn out fine.) There wasn't very much of what Marco was explaining

Welcome to New York - 1962

about the campus that I liked – actually, there was nothing he said that I liked. It sounded like a prison facility run by strict nuns who could substitute for drill sergeants. In fact, it sounded more like a facility for troubled orphaned New York boys who could not be placed in foster care due to behavioral issues. I had the urge to reach for my luggage in the back, open the car door, and make a run for it while we were stopped in traffic. I would have found shelter somewhere or spent the night homeless. At the time, that sounded like a better situation. Maybe we could call Isabelle and have her pick us up. I knew I was being unrealistic. Yes, I eventually calmed down and decided not to make any judgment until we arrived, had a chance to get settled, and taken a few days to get used to our new surroundings.

It took the driver over two hours to arrive at St. Agnes from the time we left La Guardia. He pulled into a long driveway beside a small pond and parked next to one of the Gothic-styled buildings on the campus. The rain and sleet were still coming down hard. It was dark outside, and the few lampposts on the driveway did not provide enough light to get a good look at the outside of our new home. Two lights by the entrance door to the building were turned on as soon as the car stopped. Just then, three nuns in perfectly starched full penguin costumes displaying huge smiles came out to greet us. One of them spoke Spanish, the other two just smiled a lot and shook their heads up and down.

I knew I was being overly dramatic but based on the limited conversations in the car with Marco, I was not expecting anything good to come out of this move. I was trying to convince myself to give it time and not to overreact. Easier said than done. We got our luggage and walked inside with the nuns to an office by the front door. It was now almost 6:00 p.m. and I was hungry. I had an empty stomach since I left my lunch in an air sickness bag on the plane.

After a few formalities and introductions, we were asked to turn in our passports and any legal documents we were carrying. If we had jewelry, we had to store it all with the passports in a safe. Having jewelry was highly improbable due to the restrictions we

Welcome to New York - 1962

had for leaving Cuba. Because of our ages, all four of us would be placed in separate sections. Each section had somewhere between 40 and 50 children. I told Sister Margarita, the Spanish speaking nun, that the separate accommodations were not acceptable to us and I wanted to be with my brother. Without batting an eye, she looked at me directly and responded, *"Nosotros hacemos las cosas a nuestra manera aquí en St. Agnes."* (We do things our way here in St. Agnes.) In other words, I had no say in the living arrangements – I should just shut up and follow instructions. I should have known better and kept suggestions to myself. I expected that the nuns will now consider me a "problem child".

After the somewhat "pleasant" formalities and brief introduction, the four of us said goodbye to each other and were each escorted to separate locations in the dormitory building. I immediately thought I would never see my brother again. It was not a good initial introduction for an eight-year-old spending his first night in an orphanage.

Just as I expected, I walked into that dark room, unable to see anything in front of me, finally somebody turned the lights on. I did not like what I was seeing.

Welcome to New York - 1962

CHAPTER 26

Life in the Orphanage 1962

When I walked inside the dormitory, I got the same feeling I experienced when I boarded the plane earlier this morning in Miami. The feeling of going inside a dark cave with no opportunity to exit. I felt that once I got inside, I would never see the sun again and the outside world would never hear from me. Everything inside was dark and poorly lit by gloomy florescent lights. Some of the bulbs were not on, others were gray and dark on the ends. The furnishings matched the style of the building: old, Gothic, and dreary. My initial reaction walking inside the dormitory was perhaps overly dramatic back then but I truly believed it was close to the end of my life. I asked myself how I got convinced to come here? How do I get out? It was less than an hour since my arrival and I was already feeling regret about this move. Maybe I wasn't giving it a chance. Was it fair to judge St. Agnes in less than an hour? First impressions are usually on target. A voice inside my head was telling me to turn around, find the exit door and make a run for the outside world.

That main building at St. Agnes, where the majority of the residents lived, was exactly the vision I was afraid to find. It was a facility for more than 300 troubled boys from broken homes in and around New York City who could not be placed in foster care due to behavioral issues. The worst-case scenario of what I expected became a reality. I turned nine years old during my stay at St. Agnes, and after almost 60 years, I can still feel the pain. I am marked by those experiences – I remember them vividly. I have learned from them, but I also learned to deal with them.

To say it was "not a pleasant place to live" is a gross understatement. No one should have to experience life in a facility like St. Agnes. That is a strong statement for me to make but it was exactly how I felt back in 1962 and still feel today. I'm not sure what the Catholic Church could have done to improve the situation. Today, I feel their pain when I hear of kids being placed in orphanages.

To survive a normal day, you had to force yourself to mind your own business, constantly watch your back, know the designated and self-appointed bullies, and stay away from them. I know my time there changed me and forced me to become aware of dangerous confrontations. That was a learning experience. But it also stole the remaining part of my childhood because I had to constantly protect myself and act tough like an adult. I did not trust anyone. Everyone was out for themselves. It was an exercise in survival for children. I did not have my older brother to protect me 24/7. I had to make decisions on my own. I just turned 9 years old and felt like an adult.

St. Agnes was not what the team from Operation Pedro Pan in Florida City represented to us, I don't believe they purposely meant to misrepresent the facility. I am sure you will find some past residents of St. Agnes who will tell you a different story. If you came to St. Agnes from a broken home, from an abusive

Life in the Orphanage - 1962

relationship with family, from the streets, or after experiencing trouble with the law, yes, your experience at St. Agnes would have been an upgrade and different than mine.

****

The living arrangements for my assigned group were in an enclosed, segregated section of the third floor. They included a large room with about 30-40 squeaky metal beds lined up along the perimeter and in the middle of the room. The sleeping quarters were immaculately clean and all the beds were dressed in military-style to look identical. On one side of each bed, there was a small and narrow nightstand. On the other side, there was a small dresser about 4 feet wide with four drawers to be shared equally with my neighbor. At the foot of the bed, there was a laundry bag where I would place my dirty laundry to be picked up periodically and returned the following day, if it was not lost or included with someone else's laundry. Across the hall, there was a smaller room with folding chairs and a small television on a shelf. Next to this room, there was another smaller room with a few folding card tables and chairs and a pile of board games spread out on the counter against the wall.

Continuing down the center hall, there was a door that led to a bathroom with about five stalls an equal amount of urinals and an equal number of sinks. The hallway that separated the bedroom from the other rooms had an industrial-size sink and a metal cup tied with a long chain securing it to the wall so you could not walk away with the cup. That was our designated source for drinking water – everyone drank from that same cup unless you were fortunate enough to hide your own cup in your dresser or nightstand.

****

When I arrived at my assigned section of the dormitory, there was no one around because it was the scheduled dinner time for

Life in the Orphanage - 1962

my group. One of the nuns escorted me to the dining room in the basement of the building. She gave me a tray and a plate with what looked like a slice of meat, perhaps meatloaf, mashed potatoes, and carrots, all drowning in a gelatinous gravy barely suitable for a pet pig like Pedrito. A small container of milk and a tiny piece of a very dry cake for dessert were by far the best items on my tray.

The nun who escorted me walked me over to a section where my new roommates were sitting in organized silence and introduced me to the group. There was and unwelcome stillness in the group, nobody said anything. I sat down and ate. All I heard was kids chewing their food. Why did I feel like a convict when I arrived at St. Agnes? I did not commit a crime. I did nothing wrong.

After dinner, we were all escorted, single file, to a room where we were given a small towel and told to strip naked and hang our clothes on the hooks. Adjacent to the dressing area there was an entrance to an open tiled room with about a dozen shower heads. There weren't enough showers for all the kids to use at the same time, so some of us had to wait in line, naked and cold, (the room was barely heated) until a shower head was vacant. A small bar of soap was shared and left behind in each soap dish for the next kid to use. Out of the showers, we all got dressed and stood in line until everyone was ready to go back to our dormitory. The strict discipline, the line-up to go anywhere in the building, the silence during dinner, and the nuns barking orders made my first night at St. Agnes feel like I was sentenced for a crime I did not commit. I felt the discipline at the orphanage was comparable to what anyone would experience at a detention facility.

****

Supervisory responsibilities for my group were assigned to several nuns, each covering a portion of the 24-hour day. The leader was Sister Alfreda who had a huge wart on her nose that complemented the angry look she had forced on her face. Sister Alfreda never seemed to crack a smile and was always yelling at

Life in the Orphanage - 1962

someone. I suppose she needed to demonstrate her authority and power. Her style of management was very insecure and unreachable. Her clothing was always impeccably clean and perfectly starched and stiff.

A small blackboard next to the television listed a schedule that was always changed after dinner to announce our activities for the following day. This is how we were kept us informed of what was to come, including school hours during weekdays. I sat in the TV room for a while by myself on that first night and, finally, some of the kids walked over to me to introduce themselves. When they realized I did not speak English and therefore could not communicate with them easily, they walked away in silence. I tried to reach out with my limited knowledge of the language, but I was not very successful. Most of the time, I would sit in that room by myself, watching television and tried to understand the conversations on the television.

At 9:00 p.m. sharp, after changing the schedule on the blackboard for tomorrow's activities, and without any warning, Sister Alfreda walked in front of the television and turned it off. Nobody complained, everyone got up quietly and quickly moved into the bedroom to change into our sleepwear, kneel by our beds, and say our prayers as directed by Sister Alfreda. As soon as we got under the covers, the lights went out.

Before I fell asleep, I made a promise to myself that I would find a way to get out of this situation as soon as possible. I was not going to live here under these circumstances. My experience during the first night at St. Agnes was depressing. I felt like a prisoner of the revolution.

****

I did not sleep much during that first night at St. Agnes. Without any warning, all the lights in our sleeping quarters were quickly turned on at the same time and a different nun clapped her hands and yelled, "Everyone up and out of bed!" It was very

Life in the Orphanage - 1962

early in the morning, still mostly. dark outside, and the sun had barely risen. There was a long line to the bathroom, so I went back to make my bed and search through my drawer in the dresser for clothes to wear to school. The kid next to my bed demonstrated how the nuns wanted the beds made up so there was conformity in the room. I finally got my turn in the bathroom but I was running behind and still needed to get dressed. Everyone waited in the hallway while the nun in charge of the morning schedule inspected the quality of how the beds were made. She yelled something at me that I assumed translated to *"¡Más rápido!"* (Faster!) I ran and grabbed my coat that was hung by a hook in the hallway alongside everyone else's coats.

We walked single file again back to the dining room for cereal and a small container of milk followed by a 20-minute recess in the schoolyard where I saw Segundito, Manolo, and Manuel. All four of us were in shock and shared similar experiences from our first night in each of our assigned dormitories. We all felt we were sentenced to jail.

****

Before we had time to finish comparing notes, the school bell rang, and everyone lined up in the schoolyard to march like a hypnotized youth squad towards the schoolhouse. The four of us needed to be assigned a classroom, so we entered a small office near the entrance for directions. The classroom I was assigned was large and depressing with many empty desks in the rear, dark walls and a huge oak desk for the teacher in the front center of the room. The windows were stained glass and reflected a variety of colors onto the surface of the old fashion wooden desks. Most of the window shades were partially torn and could not prevent the sun's rays from piercing through the stained glass and into the room. You can see that repairs were attempted with tape and staples. The surfaces of the desks were hinged, so you could lift the top to store books and your personal school supplies inside. I

Life in the Orphanage - 1962

could hear the whistling sounds coming from the radiators at the base of each window. Between the heat from the sun and the heat from the radiators, it was very warm in the room. The darkness, the reflection of colored lights from the stained-glass windows, and the heat made me want to go back to sleep. I looked around the room and recognized a few of my classmates from the dormitory but the rest seemed to be new faces.

The teacher for my class (another nun in a perfectly starched outfit) was probably about 80 years old and sat behind her huge oak desk nearly the entire time we were in class. I did not understand most of what she said in class. Her speech pattern was mostly incoherent mumbling. There were a few books inside my desk, and unless I looked at my neighbor next to me, I did not know which book to bring out. The discipline in the classroom was frightening. Nobody said a word unless they were given permission to speak. Why did everyone seem terribly afraid? Perhaps it was the wooden paddle that was sitting on top of that oak desk close to the teacher's hands. I wondered if she felt she needed to display it for her own protection.

I tried to follow the lessons in class that first day and tried to concentrate on expanding my English vocabulary. It was not easy. At times, out of frustration and boredom, I would just close my eyes and put my head down on my desk. But every time I did that, within a few minutes I would hear the teacher say, "Antonio, sit up and follow the lessons." It was impossible to hide from her. I would swear she had four eyes and two of them were directed only at me. That wooden paddle did not make me feel comfortable either. I was not going to give her an excuse to use it on my butt or anywhere on my body. I knew my time was being wasted in class, and what I really needed were lessons that would teach me to speak, read, and write the English language. St. Agnes did not know how to handle kids who did not speak English. I was their new problem; they were not prepared so they chose to ignore it.

That afternoon during recess in the schoolyard, the four of us got together and met two other Pedro Pan boys who were sent

Life in the Orphanage - 1962

from the Florida City campus and had been living at St. Agnes for about two months. Oscar and Pedro were not related but because they were both about the same age, they stayed together in the same dormitory and became good friends. Oscar and Pedro told us some horrible stories they experienced, including a fist fight Oscar got involved in with another boy his age. The boy called Oscar a "spik," pushed him into a snowbank, for no reason, and proceeded to punch him in the stomach. One of the nuns broke up the fight, and both of them were spanked with a wooden paddle on their buttocks.

I was young, inexperienced, and an amateur compared to some of the residents at St. Agnes. I had never heard the word spik before. Oscar told us that it was a derogatory word used to describe a person of Spanish descent. They were both very discouraged and unhappy at St. Agnes but did not know what they could do since neither of them had any relatives living in the U.S. They would not tell their parents that they were unhappy. They were hoping it would not be long before their parents left Cuba and they would be able to leave St. Agnes and reunite with them.

****

I spent the first few days of my stay at St. Agnes with minimal contact from my brother. The only times I got to see him was outside in the schoolyard during recess or after class for a short period of time. Towards the end of the first week, he was able to get permission to periodically visit me in my dormitory, sit with me after dinner, and watch television with my group.

The second week of our stay at St. Agnes was not any better than the first. Although I was adjusting to the strict disciplinary style of everyday living, I despised the surroundings, the lack of freedom, and the tension between the designated bullies and the rest of the kids. During that second week, I developed a severe cough that was preventing me from sleeping at night. After the third sleepless night, I was sent to the infirmary and was given a bottle

Life in the Orphanage - 1962

of cough medicine to take three times a day. My lungs ached from the persistent coughing. The medication seemed to help calm down the coughing fits but then I started to develop chills and sweats and was sent to the infirmary again, this time for a three-day visit so the nurse/nun could monitor my illness and reduce my fever. All the symptoms of pneumonia. I now felt like I was at a country club compared to my living quarters in the dormitory. As soon as she felt I was cured, I was sent back to my group and continued my routine as if everything was back to normal. I was fortunate that during my stay in the infirmary, I was allowed to have visits from Segundito, Manolo, Manuel, Oscar, and Pedro. We started to call ourselves *"Los Seis Spiks"* (The Six Spiks) and felt that if we stayed together during recess, the bullies would avoid us.

****

Sometimes we meet strangers under unusual circumstances that can help us at a future point in our lives. Segundito still had Isabelle's phone number, and one day after school we went over to the administration office to meet with the Spanish speaking nun, Sister Margarita. We asked for permission to call Isabelle, and she immediately wanted to know who Isabelle was and how we met her. When we told Sister Margarita that Isabelle was someone we met on the plane to New York and that she wanted to visit us here at St. Agnes once we got settled, she took the note card with the phone number away from Segundito, ripped it up in small pieces, and told us with her index finger pointed at us, *"No debes tomar números de teléfono de personas que no conoses."* (You should not take phone numbers from people you do not know.) We were both stunned by her response. Perhaps Isabelle was our "lifeline" to get out of St. Agnes. Now that opportunity simply vanished into her waste basket. What was the purpose of denying us a call to Isabelle? What harm could it do? I could not understand her reasoning for preventing any communications with Isabelle. We

Life in the Orphanage - 1962

lost contact with her. I hoped she knew how much comfort she gave us during our flight to New York.

****

Life at St. Agnes was not getting any better. Although we were learning and accepting the militaristic policies and procedures, the school and living conditions were not what anyone would consider ideal for a safe learning institution. Just when I thought it could not get more complicated for us, during the third week of our stay there, I woke up in the morning and could not open my right eye. It was swollen with a thin layer of dried crust covering the eye under the eyelid. I never had any issues with my eyes in the past, so I assumed it was just an infection or a new allergy. The hygienic practices in the dormitory and dining room were not ideal. I walked over to the nun-in-charge that morning, and she asked me to get dressed and go to the infirmary again. I was getting used to going there, so this time I did not need directions and walked across the schoolyard by myself with one eye partially closed and my vision blurry.

Inside the infirmary, the nurse/nun examined my eye for a long time (I was not convinced she knew what to do), placed eye drops in both eyes, and told me to come back three times a day for the next several days to repeat the medication. Before I left, she placed a patch on my eye, secured it with a large "X" of medical tape, and sent me to school. Just what I did not want – my bandages would attract attention from bullies. They had a special magnetic reaction towards the weak kids in the schoolyard. Now I needed to act extra tough to overcome any sign of weakness.

I went to school that day still not understanding most of what was being taught in class. Now, I had only one eye to see the blackboard and my books. If only I could close the good eye and take a nap during class without the teacher's knowledge.

After three days of three visits per day to the infirmary for eye drops, the nurse/nun did not replace my bandages and told me not to come back. My eyes returned to normal, and I survived another

Life in the Orphanage - 1962

illness at St. Agnes. What could I expect next? I am sure that the sanitary conditions in the dormitory and dining hall were less than acceptable by the Board of Health in Sparkill. Did Sparkill have a "Board of Health"? Did they ever inspect St. Agnes?

****

The same evening I had my eye patch removed, I was standing in line waiting to enter the dining room when one of the kids from a different group cut in line in front of me. He was taller and slightly bigger but I still motioned to him that he needed to go to the back of the line. Before I could even finish getting my message across, he turned around and punched me in the face. The nun who was in charge of escorting our group to the dining room that evening saw what was happening and immediately pulled the bully out of line. She grabbed my hand and signaled me to slap his face for what he did to me. I thought she was kidding but she insisted that I slap his face. I wasn't sure what to do, so before I got her angry at me, I slapped his face. *"Do unto others as you would have them do unto you."* I was shocked that she was adamant about me slapping his face. I just did not understand the purpose or what that reaction would solve. Especially since I was slapping a bully with many other bully friends just like him in the school. I knew I would run into him again somewhere. Perhaps next time, it could be worse for me. My mistake, I should have let him get in front of me. I forgot the phrase *"mind my own business,"* and now I had to face the consequences.

We were almost finished with our dinner. When the nun in charge of our group was not looking, the same bully approached me at my table, called me a spik and hit me very hard in the back with a closed fist, emptying my lungs for a split second. I fell off the bench, covered my face with my hands, kept my mouth shut, and waited for the pain to subside. The boy sitting next to me helped me back on my seat and wanted me to tell the nun what had happened. I shook my head, and he understood exactly why I

Life in the Orphanage - 1962

wanted to keep this new incident quiet. He sat with me and rubbed my back until I was able to breath normally again. I was hoping that the bully considered the score even and would not attempt to continue attacking me in the future.

****

Staying together during recess and protecting each other helped us avoid many confrontations at St. Agnes. We had no access to any political news about relations between Cuba and the U.S. and did not receive mail from home often. Any mail from Cuba could have been opened and monitored by the Castro regime on that side of the map and by the nuns on this side. My parents were careful about what they wrote to avoid any retaliation by Castro's government. Saturdays was a special day for us because we had extra time to spend together, support each other and share any news about Cuba we may have heard from letters received. In just a few days, we all experienced difficulties getting acclimated to our new environment but we didn't know what to do to improve our situation or, if possible, get relocated. At one point, we were so desperate that we even discussed escaping through the woods behind the infirmary. We didn't have a clue what we would find on the other side of the hill but felt it had to be better than our current situation. Unfortunately, the nuns had all our passports and legal documents locked up in the safe, so if we escaped, we would have no identification to bring with us. Manolo thought we could break into the office at night and try to open the safe. I thought Manolo watched too many movies. There wasn't much we could do to expedite our exit from St. Agnes.

****

Segundito received a notice on Sunday morning from the administration center that we should expect a friend of the family

Life in the Orphanage - 1962

to visit us in the early afternoon. Immediately after church services, we were asked to come to the office. In the waiting room was a lady named Magda and her husband Bernie. Magda was Tio Frank's sister. Unlike Tio Frank, Magda despised Fidel Castro. She and Bernie got permission to take us out to lunch nearby, so we got in their car and drove a few miles to a local diner. While we were having lunch, we shared with Magda and Bernie our experiences at St. Agnes, our unhappiness, and disappointment with the living conditions and school. Surprised at our stories, they were seriously concerned about our future there and assured us that they would do what they could to help, including returning for a follow-up visit the next Sunday.

After lunch and a brief ride through a public park, Magda and Bernie brought us back to St. Agnes. We said goodbye and walked towards our dormitory. I turned around and noticed they walked back inside the administration center. The following day, Sister Margarita asked us why we were so unhappy and why we would tell our problems to our visitors. It was obvious that Magda and Bernie spoke to Sister Margarita privately after we returned from lunch and expressed their concerns about our stay. I was now afraid of retribution from the nuns for complaining to Magda and Bernie. Sometimes it felt like the nuns were also the bullies at St. Agnes.

****

News traveled surprisingly fast in the early 1960s without email or Facebook. A few days passed, and we were asked to come to the administration office for a phone call. It was Susanna from Miami who was notified by Magda that we were extremely unhappy at St. Agnes. While talking to Susanna on the phone, I could see that Sister Margarita was sitting at her desk across the room listening to our conversation on her own phone. Knowing that she was listening to everything we discussed with Susanna did not hold us back. We told Susana the same stories we told Magda and Bernie. After a few minutes, we were asked to say goodbye to

Life in the Orphanage - 1962

Susanna and return to the dormitory. Sister Margarita continued the phone conversation with Susanna. As we walked back to the dormitory, I shared my concern with Segundito about potential retribution from the nuns because of what we told Susanna and Magda. He was not worried and told me there was nothing we could do to stop it now. We did not lie to Susana and Magda, so everything should be fine. I hoped he was right.

****

Just before the start of the weekend and while we were in school, we got another request to come to the administration office for another phone call. It was unusual for any one of the kids to get this many phone calls. We walked inside, and Sister Margarita told us it was our parents on the phone from La Habana. My eyes widened, and I immediately sat down at the desk and picked up the phone. I was very surprised to hear their voices. I could not hide my emotions – I cried talking to them, which made my mother cry on the other end.

Looking back, I realize that having my parents hear me crying on the phone must have been extremely painful for them. I missed them very much and was grateful to hear their voices on the phone even if it was just for a few minutes. They wanted to let us know that they knew we were not happy about the school and that they were doing everything they could to get us into a better environment. Meanwhile, Sister Margarita was on the line listening to our conversation again. She signaled to me across the room not to cry on the phone. It was a very emotional few minutes on the phone and extremely difficult for me to control my feelings. The tough kid in me vanished while I was on the phone. The bullies broke me down.

After we said goodbye, I put the phone down and wiped my tears with my coat sleeves. My eyes were still wet, swollen and my nose was runny. I was in no condition to return to school. Sister Margarita stayed with us for a few minutes. After I calmed down, she walked us back to our classrooms. I could not stop thinking about our conversation on the phone with our parents. I had no interest in what the teacher was saying, nor could I bother to pay attention to class. This school was not important to me. Getting out was now my number one priority.

****

Our disappointment with St. Agnes continued after the phone call from our parents. Nothing changed, and I was becoming unreasonable and impatient. There was nothing we could do to change our surroundings and we could not attempt an escape without our passports and identification which were stored in the office safe.

Perhaps I was not trying hard enough to adjust. Maybe after a few more days, my feelings about the school would change. I was open to the idea of just adapting to my new surroundings. I gave it a chance, multiple times. I still had to avoid the bullies. I was not improving in school. And the military style of management by the nuns made me feel like a prisoner. The good news was that I finally found a paper cup that I kept inside my dresser to avoid using the communal cup for water. The quality of the food seemed to be getting worse every day. I gave it more than a reasonable chance. This was not the place to be. We needed to leave soon.

****

A week after the phone call with our parents, Segundito came to my dormitory to watch television with me and told me we were leaving St. Agnes in a few days and returning to Miami. Freddy, Susana's husband, was flying to New York to pick us up and fly back to Miami. They made arrangements with my parents for me to move in with Susana, Freddy, and their children. Segundito would go and live with another family friend in Miami. It was the best news I heard since arriving in The United States over two months ago. Another move, another school, another change of scenery, and new friends to meet. I was confused, but this time, I started to feel positive about this sudden change and looked forward to the next step in our lives – outside of St. Agnes. Finally, a smile returned to my face.

****

We spent about 50 days at the orphanage in Sparkill, New York. Anxious to leave quickly, I was counting the hours before Freddy arrived to pick us up and take us back to Miami. Our time there was not an experience similar to life at the Florida City campus. Yes, there was more living space, and our surroundings were not as crowded as in Florida City, but the quality of life at St. Agnes was not something I would have recommended. I don't know if more Pedro Pan children were sent there after we left. I don't know if our other Pedro Pan friends who were there with us ended up staying for a long period or if they managed to leave shortly after we left. We lost contact with them and, sadly, after leaving St. Agnes, we lost contact with Operation Pedro Pan.

Life in the Orphanage - 1962

CHAPTER 27

A Merry Christmas
2018

It was a special Christmas morning, December 25, 2018, in Cienfuegos, Cuba – 57 years after spending my last Christmas in Cuba. The early morning sunrise peeking over the mountains that surround the city was an amazing sight to watch sitting on our verandah with a hot cup of coffee and steamed milk just delivered by our butler. My memories returned to Christmas in 1961 – No Christmas tree because it was almost impossible to find one and if you did, they were very skinny, extremely dry, and expensive. Our presents that year were items needed for our expected trip to The United States, such as luggage, a Dopp kit with a comb, toothbrush, and a nail clipper, new shoes, and some new clothes. Jorge was only 5 years old at the time, and my parents managed to find a few toys for him to place by the manger my mother always set up. It was a quiet Christmas, and we all understood the situation well. We were fortunate that my father was still employed by Arechabala even though the company was now nationalized. Today felt starkly different than Christmas morning 57 years ago.

Cienfuegos was our last city to visit on this cruise before we began our journey back home to South Florida later that night. The town is located only about 160 miles southeast of La Habana and has a small population of about 150,000 residents. It is named after José Cienfuegos, a Captain General of Cuba from the early 1800s. It was originally settled by French immigrants, that is the reason so many of the streets in the old town reflect French origins in their names. Despite having a great safe harbor and a town with many acres of fertile farmlands, Cienfuegos does not seem to take advantage of its location and surrounding natural resources. During the two days our ship was docked in the port, there was no other activity at the docks. Back in the late 1800s, Cienfuegos grew to be a powerful center due to its position for trade between other Caribbean Islands and South America. It was a major sugar cane, tobacco, and coffee trading center. Today, it appears that its once lucrative trade business has been reduced substantially.

In 1957, during the Cuban Revolution, Cienfuegos revolted against Fulgencio Batista, and was heavily bombed in retaliation. Many of Castro's armies hid in the surrounding mountains of Cienfuegos during the late 1950s before invading the city and later moving northwest towards La Habana.

Since we traveled a good part of our day yesterday on a bus to and from Trinidad, we all felt it was better to go out into town on our own and walk the streets of Cienfuegos. The ship was docked only about a half mile from the Jose Martí Park between Calle San Carlos and Calle San Fernando, so it would be an easy walk to the center of town, especially today – The weather outside on this Christmas morning could not have been more perfect. It was a great day for a walk through the city.

Cienfuegos has an important and significant Cuban history. In 2005, UNESCO inscribed the Urban Historic Centre of

Cienfuegos on the World Heritage List due to its preserved early 19th Century Spanish urban planning. My photographic goals when we disembarked the ship were to capture the mood of the people and use the architecture as my background scenery.

As soon as we exited the terminal, we began our walk north on Calle Bouyón to Jose Marti Park where we found the town's "Arco de Triunfo" (triumphal arch) and a beautifully restored neoclassical bandstand. In the center there was a statue of Jose Marti, a Cuban national hero who played a significant role in the liberation of Cuba from Spain in the late 1800s. The buildings that surrounded the park were also designed in the neoclassical style of Spanish architecture and were mostly well maintained. Many retail stores at the street level were open on Christmas Day, but the interiors displayed limited merchandise with plenty of empty shelving. Many of the stores would be considered secondhand stores or consignment shops in the U.S. since a lot of their merchandise, especially household items such as appliances, beds, and furniture, were labeled as *"USADO"* (USED). Or, as we would say here in the States, "previously owned" by another resident.

The architecture of many buildings included a colonnade-style covered sidewalk intentionally built to protect shoppers and strollers from the heat of the direct sun. We walked through the park and did not see any kids playing or riding their bikes. There were no musicians playing their favorite classic Cuban music either. It was a quiet stroll. A few residents were sitting on park benches, some partially asleep, some simply strolling with their families, others just staring into space. From the park, we could see some of the residents entering the stores on Christmas morning, perhaps to find last-minute bargains. The main street had its share of occasional street vendors standing next to their homemade kiosks, selling their personal works of art, handicraft items, or anything they felt could be marketable to tourists at the moment.

There was an atmosphere or perhaps a "community personality" here in Cienfuegos that was sharply different than what we found in La Habana, Santiago de Cuba, and Trinidad. Cienfuegos seemed to be a much quieter and conservative town. We did not see many street musicians or the bands playing at the cafes, or the happy faces of residents greeting the tourists disembarking from the ship. Instead, everywhere we walked through the neighborhoods, there were people sitting outside of their homes with lonely looks on their faces just watching the world pass by their front door with little, if any, expression or interaction. The mood in the air was somewhat subdued. I was beginning to believe they were afraid to communicate with the tourists or had been threatened not to interact with visitors or barely with each other. It was not like the other towns where we found the residents happy and ready to chat and pose for pictures. Today, there was definitely a sad tone in this town, and I could not understand their reaction.

The sadness I was seeing in Cienfuegos brought me back to St. Agnes. It seemed to me the residents of both did not want to be there – an unhappy feeling. As I walked through the neighborhoods of Cienfuegos I could not help the continuous reminder of my life in Sparkill, NY, an unpleasant time of my life. I still don't understand why I connected the two during my walk. Perhaps the expressionless faces I was seeing in Cienfuegos connected me of the sadness I witnessed and personally experienced at St. Agnes. Both had unhappy residents who could do nothing to change their situations. This was not what I would expect on Christmas morning in Cuba or anywhere in the world.

I wondered about the conditions of orphanages in Cuba. An interesting observation, orphanages are called, *"casas de niños sin amparo filial"* (homes for children without family protection), and the orphaned children are called *"niños de la patria"* (children of the motherland). It sounded to me like typical socialist propaganda labeling.

****

We continued our walk in Calle San Fernando towards an elegant boulevard, Paseo del Prado, with a wide walkway in the middle of the street lined with trees and benches. The famous street stretches from the Rio Inglés in the north to Punta Gorda in the south of the town. It was a great place for people watching with more neoclassical buildings and pastel-painted columns with colonnades protecting the strollers from the sun. It was the perfect location to just wander and see how the lives of the locals unfold. Many residents came out on Christmas morning to sit on the shady sidewalks by their doorway or they simply brought out a chair to sit and enjoy the views of folks passing through. Some gathered around and sat on wooden boxes to play dominos with their neighbors or to discuss politics, their grandchildren, the latest neighborhood gossip, or whatever came to their minds on this holiday. This section of town is where I was able to capture several of my best portrait shots of the residents in Cienfuegos. The background architecture was classical. The mood of the people was subdued.

In the southern portion of the boulevard, the street turns into El Malecón (the esplanade), offering amazing views over that beautiful huge bay where our ship was docked. People were walking El Malecón and enjoying the breezes from the bay. I was still experiencing sad looking faces everywhere we walked, even on this Christmas morning. Why did I see so much sadness in Cienfuegos? Was it just my impression? Maybe it was because our trip was getting closer to the end.

****

I saw a lot of Cuba on this trip, including cities I had never visited during my childhood. Our trip was getting close to completion and my sadness that the end was near might have been reflected in my photography. Maybe today I could not see the liveliness of the Cuban people because I couldn't ignore my personal feelings about leaving the country again. I know that photography usually reflects the mood of the photographer. Maybe there was a lot of happiness in the town that morning I did not see. What I was capturing may

A Merry Christmas - 2018

have been a response to the personal feelings I was having about the suffering the Cuban people have experienced in the past and still today.

Later in the day, when we returned to the ship, I took a quick look at my photos and confirmed that I had clearly captured a sad and dark atmospheric mood around town. When Arthur looked at my preliminary photos, his comment was "Why did you capture only sad looking folks?" I responded by telling him, "I didn't see anyone smiling." His quick reply made me think more about my day in Cienfuegos "You were not smiling and therefore not interested or attracting anyone with a smile".

CHAPTER 28

Return to Miami
1962

The lights were turned on, and I heard, "Everyone up and out of bed!" one last time. It was Sister Alfreda on my final morning at St. Agnes, still playing the role of drill sergeant and belting out orders, as usual. My routine for most of my last day at St. Agnes was the same as other days: get in line for the bathroom, make my bed, get dressed, get in line for breakfast, spend a short time outside in the schoolyard, and, when the bell rings, get in line again and go inside a classroom where I would not learn anything but stare at an eighty-year-old nun who never gets up from behind her desk. The difference today was that after school ended in the afternoon, Freddy would be arriving from Miami to pick us up, take us for a stay an overnight stay in Manhattan at a friend's apartment, and bring us to La Guardia airport early the following morning for our return flight to Miami.

I was in a different mood than usual from the moment I opened my eyes, feeling excited to leave behind my life experiences from St. Agnes. I was confident and anxious to get the day started. At the same time, I was somewhat distressed and concerned about leaving behind our friends, Manolo, Manuel, Oscar, and Pedro. They felt certain that their parents would be arriving soon, and then it would be their turn to leave St. Agnes.

During our last lunch recess in the schoolyard, the *Seis Spiks* got together as always and said our goodbyes. Segundito gave them each our new addresses in Miami in hopes that they would write and keep us updated. Perhaps they would settle back in Miami when their parents left Cuba and we would be able to meet again and commiserate about our experiences at St. Agnes. Maybe it was better for those experiences to be forgotten and not discussed again.

My last day in class, it was even more difficult to concentrate on my studies than on other days. All I did was think about our new life in Miami and hope that our parents and Jorge would meet us there soon. When class ended, we both returned to our separate dormitories and picked up our luggage. Before I went out the door to wait for Freddy in the administration building, I received a warm hug and blessings from Sister Alfreda. It was surprising to experience a genuine and heartwarming farewell from her. I did not believe she had it in her. Maybe she felt she had to play the role of a strict and rigid authoritarian to control the resident bullies of St. Agnes. I thanked her and walked over to the administration building to meet Segundito. Now it was time to wait for Freddy's arrival.

We sat in the waiting room looking out the window for Freddy's taxicab to pull in the driveway. Every time I saw a car, I would run to the window to look outside. I started to fear there was a change of plans and we would have to return to our dormitories. I could not imagine picking up my luggage and going back to that world I just happily left. Was leaving St. Agnes just a dream? Now that we

Return to Miami - 1962

were given our passports, if Freddy didn't show up, I was ready to convince my brother to escape and start running down the street. Our luggage was light enough to carry and run. I was certain a stranger would pick us up and provide us with overnight shelter. Then I thought about the following day after our escape. Where would we go? Reality becomes obvious when you carefully plan day two of your escape.

While we were sitting there (somewhat patiently) with nothing to do, I started to visualize our arrival at St. Agnes. I was sitting in the same waiting room on the same sofa that evening, frightened because I was told that my brother and I would be separated and placed in different groups. I would be assigned to a group where nobody spoke Spanish and a few bullies were always looking for trouble. I remember that same evening being escorted to the dining room where I was introduced to my roommates and nobody spoke, everyone practicing organized silence. I felt constraint from the military-style schedule we had to keep every day, including the single file marching everywhere we went. I felt like a prisoner of the revolution who just walked into that dark room with no exit doors – not what a nine-year-old should feel.

I hated having to watch my back constantly and stay away from bullies who had nothing better to do than to look for trouble, especially with the younger kids who could not put up a fight against them. Going to class was a waste of my time. I did not learn anything. My English skills were not improving and, as a result, my education was going nowhere. I also spent a lot more time in the infirmary during my short stay in St. Agnes than most kids did during their entire time in residence.

The taxicab with Freddy finally arrived two hours after its original scheduled time. I should have expected that flight delays and traffic jams from the airport would be the cause. Freddy came inside to review and sign the paperwork the school needed. Within 15 minutes of his arrival, we received farewell hugs from all the nuns in the office and were out through the front door and inside the same taxicab still waiting outside. As we drove away onto the

Return to Miami - 1962

main road, I turned around for my last view of St. Agnes. Instead of feeling sad about leaving, I had a smile on my face. It was time to be grateful, look back and say goodbye. I was not sorry to go.

The taxicab would take us into Manhattan where we were going to stay overnight at an apartment belonging to Lucy and Jose, friends of Freddy and Susana who had lived in New York for many years.

****

We arrived at a very nice building somewhere in the Upper West Side near Central Park. The well-dressed guard at the front door of the building let us inside and guided us to the elevator. As soon as the elevator door opened on Lucy and Jose's floor, Freddy introduced us to his friends who greeted us warmly and brought us to the dining room where dinner was ready to be served. It had been a long time since I was able to recognize the food I was eating. This time, I didn't leave anything on my plate. Having dinner conversations with friendly people was a welcoming experience – there was no organized silence at this table. Segundito and I helped clean the dishes, and as soon as everything was put away, we were off for a subway ride to see the new movie, "State Fair," with Pat Boone, Ann-Margret, Bobby Darin, and Alice Faye.

It was an amazing experience riding on a subway underneath this huge city for the first time. I was certain that someday I would return and perhaps live here. I loved the excitement, the busy streets, the traffic jams, the steam coming out of manholes, and the overwhelming skyscrapers. The movie theatre was near Times Square and, as we got out from under the street, the marquee lights became blinding. The oversized billboards were overpowering, and the gift shops were jammed with tourists purchasing all sorts of gift items (some of which were not meant for a nine-year-old to see). There were newspaper and magazine stands, pretzel vendors, crowded sidewalks with constant movement, and people crushing me. Everywhere I looked, I was mesmerized by the sites of the city.

Return to Miami - 1962

I could have lost myself, never to be found, in the streets of New York.

I loved looking at the scenery around me and was not paying attention to where I was going. Segundito grabbed me by the neck and pushed me forward to walk between Freddy and his friends. I used to love the excitement of being in the middle of busy traffic in La Habana Vieja when shopping with my mother or walking the neighborhood with Tia Nena and admiring the architecture. The experience in Times Square as we exited the subway station made La Habana Vieja seem like a tiny village.

I'm not sure how much of the movie I watched. After arriving at the theatre and working our way to the balcony, I fell asleep soon after the movie began. The excitement of the day and a hot delicious dinner were way more than I could handle. Usually by this time, Sister Alfreda would stand in front of the television, turn it off without warning, and send everyone to bed for prayers and sleep.

The movie ended, and Segundito woke me up. We went back out onto the exciting streets of Times Square, reversing our earlier route. Once we got inside the apartment, Freddy went to sleep in the guest room, and Lucy prepared the couch for Segundito and me, where he slept soundly until the following morning. I was up for a good part of the night listening to the outside traffic noises before I was able to ignore them and fall asleep sometime after 2:00 a.m. It was our first night outside of St. Agnes. I finally felt free again.

****

Everything seemed to happen quickly after we woke up the following morning. Before I knew it, we dressed, hailed a taxicab, checked luggage at the airport terminal, and boarded the plane to Miami. By mid-afternoon, we had arrived at my new home and were greeted by Susana, Susie, and Howard (Freddy and Susana's teenage son). Later in the afternoon, Julio and Miranda, friends of my parents, came over to visit for a few minutes and pick up

Return to Miami - 1962

Segundito who was going to live with them a few miles away. I didn't mind this separation from my brother knowing that we were both going to be living with families who would take care of us until our parents arrived.

Now that we were living in Miami, it was much easier to obtain news about relations between the U.S. and Cuba – it was constantly reported on television news stations. Susana and Freddy always watched the evening news, and I would sit with them and try to understand what was being said in English. Television is a great way to learn a new language. Unfortunately, much of the news about Cuba was not encouraging and made me worry about the safety of our parents and Jorge. Freddy and Susana tried to protect me from all the negativity by telling me, *"No se preocupe por lo que digan. Siempre les gusta exagerar."* (Don't worry about what they say. They always like to exaggerate). Their observations were helpful, but I still listened, evaluated the facts, and tried to process what was happening in the world and, more particularly, in Cuba.

Susana took me to a nearby elementary school the day after arriving in Miami to register for classes. I was placed in a classroom with Cuban kids who were also learning to speak a new language. It was a mixed group of ages in the same room and, depending on your age, your assignments would vary. Some of the kids were living with their parents, others with relatives or friends as they waited for their parents to leave Cuba. Math, history, geography, penmanship, civics, and a strong emphasis on learning the English language were the priorities. As soon as our English grammar skills improved, we would be transferred to regular English-speaking classes. The new curriculum was ideal for kids learning a new language in a new country.

After meeting new friends in school and in my new neighborhood, some of us would walk to school together, approximately one mile in each direction. The semester ended in mid-June but I continued attending summer classes with several other friends to keep busy and catch up with studies.

Return to Miami - 1962

I had plenty of new friends in the neighborhood. Many would stop by the house on weekends or after school and we would go to a playground nearby to play volleyball or just hang around. There were several fruit trees in the backyard of the house, including guava, mango, orange, lemon, and banana. I learned to climb the guava and mango trees to grab the ripened fruits before they fell on the ground and rotted. Sometimes, I would climb the tree and sit there by myself for hours just staring at the fruits, the leaves, and the ground below. I soon realized that spending time up in the tree was relaxing for me and a great escape.

Early Saturday mornings, Pablo, a neighborhood friend of Freddy and Susana, would go fishing under a bridge in Miami Beach. He always asked to take me along to help him with the fishing gear. That's where I learned to fish and, unfortunately, I never fished again in my life. I enjoyed going with Pablo and felt fishing, like sitting in the guava tree, was a great relaxing experience. Spending my early Saturday mornings under the bridge was peaceful and quiet, except for the noises from the cars crossing the bridge. Once we got the fishing lines out, we could sit back and stare at the horizon and just meditate or chat. I never expected to enjoy fishing as much as I did during that time. I regret not continuing with this sport.

After a couple of months living in Miami, I started to feel very comfortable, and was building my confidence level at school. The only setback was the negative news coming out of Cuba. Even if Freddy and Susana tried to protect me by filtering the news, my neighborhood and school friends would always have information they wanted to share with everyone else. It was obvious that my life had improved substantially after returning to Miami from St. Agnes but the news out of Cuba and the rumors in our community just kept getting darker and darker. The thought that I would never see my parents again remained in my mind.

****

Return to Miami - 1962

Thinking back to our days at St. Agnes, I am sure we would have survived if we had stayed there until our parents were able to leave Cuba. But at what cost? We had no assurance our parents would be able to leave Cuba and, therefore, did not know if we would stay there for another month, a few months, a few years, or longer. If we were forced to spend more time watching our backs and steering clear of the bullies, the school should not be considered a learning institution. It was more of an experiment in the survival of the fittest.

While we were living at St. Agnes, the friction between The United States and The Soviet Union continued to increase. The U.S. was perceived to have long-range missiles aimed at The Soviet Union. The Soviets did not have the capabilities for missiles to reach U.S. soil. At that time, Nikita Khrushchev, The Soviet Union's First Secretary, was concerned about The United States' growing lead and decided to place Soviet intermediate-range nuclear missiles in Cuba, just 90 miles away.

Fidel Castro had already begun friendly trade conversations with the Soviets. Since Khrushchev wanted to show support for Cuba and the Cuban people who were convinced by the Castro regime that The United States was a threatening force, he stepped further inside Cuba. He convinced Castro to secretly install short-range soviet missiles aimed at the U.S. since the Cuban leadership had strong expectations that the U.S. would invade Cuba again. Castro was enthusiastic about the idea because he knew it would be an irritant to the U.S. Khrushchev knew that a U.S. invasion of Cuba would lose Cuba to the U.S. and do great harm to the communists, especially in Latin America. The U.S. became aware of the missile installations on Cuban soil later in August 1962.

We did not know all these talks and negotiations between the Cuban and Soviet governments were going on while we were trying to leave St. Agnes and find a better environment until our parents were able to join us. There was fear that freedom flights from Cuba to the U.S. could be canceled with continued friction between the two countries. Many negotiations between the Soviets and Cuba

Return to Miami - 1962

and between Cuba and the U.S. were considered classified and not disclosed to the public at the time. The possibility of a nuclear war between the Soviets, Cuba, and the U.S. was soon to be made public. The Cuba advantage was important for the Soviets and for the U.S. If the freedom flights from Cuba were canceled, who knows when we would see our family again.

Return to Miami - 1962

CHAPTER 29

Cuban Missile Crisis 1962

After the failure of the Bay of Pigs Invasion in April 1961, President Kennedy was seen by the Soviets as weak and ineffective due to the way he managed the situation. Khrushchev now believed that President Kennedy did not have the power to mount an effective military response against any Soviet military build-up in Cuba or perhaps anywhere in the world. Khrushchev's opinion was also based on the events in Berlin during the same year when the East German government constructed the Berlin Wall, preventing many East Berliners from fleeing to the West. President Kennedy criticized the construction of the wall but did not take military action. Perhaps his response may have led Khrushchev to doubt any future military action by the U.S. towards Cuba.

Cuban Missile Crisis - 1962

When we returned to live in Miami, the secretive and classified first phase of Operation Mongoose was still in process. The C.I.A. continued to gather intelligence and to participate in covert actions designed to entice an internal revolt. The intelligence being gathered was critical and provided the U.S. with the advance knowledge of missile sites being built by the Soviets. The covert actions were not sufficient or effective enough to entice the internal revolt from the Cuban people the C.I.A. had predicted. Operation Mongoose's plan for U.S. intervention in October 1962 was still on the table and every covert action being planned for now would lead up to a U.S. invasion.

The rumors and speculations shared by my summer school classmates sounded like a dysfunctional United Nations meeting. Everyone strongly believed in their own opinions about what was happening behind the scenes between Cuba, The Soviet Union and the U.S. Most of what was shared in the schoolyard came from comments and speculation my classmates must have overheard from their parents or others at home. I did not believe most of what was discussed; I felt it was only speculative. How can nine-year-old kids obtain classified information not available to the news media? The stories that were being spread began to upset some of the kids in class, including me. Even though I felt these stories were just rumors, the idea of war was planted in my mind. I tried not to show my concerns about a future war with Cuba and the effects it would have on my family. But I still privately worried about them and still hoped that someday everything would return to normal.

In mid-summer of 1962, Fidel Castro publicly announced that any direct U.S. attack on Cuba was the equivalent of starting a World War. Today, the declassification of certain C.I.A. documents on this topic has given us direct knowledge of the secret actions coordinated by the C.I.A. under Operation Mongoose. I can understand Castro's strategy to side with The Soviet Union and request military assistance from them. He did not have access to the resources needed to resist a massive invasion from the U.S. by himself. If he aligned Cuba with the Soviets, perhaps the U.S.

Cuban Missile Crisis - 1962

would walk away and leave the island in Castro's control with a somewhat indirect control from The Soviet Union. Today, it would seem that Castro had direct inside knowledge of the workings of Operation Mongoose, even though it was labeled as a top-secret, classified initiative of the C.I.A.

****

My summer of 1962 was mostly enjoyable and educationally satisfying. I spent a lot of time with new friends and was happy to continue my studies in summer school, since it got me out of the house and helped me catch up on my education, including English lessons. All the kids in class were Cubans but the instructors always insisted that everyone in class speak English or, at the very least, try. The school organized several summer field trips, including visits to Jungle Island, the Miami Seaquarium, and other famous tourist sites. The field trips gave me the opportunity to see the important highlights of the city with kids my age.

Periodic visits to the beaches of Miami Beach on Sundays brought back memories of the summer of 1960 in Varadero. Although, I found the Miami Beach seashore to be way too crowded. We also enjoyed going to the Venetian Pool in Coral Gables nearby. A favorite place for me to hang out with friends, it was one of the first public pools in South Florida created in 1924 from a coral rock pit. The pool was designed as a picturesque cooling-off spot for the locals in the summer. It was fed by an underground aquifer complete with man-made caves, bridges, and a sandy beach. We spent a lot of hours in that pool during the summer. It seemed from the outside that my life was beginning to return to normal. Everywhere I visited, I still thought about my family in Cuba, wished they were with me at that moment, and worried for their safety.

A few weeks before returning to school in September, Tia Maria Luisa (my mother's eldest sister), her husband Tio Mario, and their 18-year-old son Juan arrived in Miami from Cuba. I was happy to see them here and their arrival gave me hope that our parents and Jorge would soon follow. Close friends of Tia Maria Luisa hosted them in their home upon their arrival. As soon as Tio Mario and Juan were able to get jobs and rent an apartment, Segundito and I would move in with them. I understood the arrangements and supported the eventual move with them. But at the same time, that meant a new school, a new neighborhood, and new friends - again. I hoped they would find an apartment nearby so I could stay in the same school and keep my current friends.

Just around the time Tia, Tio and Juan arrived in Miami, U.S. Senator Kenneth Keating from New York State told his colleagues in the senate that several Soviet missile installations were being built in Cuba. The Senate urged President Kennedy to launch an investigation and act if needed. The source of the information presented by Senator Keating of New York is still a mystery; the Senator himself never divulged his sources prior to his death in 1975. It was ironic that my neighborhood and school friends would talk about the dangers of atomic weapons in Cuba and the possibility of World War III before any information about missiles in Cuba was confirmed and made available to the public. Was there anyone in my small group of friends who may have had family connections to the C.I.A. and overheard discussions at the dinner table? It's hard to believe anyone with classified information would discuss it at the dinner table with their family. Perhaps it was just their prediction that turned out to be accurate. I will never know.

I had already started a new semester in school in the fall of 1962 when the C.I.A. obtained limited photographic evidence from U-2 spy planes that medium-range ballistic missiles were, in fact, unloaded from Soviet cargo ships on the evenings of September 8 and 16, 1962. These missiles had a range of up to 2,800 miles, enough to reach not just Miami but also New York City, Chicago, and the West Coast of the U.S. It was also found that the Soviets were building multiple missile launch sites in numerous locations around Cuba. Additional intelligence gathering was requested, which led to the establishment of the Executive Committee of the

Cuban Missile Crisis - 1962

National Security Council (ExComm) in early October 1962 to advise President Kennedy on issues related to the missile crisis.

On Sunday, October 14, 1962, a U.S. U-2 spy plane returned to Cuba and took hundreds of photos of newly built missile launch sites in the countryside. That same day, early in the evening, after spending a day on the beach, we received a telegram from my parents in Cuba to let us know that Abuela Balbina had died. I don't know why the news caught me by surprise, she was already frail and weak when I left Cuba eight months before. It was the first time in my life I experienced the death of a close relative. I was sad that I was not there with the rest of my family and wasn't sure on how I should react to the news. Shortly after dinner that evening, I returned to the guava tree to think about Abuela Balbina and the times I spent with her before leaving Cuba. I didn't know what else to do. Mourning the loss of a close relative was a new experience for me. I desperately wanted to be with my family.

Two days after the U-2 spy plane returned from Cuba, at the October 16, 1962 meeting of ExComm, the C.I.A. presented photo evidence of missile sites on Cuban soil taken by that U-2 spy plane. All this information was classified at the time, and the media was not informed. But somehow, discussions with my classmates continued to center around bombs in Cuba and the devastation nuclear war would cause. It was hard to escape the conversation. Every time someone brought up the subject in the schoolyard, I would try not to listen or to walk away unnoticed. I could not understand why some of the kids were so persistent on scaring others with information that was, at the time, simply rumor. I needed to hear some positive news about the U.S. and its relations with Cuba. Instead, all I was getting at school and on the evening news was negativity. Sometimes, I would just walk away from the television and climb the guava tree to hide, sit, and relax on a branch. That guava tree became my only escape from the problems of the world.

The following day, C.I.A. analysts reviewed additional photographs taken by the other U-2 spy planes. They found

Cuban Missile Crisis - 1962

launchers, missiles, and transport trucks that led them to conclude that the Soviets were already building sites to launch missiles capable of striking anywhere in the U.S. President Kennedy scheduled a meeting with ExComm to discuss three options presented by the Secretary of Defense Robert McNamara. The first was to pursue diplomacy with Castro and Khrushchev. The second was to surround the island and create a blockade to prevent future deliveries of missiles and supplies to build the launch pads. The last and most severe of all three options was an air attack to destroy all the missile sites, killing thousands of Soviet personnel. The air attack was guaranteed to trigger a Soviet counterattack somewhere around the globe, perhaps in Berlin. Kennedy rejected the attack and favored a "quarantine" to buy time to negotiate a missile withdrawal. It was important to call it a quarantine and not a "blockade," which could be interpreted as an act of war. President Kennedy insisted on additional time before he made his decision. The meeting ended without a follow-up date.

On Sunday, October 21, 1962, one week after the U-2 spy plane took photos of the missile sites, President Kennedy decided on a naval quarantine of Cuba. On the following day, Monday, October 22, 1962 at 7:00 p.m., he addressed the American public in a dramatic 18-minute live television speech, shocking viewers by revealing the evidence of the missile threat and demanding that the Soviets remove their missiles immediately.

I remember that day very clearly. The regular program on television was interrupted for a "special announcement." As we all stared at the screen, the President appeared live for his speech. Everyone in the house was glued to the television set. Susana had her hands covering her mouth in disbelief of what we were all hearing. The look on everyone's faces reminded me of our neighbors in Cuba sitting around our radio listening to the news about the defeat of the Cuban exiles in the Bay of Pigs. My worst nightmare became a reality. What my classmates in school were saying during the past several months became fact. I immediately assumed that I would never see the rest of my family again.

Cuban Missile Crisis - 1962

****

The day after President Kennedy's speech on national television, my classmates in school were all buzzing with "what if" scenarios that frightened many of the kids who still had family in Cuba. It was an ugly scene that morning before going inside the classroom. Several kids began to cry, others wanted to leave and return home. The teacher, Miss Fernandez, realized what was happening and brought us inside quickly and attempted to calm everyone's nerves. It was not easy for her either; she told us she also had family living in Cuba. She said it was important for everyone to support each other and remain optimistic for a peaceful solution. Discussions about the missile crisis continued in class for most of the morning. Nobody had any interest in the regular schoolwork. But eventually Miss Fernandez was convincing enough to make everyone feel more comfortable. Soon, we returned to our studies. Concentrating on our regular schoolwork eventually got our minds away from the crisis until it was time for recess.

Today, I look back at that scene outside the classroom the day after President Kennedy's speech, and I can still see the fear and sorrow in my classmates' eyes. It was distressing. I think I had the same look on my face but I tried to hide my feelings. Everyone needed to share their concerns and fear with each other. I avoided contact with anyone discussing the missile crisis. I just stood there, listened, and kept my mouth shut. I kept all my emotions locked up inside my mind and tried to convince myself that everything would work out fine and the war would be avoided.

At the end of class that day, Miss Fernandez asked me to stay behind for a minute. My group of friends, who usually walked with me to and from school, continued without me. Miss Fernandez waited until everyone left the room and told me that she was concerned about me because I did not participate much in class today and I was not acting like my usual self. She knew my parents and younger brother were still in Cuba and wanted to be sure someone was there for me if I wanted to share my thoughts

Cuban Missile Crisis - 1962

or just chat. She held my hand and then gave me a big hug. I could not control myself any longer. I cried on her shoulder as she rubbed my back and kept telling me that everything would be fine in the future. She looked directly at me and told me not to worry, a peaceful solution will prevail. I noticed tears running down her cheeks and realized that she was hurting just as much. I walked home by myself that afternoon thinking about my parents and the confrontation between the U.S., Soviet Union and Cuba. I cried almost all the way home.

****

Reconnaissance photos continued to reveal that Soviet missiles were up and ready for launch. Secretary of Defense McNamara and President Kennedy reviewed the new photos and discussed options that were available at that time, knowing that if the U.S. invaded in the next few days, Cuba would most likely fire missiles at U.S. targets. The crisis dominated most discussions at home and at school. The television was on all the time at home, with periodic interruptions updating the viewers on the status of the missile crisis. Schoolmates would bring portable transistor radios to school to hear the news during recess. It was impossible to escape the media blitz – and I did not want to hear it anymore. Whenever the news was getting to me at home, I would just return to the guava tree, my best and only escape from the world.

The tree was not completely void of the missile crisis because my mind would occasionally still go back to my family in Cuba and think about what they were doing while I was just sitting on a tree branch in the backyard. In school, we began to rehearse bomb drills and practice getting under our desks in the event a missile was launched to hit Miami. It was difficult to escape the thought of war. It was all around us.

During the week of President Kennedy's live television speech, there were barely any communications with Soviet officials until Friday, October 26, 1962 when U.S. officials received a letter from

Cuban Missile Crisis - 1962

Khrushchev stating that the Soviets would remove their missiles if President Kennedy publicly guaranteed the U.S. would not invade Cuba. At the same time, the C.I.A. reported that construction of the missile sites continued and accelerated. Earlier that day, Attorney General Robert Kennedy secretly met with the Soviet Ambassador and agreed that the removal of U.S. missiles from Turkey could be negotiated as part of the settlement.

Castro felt that the Soviets may back down from a confrontation with the U.S., so he sent a cable to Khrushchev before the end of the day, urging a nuclear first strike against the U.S. immediately, even if the U.S. did not invade Cuba. He was truly obsessed with starting a war with the U.S. as long as he had The Soviet Union supporting him.

It was impossible to make calls to Cuba during this time. Every Cuban in Miami was trying to reach relatives, and the international telephone lines were constantly busy. Finally, we were able to get through while Segundito was visiting, and we spoke with our parents. There was not much they could say in fear that the government was listening to our conversation. It was a sad moment, but we kept our spirits up and tried to give them comfort, assuring them that diplomacy would find its way through the ordeal.

On Sunday, October 28, 1962, Radio Moscow announced that the Soviet Union had accepted the proposed solution from the U.S. It released the text of Khrushchev's letter affirming that the missiles would be removed in exchange for a non-invasion pledge from the U.S. Sadly, Operation Pedro Pan ended when all air traffic between The United States and Cuba ceased due to the crisis. The influx of Cuban children had been reported on locally, but details of the program were not disclosed nationally, so few news outlets outside Florida realized it was happening.

Now that air travel between the two countries was terminated and there was no discussion of restarting it, Cubans who still wanted to leave the country and reunite with families here needed to travel via Spain or Mexico first to reach the U.S. This process was much more difficult and expensive, and it required significantly more

Cuban Missile Crisis - 1962

time. The opportunity for our parents to leave the country had just about completely disappeared.

The quarantine continued until December 1, 1962, when President Kennedy was assured that the Soviets had removed all the missiles. On that day at 9:00 a.m., a large Soviet cargo ship quietly left the Cuban port of Mariel carrying the last of the nuclear warheads that The Soviet Union had deployed just a couple of months ago. Now the ship was headed east across the Atlantic back to The Soviet Union. This inconspicuous departure represented the end of an extremely dangerous crisis in our lives.

One of the very few positive outcomes of Operation Mongoose was that it generated the intelligence that tipped off Washington about the Russian nuclear missiles in Cuba. However, leaks about Mongoose had also encouraged Nikita Khrushchev to send missiles in the first place to safeguard the Castro regime from *yanqui* aggression. After the crisis ended, Mongoose was formally disbanded early in 1963. Efforts to overthrow Castro resumed shortly thereafter.

It was not a completely happy ending to the crisis.

Cuban Missile Crisis - 1962

CHAPTER 30

Another Move
1963

During the time that the U-2 spy planes were flying over Cuba and the U.S. was discovering the Soviet missiles, Tio Mario and Juan were able to secure jobs in the restaurant business. Tia Maria Luisa was also able to get some housecleaning assignments. Within a few weeks after their arrival, they rented an affordable apartment in a northwest neighborhood of Miami. Unfortunately, it was not close to my current school district. They were also able to purchase an old car for their transportation.

Now that the missile crisis was over and they were settled in a new home, Segundito and I moved in with them in late October 1962. Another moving experience – our new home was a very small two-bedroom street level apartment in a neighborhood that had a higher than normal level of crimes. Actually, the apartment was only a one-bedroom with a fabric curtain dividing the room so the landlord classified it as a "two-bedroom". Tia and Tio slept on one side of the curtain. Segundito, Juan, and I slept on three small twin sized beds jammed on the other side of the curtain. The only way to access the bathroom in the apartment was to climb over one of the twin beds. The landlord restricted the occupancy of the apartment to no more than three residents, so Segundito and I had to hide inside most of the time to avoid being seen by the landlord in case he drove by the house.

Tio Mario and Juan worked in a trendy Miami Beach restaurant, so they kept late night hours and did not come home until after midnight. Because of their late hours, they did not get up in the morning until we left for school. Our morning routines of breakfast and getting dressed and ready for school were done in complete silence. I got used to the new sleeping arrangements quickly. I did not mind the small apartment. I was comfortable and happy to be living with my brother and other family members.

The multiple changes of schools during the past year were obviously annoying and disruptive but necessary. I started another new school on November 1, 1962. This time, I walked about a mile and wait in the school auditorium for the bus to take a group of Spanish-speaking students for a 30-minute drive to another school that provided classes for Spanish speaking students. After classes were finished, another bus would take us back to my neighborhood school, and I would walk home by myself. This was necessary because my neighborhood school had reached maximum capacity and was not equipped to handle students who were not proficient in English. It seemed like a lot of time was wasted getting bussed to a different location daily.

Segundito attended a middle school nearby and did not have the travel issues I experienced. At times, he would meet me after school, and we would walk home together. Our new neighborhood did not have the reputation of being the safest place in the city, so it was good to have company on the way home. I was never able to

Another Move - 1963

make new friends in this neighborhood, and the kids I knew from school lived in different and better neighborhoods.

****

During the time that Segundito and I lived with Tio, Tia, and Juan, I couldn't help but feel the stress that came from having limited financial resources. Tio and Juan always commented that they were not making enough money for the hard work they were doing at the restaurant. They realized it was not easy to find work, so they were forced to stay until the job market improved and a better paying job could be found. Tia's housecleaning assignments were sporadic and unreliable. It seemed like they were always trying to figure out how much money was available for groceries, gasoline for the car, and the monthly rent. Segundito and I were too young to find a job but I was willing to go around the neighborhood and help anyone with their gardening chores. Tio Mario would not allow it – It was not the type of neighborhood where he felt comfortable letting me do a few gardening chores on weekends to earn a few dollars.

There wasn't much I could do to help except for trying not to be a financial burden to them. Five people living under one roof in an extra-small apartment was confining. Staying out of everyone's way was not an easy task. We were able to get assistance from government agencies and family friends, and I was just as happy searching in thrift stores with Tia for clothes that fit and were suitable for school.

The holidays were approaching. We were all invited for a Thanksgiving feast at the home of a friend of Tia and Tio. The restaurant was closed for this holiday, so Tio and Juan were able to join us. Besides being a time to give thanks for what we had, we learned that it was also a Thanksgiving tradition to stuff yourself with a delicious meal on this day. We did not disappoint our hosts who were gracious to provide us with "to go" containers when we left their home.

Another Move - 1963

My first Christmas in the U.S. was approaching, and I knew a Christmas tree was not going to be a wise investment for us. I did not ask for one that year. Instead, the same family that invited us for Thanksgiving surprised us and brought us a small artificial tree with a few lights, ornaments, and a nativity set to place under the tree. It was a kind and memorable gesture during a financially difficult time for us.

****

On Christmas Eve 1962, just over 1,000 men who were taken prisoner at the Bay of Pigs Invasion returned to the U.S. in accordance with an agreement between the two countries that required the U.S. to make a payment of $53 million in food and medical supplies. The U.S. government coordinated the payment by getting companies all over the U.S. to donate. Because the delivery would take time to arrange, only a small portion of the total amount was sent to Cuba via a Red Cross freighter prior to Christmas Day. The remainder was expected to take several months and at least four more trips. This presented an opportunity for Cubans who wanted to leave the island. The freighters would be returning to the U.S. empty after their deliveries, so Castro allowed Cubans the opportunity for passage to the U.S. on the return trips. There were specific requirements the passengers had to comply with, including assigning all your assets such as real estate to the Castro regime. In just a short amount of time, the list to leave the country on a future Red Cross freighter became extremely long and almost impossible to access. Most of the Cubans on the list were family members of the men taken prisoner at the Bay of Pigs Invasion. My parents were still determined to be part of this exodus effort, which would expire once all the food and supplies that were promised reached the island. It was extremely difficult to get on the list and it was doubtful they would be able to leave Cuba on one of the freighters.

It was later revealed that the deal to exchange the prisoners for food and medical supplies almost fell apart after Fidel Castro's last-minute demand for an additional $2.9 million in cash. He made this request just as the prisoners were preparing to leave on transport planes. The additional money was raised in a frantic day of fundraising on Christmas Eve by President Kennedy's brother, Attorney General Robert Kennedy, and General Lucius D. Clay, an advisor to the Cuban Families Committee of the prisoners' relatives. The largest donation was $1 million, given by a donor who wished to remain anonymous. According to the government, the donor was not part of the Kennedy family.

On Christmas morning, we were lucky to be able to get an international phone line and call Cuba to speak with our parents and Jorge. Even though there were no more flights from Cuba to the U.S. since the missile crisis, they told us they were still determined to find a way to join us quickly. Having the opportunity to speak with them on Christmas morning was the best and only present I received that day.

New Year's Eve was quiet and uneventful. Tio Mario and Juan had to work that night, and Tia Maria Luisa went to bed early. Segundito and I stayed up and watched the ball drop in Times Square on an old black and white portable television with a rabbit ears antenna wrapped in aluminum foil. The scene on the television screen brought back memories of our overnight visit to Manhattan where we visited Times Square to see the movie, "State Fair." It was exciting to see Times Square on television filled with New Year's revelers and to recollect my astonishment at the size of the buildings, billboards, and illumination generated by the marquees.

****

A new year had begun: 1963. A week after New Year's Eve, Tio Mario and Juan were both terminated from their restaurant jobs due to a slowdown in business, a sad beginning to a new year. Within a few days, Juan was able to get another restaurant job but Tio Mario had to keep looking for work. The unemployment rate in Miami was high, and the job market was extremely competitive.

Another Move - 1963

The influx of Cuban families looking to settle and find employment had increased significantly over the past two years. Government, other non-profit assistance and help from local friends we received during this difficult time was helpful to get us through financially, but it was not to be expected in the long term.

Because of the significant population of Cuban refugees looking for jobs in the Miami area, the National Catholic Welfare Conferences Resettlement Program for Cuban refugees encouraged us to consider moving to another city or state where jobs would be easier to find and the unemployment rate would be significantly lower. Our assigned case manager explained to Tia and Tio that jobs in the Northeast were plentiful and paid a higher rate than the market could sustain in Miami. The agency, along with several local Catholic churches in the Northeast, would cover most if not all of the basic relocation expenses such as travel and meals. They would also work with us and the churches to find suitable housing and provide limited financial assistance to get us settled at our new location. The case manager preferred for Tia and Tio to consider a move later in February to avoid the severe January winter the Northeast was experiencing. Since there was no reason to make an immediate decision, they decided to continue to look for employment in Miami and reconsider the case manager's suggestion later in February.

I was aware of the case manager's recommendation and this time, I was not particularly concerned about another move. I was now an experienced mover, so this one would not be a shock to my system. Perhaps it would be a better location for employment and schools. The cold winter would not bother me after spending time in Sparkill, New York. If my parents were able to leave Cuba soon, they would likely join us up north since the shortage of professional jobs in Miami for my father would make it difficult to stay here and find work to support the family. Maybe there would be more positives about this move than negatives. I was supportive of the decision. Tio and Tia had the last word.

Another Move - 1963

****

The start of the New Year was uneventful for me. Not having any neighborhood friends forced me to stay home a lot after school. We were afraid to be seen outside on the front porch by the landlord, so that area became off-limits for us. There were no trees to climb in the backyard either. The only entertainment after school was watching television, especially the "I Love Lucy" show and "American Bandstand" with Dick Clark on Saturday afternoons. Our television set was always temperamental, and the rabbit ears antenna always seemed to need constant adjustment.

The freighter ships delivering food and medical supplies to Cuba continued. On their return trips, the ships were full of Cuban refugees. We waited patiently to hear if our parents and Jorge were able to get on board, but by the end of February 1963, there was still no news of their departure. On the 17th of February, we celebrated the one-year anniversary of our departure from Cuba. Perhaps "celebrated" is not the proper description. Let's just say the anniversary was remembered and acknowledged. I was happy to be in the U.S. but sad that we could not get any information on how much longer it would take to see the rest of my family again.

During the beginning of the New Year, Secretary of State Dean Rusk warned the Senate Foreign Relations Committee that the Cuban crisis was far from over. President Kennedy still felt that Cuba should remain a focus of the U.S. He was primarily concerned about the potential spread of communism in the Caribbean Islands and Central and South America. There were persistent rumors that The Soviet Union was still hiding missiles on the island because there were several thousand armed Soviet troops that remained in Cuba after the official end of the Missile Crisis. President Kennedy had hoped that after the official crisis ended, and with Castro's disappointment of how Khrushchev handled the negotiations, Castro would be interested in developing some type of relationship with the U.S. which would get the Soviets out of Cuba.

Another Move - 1963

In late March 1963, another freighter trip left South Florida and arrived in Cuba with food and medical supplies. The freighter returned filled with Cubans wanting to leave the island. There was still no word from our family. The opportunities for their departure from Cuba were slowly diminishing. Sadly, there was nothing we could do to help them get on the list. Time was slowly running out.

Another Move - 1963

PART THREE

One cannot and must not try to erase the past merely because it does not fit the present.

- GOLDA MEIR

CHAPTER 31

A Move to Connecticut 1963

The absence of any news about my parents and Jorge getting on the list to board the next Red Cross freighter leaving Cuba was disheartening. By now, Tio, Tia, and Juan were discouraged about the lack of employment opportunities in Miami. They met with the case manager again at the National Catholic Welfare Agency around the end of February 1963 to discuss options for jobs and housing outside of Miami. They also discussed the process they would have to follow if they decided to leave Miami.

The case manager informed them about an opportunity that was available through the Spanish Speaking Center at St. Cecilia's Church in Waterbury, Connecticut, which expressed interest in sponsoring another family. The Center had already successfully hosted a Cuban family of five several months ago, and the husband began working almost immediately upon their arrival. She informed Tio and Tia that the City of Waterbury had many opportunities for manufacturing jobs that paid more than what Juan and Mario could earn in Miami. The city had a low cost of living, good schools, and a low unemployment rate.

There was also potential employment for non-manufacturing and professional jobs. This was important since Juan's schooling was in office management and accounting. St. Cecilia's Church and other donors coordinated by the church would provide us with a furnished apartment, food, and rent until we were settled and the adults were employed. In addition, Segundito and I would enroll in a local private Catholic school that would give us an excellent education beyond what we could have in Miami. Since our English had improved substantially, we would be eligible to enroll in all English classes.

I couldn't see any downside to the proposal. The case manager was still concerned about the weather in the Northeast, and suggested we target mid-April for our move. Tio and Tia were concerned about the cold weather and the winter snows. We had several days of discussions, and Segundito and I assured them that we were in agreement for a move back up North if the economics and schooling were to our advantage. The following week, Tio and Tia met with the case manager again. After obtaining confirmation from her that we would receive the initial assistance needed to get settled, they agreed to move to Waterbury, Connecticut.

We had to travel to Waterbury by train. We were scheduled to leave on April 15, 1963. It would take us just over a day and a half to arrive in Waterbury and had only about a month to prepare for the move. The only personal possession that needed to be sold was the old used car Tio and Juan bought for transportation. The apartment in Miami was rented fully furnished, so all we had to do was leave the furniture and kitchenware as we found them.

There wasn't a lot for me to prepare for this trip. I was used to moving and knew how to quickly pack my clothing and my limited personal belongings. I did not get the opportunity to develop any

A Move to Connecticut - 1963

close relationships with my schoolmates. Making the move to Waterbury now was easy.

We were warned that meals on the train were expensive and of poor quality. So, as part of our economizing strategy, the night before we left, Tia made sandwiches for the five of us to last us for the entire trip. Almost 36 hours of sandwiches! The train was scheduled to leave Miami at 8:30 a.m. and to arrive in Waterbury at 6:00 p.m. the following day, with a station transfer from Penn Station to Grand Central when we arrived in Manhattan.

On the morning of April 15,1963, about a week after my 10th birthday, I was up early and ready by the front door while everyone else ran around the apartment trying to squeeze last-minute items in their luggage and close it tightly. We needed two cars to take us to the station, so friends of Tia and Tio gave us rides. Upon our arrival at the station, I looked at all of us and saw images of "The Beverly Hillbillies." We had to carry two bags each, find the track number, and board the train for the next two days.

Finally, the train pulled away from the station. I looked out the window and was reminded of previous departures from La Habana, Miami, and St. Agnes. After moving several times in Miami, now we were headed back up north, this time to Waterbury, Connecticut. All these changes in just over one year. I was starting to feel like an experienced world traveler! I stared out the window and said my goodbyes to Miami again.

****

The train ride was boring and uneventful. There was not much to do except look out the window and watch the towns fly by. I kept getting out of my seat to walk up and down the aisle to visit other cars. Those walks began to get boring also. The train was scheduled to make multiple stops in some major cities, including Savannah, Charleston, Washington, D.C., and Philadelphia. When we stopped in Washington, D.C., we were allowed to get off the train for 30 minutes. Tia and I stayed inside while the others

A Move to Connecticut - 1963

went out to the station to see if they could find refreshments and something to eat besides sandwiches. Not surprisingly, we were all tired of the sandwiches. As we were getting close to the end of the 30-minute time frame, we kept looking out the window and did not see Juan, Tio, and Segundito. Now we started to panic and wondered what we would do if the train left without them – Should I pull the emergency cord? As far as I was concerned, it would have been an emergency if we left them behind. I was young and did not realize the implications of pulling the emergency cord. Finally, just as the train was ready to start moving, the three of then came running down the stairs of the terminal and jumped inside the car closest to the stairs. They brought back hamburgers, fries, sodas, magazines, and Spanish-language newspapers. Enough food and entertainment to last us until we arrived in Waterbury.

As we got close to Penn Station in Manhattan, Juan reviewed the plans to transfer to Grand Central Station with us. He warned us to stay close together because it was the start of rush hour and the station would be filled with commuters running for their trains. We were expecting to meet with a man who would identify himself as a private investigator. He was hired by the Agency to take us from Penn Station to Grand Central Station by cab. Now we had to pin to our coat lapels a small sign that read "CUBAN REFUGEES" so the PI could find us. I don't think the signs were needed. He just had to look for five people walking together with luggage they could barely carry.

We met with the PI just as we got off the train. He grabbed Tia's luggage and told us to follow him to the waiting room. As soon as we exited the tracks and walked into the terminal, I was struck by the architectural grandeur of Penn Station. The interior was something I had never seen before. There were huge columns and windows that provided an amazing light to complement the design details. All I could do was look up to the ceilings, the walls, and the massive windows. People everywhere tried to get around me as I stopped and simply stared at the ceiling, the walls, and the marble floors. It only took me less than 30 seconds to realize that I

A Move to Connecticut - 1963

was now alone, by myself, and very lost. My family did not noticed I wasn't following them any longer – I was left behind in the center of complete chaos. I was sinking deep in a sea of people who all looked the same: They were twice my height wearing dark grey suits under long winter coats and hats. Everyone was walking in different directions, crisscrossing each other without bumping into each other. How did they do it?

I stood in the middle of Penn Station with two pieces of heavy luggage, all my myself. Nobody noticed me. I wondered what my next step should be. If I stayed here and hollered for help, nobody would hear me. The noise inside the building was much greater than the power inside my lungs. If I didn't move, someone could accidentally knock me down on the marble floor and step on me. If I walked over to the side wall, perhaps the others would not think to look for me there. I stayed where I was, placed the luggage on either side of me for protection, and waited for someone to rescue me. It took less than two minutes but felt like hours. Suddenly, a hand grabbed me by the collar and another hand grabbed one of my bags. It was Juan who whisked me out from the center towards the waiting room where the PI had gathered the rest of my group. I think if the PI had his way, he would have smacked me in the head or belted me for getting lost. I was simply acting like a tourist – I felt I did nothing wrong.

Watching all the commuters rushing by us trying to get home was exhausting. Now that we were all together, the PI gave us instructions on our next step. He was going to put us in two cabs to get to Grand Central Station's main entrance. There, we would board another train that would make its last stop in Waterbury, Connecticut. Inside the first cab would be Juan, Tia, and Segundito with most of the luggage. The second cab would be Tio, the PI, and me with the remainder of the luggage.

We were out of the building and I was still staring at the grandness of the architecture. This time, it was the façade of the building that entranced me. Suddenly, the PI grabbed me by my collar and pushed me inside the cab. He said something under his

A Move to Connecticut - 1963

breath that I did not understand. Today, I can easily imagine what he said.

The ride to Grand Central was the equivalent of riding bumper cars at an amusement park. The only difference was the number of people in New York City crossing the streets in front of the moving cars. Were all these people trying to commit suicide? We reached Grand Central Station where we were relieved to be reunited with Juan, Tia, and Segundito. We walked inside the terminal where I stopped to admire another beautiful structure. I had to slow down to experience what I was witnessing. Unfortunately, the PI grabbed me by the collar again and almost choked me as he pushed me along to the designated track to board the train. I wondered if New York was filled with buildings like the two I just experienced. I knew back then that I would return to New York someday in the future and spend a lot more time there on my own. I loved the atmosphere of the city and the excitement that the people generated. I hoped that Waterbury was not too far away to be able to return often.

The train left the station and traveled underground for several miles. After a few minutes, we were out in open air. There were buildings everywhere I looked. This was one of the most exciting places I had visited. Tio had a different opinion. *"No sé quién quiere vivir en una ciudad como esta."* (I don't know who would want to live in a city like this.) I quickly figured out he would not be taking me back here anytime soon. I could not wait to reach Waterbury and get off this train. After spending over 30 hours inside a train car, I felt like a wild animal inside a cage. I was ready for a change and I hoped it would not be much longer.

****

As we got closer to our last stop, the pace of the outside world seemed to slow down substantially. Buildings were not as tall, the traffic was not congested, the noise level was down, and there were only a handful of people walking the streets. The train began to travel north from the Bridgeport stop. The spring scenery going

A Move to Connecticut - 1963

north from Bridgeport was a memorable site to see. The rolling hills, blossoms on trees, and riverbeds were encouraging to see from the train's window. Finally, our train began to slow down as it reached its final stop. We climbed down the steep stairs with our oversized and overweight luggage. Now, I could breathe fresh spring air that was absent in New York City. Just in front of us there was a man dressed in a "priestly" outfit approaching us with a friendly and welcoming smile. *"Hola, yo soy Padre Blackall."* (Hi, I am Father Blackall).

The friendly priest drove some of us to our new apartment followed by a cab with the rest of us and the remainder of the luggage. We stopped right in front of a six-story building where he said, *"Bienvenidos a su nuevo hogar."* (Welcome to your new home.) There was no elevator and a lot of luggage. Of course, the apartment was on the top floor. It was worth the exercise after a long train ride just sitting on my butt. I wasn't sure Tio and Tia felt the same way. Tio was a heavy smoker, so he had difficulties climbing the stairs without stopping to rest. I raced up to the top floor, dropped off the luggage I was carrying and walked down to meet Tio and Tia to help them with their luggage.

When everyone finally arrived at the top floor and opened the door, the apartment surpassed our expectations. Located just around the corner from the main street in the downtown district, it had four bedrooms fully furnished with extra linens and towels in the closets. The large kitchen was fully stocked and had a door to the back porch. At the opposite end of the apartment, a large living room in the front facing the street. The four small bedrooms between the kitchen and living room meant that each of us had our own private space. It was hard to believe we walked into a fully furnished apartment packed with groceries in the pantry and milk, eggs, bread, and other food staples in the refrigerator.

While touring the apartment and its contents, there was a knock on the door. Neighbors from the floor below us, also Cuban, brought a large pot with *arroz con pollo* (chicken with rice), a Cuban favorite. Zenaida lived downstairs with her husband Higinio, his

A Move to Connecticut - 1963

elderly mother, and two small children. They were the first Cuban family that St. Cecilia's Church sponsored. They made us dinner so we did not have to cook upon our arrival. It was a kind and generous gesture by a friendly and welcoming neighbor. We were all tired and starving after a long and tedious train ride. A home-cooked Cuban meal was a wonderful welcoming gift to receive in a new city.

****

That first night in Waterbury, Tuesday, April 16, 1963, was a late night for all of us. After eating a delicious warm Cuban meal, we began to unpack. Each of us took turns bathing. The following morning, we got a late start. Tio, Tia, and Juan walked over to St. Cecilia's rectory, which was just about two blocks from the apartment. They were going to meet with Father Blackall who was to provide them with information about job opportunities and where to apply. In addition, he made arrangements for Segundito and me to attend St. Anne's parochial school within walking distance of the apartment. We were scheduled to meet with the principal the following day before school started. But first, we had to purchase the school uniform at a local department store. Father Blackall had arranged for the store to bill the Church directly.

I was assigned to the fourth-grade class and Segundito was assigned to the seventh-grade class. My teacher, Sister Teresa, was extremely helpful to me during my first day, and made sure that I felt welcomed. My English had improved substantially. Now, in an all English class, I was concerned I would be lost and fail. I had to work twice as hard as the other kids in class because I needed to improve my reading and writing skills. Since the teacher recognized my effort, she continued to provide me with personal attention and encouragement. She also got me more involved with other students who tutored me. After a few days at St. Anne's, I started to enjoy going to school – I didn't remember ever having such a positive attitude about learning. That is the effect a teacher should have on students.

A Move to Connecticut - 1963

Tio Mario and Juan were able to get work within the first week of arriving in Waterbury. Tio was a salesman when he lived in Cuba, and Juan's background was in administration and accounting. Getting manufacturing jobs for both was a start in the right direction but their ultimate goals were to get jobs that would fit their backgrounds. Juan had a better understanding of the English language than Tio. That would make employment opportunities for Tio more difficult.

About two weeks after we arrived in Waterbury, Tio and Juan came home with a used car they had just purchased. We all got in and Juan took us for a ride around the city to see other neighborhoods in town. On weekends, we occasionally packed a picnic basket and drove to a local lake with Zenaida, Higinio, and their family for an afternoon of swimming and just relaxing in the open air. It was still a bit colder in early May than it was back in Miami but that did not stop me from plunging into the water. I missed the rough waves from the ocean and the smell and taste of the salt water.

After school, I would go home to change from my school uniform and walk around the neighborhood. Our apartment was located about a block away from the main street, so it was fun to walk there by myself and window shop in the afternoons. The city had three separate high schools, all of which were located just outside the perimeter of the downtown district. After school ended for the day, the streets downtown were flooded with high school kids sitting at the local soda fountains or pizza shops, walking the streets, shopping at the various department stores, hanging out at the local record store, or waiting at the bus stops for a ride home. Life in downtown Waterbury after school was fun, lively, and full of young teenagers. I could get used to living here very quickly. It seemed to be a city with a big future.

****

Shortly after we arrived in Waterbury, another Red Cross freighter returned from Cuba full of Cuban refugees after delivering

A Move to Connecticut - 1963

a shipment of food and medical supplies in accordance with the agreement between the U.S. and Cuba. My parents and Jorge were not able to get on the ship again. I sensed the fear in Tia's eyes when we received confirmation that they were not on that freighter. I was really beginning to worry. The last delivery would take place towards the end of May 1963. Tia would always tell me not to worry. *"Ellos encontrarán una manera de llegar aquí."* (They will find a way to get here).

A Move to Connecticut - 1963

CHAPTER 32

The Morning Light
1963

There was little, if any, hope of emigrating to the U.S. as originally planned. That was the feeling of many Cubans left behind after the Cuban Missile Crisis. Thousands still tried to leave only to find there was no more travel between the two countries. Many of them had sons and daughters in the U.S. sent under the Operation Pedro Pan program. Like my parents, they were now stranded in Cuba without an exit strategy, unable to reach their dream of being reunited with their families again.

The agreement between the U.S. and Cuba to exchange food and medical supplies for the prisoners of the Bay of Pigs Invasion provided a limited way out for a small number of Cubans to leave the country. The Red Cross was responsible for all the deliveries in addition to the safety of the passengers that were leaving Cuba and emigrating to the U.S.

My father immediately applied for passage for my mother, my brother, and himself in December 1962 at the start of the program. As time passed without receiving any notification, their hope of reuniting with us was diminishing daily.

After almost five months of waiting, in early May 1963, my parents were told that they may be placed on the last ship. They would have to present their documents at the police station where they would be questioned and forced to signed over ownership to the government of all their personal property, including our home, car, bank accounts, and household furnishings. There was still no guarantee that after turning over all of our assets to the government, they would be allowed to leave. It was a risk they had to take. The Red Cross S.S. Morning Light would leave the port of Mariel on May 23, 1963. If they were allowed to depart on this trip, they would be notified only 48 hours in advance.

Two days before the departure of the S.S. Morning Light, my family found out they could board the ship as long as they obtained written confirmation that all their utilities, including phone, gas, and electricity, were fully paid. They also had to show physical proof that they had paid off any other personal debts. If they did not have proof of payment with them at the dock, they could not board the ship.

They were told to arrive at the port at 6:00 a.m. on May 23 with nothing but the clothes on their backs. No money was allowed, not even loose change in their pockets. The same day they received notice, Tio Orlando called us from La Habana to keep us informed because my father had to disconnect his phone and was not able to make or receive any telephone messages. Tio Orlando wanted to be sure that we did not set our hopes too high because anything could happen. They could be denied boarding for any reason the government could create. But still, it was great news for all of us. We were optimistic, and in our minds, we were already planning a reunion.

The Morning Light - 1963

Many of our relatives living in Cuba at the time, including Tia Nena, Tia Vivina, and Tio Frank, stopped by the day before they were scheduled to board the freighter to say goodbye and wish them a safe journey. To avoid raising any concerns from the neighborhood *Comité* of a large gathering at our home everyone arrived at different times and only stayed for a short period. It was the only way to say goodbye to relatives and friends. Earlier that morning, my parents and Jorge went to visit and say goodbye to Abuela Teresa. She had begun to develop signs of dementia and did not completely comprehend that her daughter and family were leaving the country and she may never see them again. It was a sad farewell – My mother knew it would be the last time she would see her mother again.

In the early morning of May 23, Tio Orlando drove my parents and Jorge one block away from the terminal as requested by government officials and hugged them in a tearful goodbye. When they reached the check-in area and the government officials reviewed all their documents, they were told to stand in line and wait in the hot sun without food or drink until 2:00 p.m. when they finally were allowed to board the ship. No relatives or friends were permitted anywhere near the docks. Finally, several hours after boarding, the ship sailed out of the port and into the open and free waters of the Caribbean Sea. Tio Orlando could not confirm they were on the ship sailing to the U.S. He was not allowed to see them board. If they were prevented from boarding, they were most likely being detained at an undisclosed location. We still could not get confirmation that they left Cuba and were headed for the U.S.

The day the freighter sailed away from Cuba's port, we received a call from friends in Miami. They told us they heard through mutual friends in Cuba that my parents and Jorge may be arriving in South Florida the next day. They planned to be at the terminal the following morning to pick them up in case they were on the ship and would bring them to their home. As soon as they got in the house, they would call us with any news. We had hope that the news was favorable, but we were still not certain they were allowed to leave the country.

The Morning Light - 1963

The S.S. Morning Light arrived in South Florida as scheduled on the morning of May 24, 1963. After delays in debarkation and the normal immigration process, my parents and Jorge were seen exiting the ship and going down its gangway. They immediately connected with their friends who were anxiously waiting to confirm that they were on the ship. After a warm and tearful embrace, it was time to take them home and make a few phone calls to family waiting for the good news.

As soon as we got home from school that day, Tia Maria Luisa told us that she got a call from Miami and spoke with our parents and Jorge. In a few minutes, we would place a telephone call to Miami and speak with them directly. I can still remember their voices on that telephone call. They were more than 1,000 miles away but I felt they were right next to me.

It was the start of a wonderful weekend as we began preparations for a reunion.

****

My parents and Jorge had to stay in Miami for a couple of weeks to get their immigration papers settled and work with the National Catholic Welfare Agency to obtain assistance with travel to Waterbury. Father Blackall and the Spanish Speaking Center of St. Cecilia's Church were ready to help on this end. Upon their arrival, we would all have to live together in the same apartment until we had the financial resources to afford our own apartment. Father Blackall assured us it would not take long with his help. It was time for us to plan and prepare the apartment for three more residents. My parents would take over my bedroom, and Jorge and I would sleep on the couch in the living room. I knew it was going to be a temporary arrangement. I was used to sleeping on couches at this point. And if that's what it took to accommodate them, I was very happy to give up my room to make them comfortable.

The generosity of the parishioners from St. Cecilia's Church was heartwarming. During this time, we kept receiving donations of food, clothing, and housewares for our new apartment. I was no longer concerned whether I would ever see my family again. My thoughts now focused on counting down the days it would take to get them to Waterbury.

Periodic telephone calls to Miami kept us updated on their travel status. Finally, The National Catholic Welfare Agency arranged for train passage for all three leaving Miami on Saturday, June 8, 1963. They would arrive the next day in Waterbury, one week before Father's Day. There could not have been a better early Father's Day present for everyone. We continued making plans for their arrival.

****

On Sunday morning, June 9, the day of my family's expected arrival in Waterbury, we all went to an early mass. When we returned home, Tia began to cook for all of us, including Father Blackall and our Cuban neighbors downstairs who we invited to join us. Since their expected arrival would be late in the afternoon, we planned for an early dinner of Cuban *paella*. The Catholic Welfare Agency in Miami not only provided my parents and Jorge with train tickets to Waterbury but also clothing, luggage, and some spending money for the trip. I moved out of my bedroom and emptied my dresser and closet to make room for their personal items. I folded my clothing, placed it inside my luggage and forced it to fit neatly under the couch in the living room which I used as my bed at night.

It was a chaotic day waiting for their arrival. I wanted everything to be perfect for them but at the same time I knew they would be tired from the long trip since we had just experienced the same a couple of months ago. Perhaps they would like to rest and go to sleep early. I was obviously selfish and wanted to spend as much time with them as I could when they arrived.

A half hour before their scheduled arrival, we all got in two cars. Zenaida and her husband Higinio volunteered to drive their car to the train station also so we would have enough transportation to bring them back to the apartment in one trip. Just as we parked near the outdoor platform, several minutes before the train was scheduled to arrive, Father Blackall pulled up in his car and volunteered to help with the transport also. While we were waiting, we were approached by a young woman holding a notebook and pen accompanied by a man with a large camera and flashgun. They were representing the "Waterbury American," the city's newspaper. Father Blackall had informed them about the reunion, and they asked permission to write an article and take photos. We did not object.

You could feel the high level of excitement among all of us waiting for the train to arrive. It was contagious. I stood on the edge of the open-air platform and kept my eyes looking south at the tracks as far as I could see. I wanted to be the first to announce the train's approach to the station. The tracks were empty, I felt it was taking longer than I expected. I was extremely impatient waiting to see the train. The anxiety was exhausting but finally, far away in the distance, I saw a train approaching the station. Before I could open my mouth to tell the others, an announcement was made on the platform's loudspeaker confirming the train's arrival from Grand Central Station in New York City. I stood back, and as the train pulled ahead in front of us, I could finally see my father, mother, and Jorge inside looking at us through the train's window with big smiles, waving to us. It was a scene that is sketched permanently in my mind. Everyone yelled and applauded.

It is almost impossible to accurately explain how good it felt when the three of them stepped off the train, called our names, and reached out for a long overdue embrace. A lot of what happened after they stepped off the train and on the platform is blurry. I do remember that none of us wanted to let go. It was 477 days since we were all together – it was difficult to believe we were finally reunited. For a brief moment, I thought it was just a dream. Is this really happening? We wanted to remember this moment for the rest of our lives. There wasn't a dry eye on the station's platform. Even

The Morning Light - 1963

the reporter and the photographer we had just met a few minutes ago had tears running down their cheeks. Other travelers on the train stopped on their way off the train to congratulate us and wish us well. People who were standing on the platform waiting for their families and friends to disembark surrounded our group and applauded. It was difficult to leave the platform – It was an important moment in our lives and none of us wanted to let go of each other.

I felt all alone with my family, the large group that surrounded us had vanished in my mind. We were all huddled together like a bunch of football players, in the middle of the field hugging and shedding tears of joy. Shortly after we calmed down, the reporter spent a few minutes talking with my father and Father Blackall. We were all able to compose ourselves eventually and headed home for the celebration to continue. It was time for Cuban *paella* and *cervezas* that Father Blackall brought with him as a present.

We spent the rest of the day together celebrating with our neighbors and Father Blackall. Everyone was excited and happy for us, grateful for everyone's support leading up to this day. After a while, I wanted everyone to leave so we could be alone. It was a day I will always remember, a day that I know my family will not forget. I was thrilled to tell my parents all about my new school, new friends, the neighborhood, and anything they wanted to talk about. It was a long day, and I knew they also wanted all the guests to leave early so we could spend time alone. There was a lot to catch up on. We had a lot to share – And a lot of time to do it!

****

The following morning, as I was getting ready for school, Zenaida brought us the morning newspaper. Front page, above the fold was a photo from the train station of my mother and me, just as we were coming together to embrace. It appeared along with a great article about our reunion, the issues in Cuba today, and an interview the reporter had with my father. We grabbed our lunch

The Morning Light - 1963

and headed for school. I would have preferred to stay home but that was not an option that would have been allowed. When I arrived in school, I was immediately treated like a celebrity because a classmate had brought the morning newspaper to class to show everyone. The teacher showed the photo to the entire class and read the article out loud to everyone. She then shared it with other teachers in the school. I was embarrassed from all the attention we were getting but happy for the recognition and proud of my parents.

The media blitz continued that day when, just before lunch, we were called to the principal's office and told we needed to go home because the local television station was there. They arranged to have a reporter and video cameras there to record the story about our family's reunion. We raced home to find our living room filled with numerous studio lights, wires everywhere, and a movie camera facing the couch ready to film the family together. That evening, the local television network station featured our personal story and our reunion on their 6:00 p.m. news. All of the attention we were getting was overwhelming and positive. Father Blackall received numerous calls from strangers who either saw the article in the newspaper or watched the feature on the television evening news, and wanted to donate clothing, furniture, and money.

All this publicity generated additional needed donations to St. Cecilia's Church. The result was increased funding so the Church could sponsor several other families from Miami during the summer who were willing to move to Waterbury. It took a few days for the media blitz to calm down and for us to become normal residents of Waterbury. Now it was time for my father to look for employment, followed by an apartment for our reunited family of five. A lot of pressure was placed on him and my mother during this time. They were strong, just as I remembered them, and determined to work hard to provide us with a comfortable, loving home.

The stress of not knowing if we would ever see them was now gone. I hoped it was gone forever.

The Morning Light - 1963

CHAPTER 33

Leaving Cuba
2018

Our cruise ship was now sailing way from the docks in Cienfuegos. The lush tropical surroundings around the Bay of Cienfuegos combined with the mountainous backdrop provided us with another amazing late afternoon scene. It was a beautiful Christmas Day. I felt a wonderful sensation breathing that crisp, cool air from our verandah. The air, free of pollution as I inhaled deeply, provided a cleansing experience.

Cienfuegos was our last stop on this cruise. Now, we were headed home. As we admired the view from our verandah, the ship sailed through that small channel at the mouth of the bay. It headed out into the Caribbean Sea going west around the western coast of Cuba and turning north towards the port of Miami. Soon after we passed the mouth of the bay, we approached Playa Giron and the Bay of Pigs. We were seeing a historic site. Who will be the future inhabitants of those mountains? Maybe there is another group hiding there now waiting for the right moment to overthrow the government. Sailing through the Bay of Pigs reminded me of the military raid at our home and the incarceration my father experienced. All because of what happened here directly in front of me 57 years ago.

As we sat there staring at the coast, I wondered if there would ever be a reversal of the poverty and deterioration we witnessed in Cuba during this trip. It's difficult to believe that a country so rich in culture and economically strong could go so far downhill. A new generation of Cuban citizens don't remember the 1940s and 1950s and the robust presence Cuba had economically throughout the Americas. That is history I'm certain is not taught in Cuban schools today. The new generation can't compare their lives to what could have been since they are not taught the past nor how to prevent similar mistakes.

A government that suppresses and lies to its people will never be able to participate in the international economy successfully. The leadership in Cuba can't possibly care about the people they are supposed to serve. They only seem to care about themselves. They only enrich themselves personally and blame everyone else for the poverty that surrounds the people they govern.

I grabbed my laptop to view today's photos and to look at the people I photographed during the past several days. There was a significant assortment of expressions. Some were jovial (they were the models looking for the dollar bills), and some were sad. I thought about what they were thinking when I photographed them. If they had the freedom to express their thoughts, what would they tell me? If they can envision a better life for themselves, why don't they protest and build a separate government that cares about them? When did the Cuban population became so passive and afraid to fight against their current condition? I am not sure there is an answer to any of these questions. Perhaps I should just sit, take in the views, and just enjoy the portfolio of photographs taken during the past few days.

Leaving Cuba - 2018

****

It was sad to say goodbye to Cuba again. This time, it was a different goodbye than when my brother and I left in 1962. This time I was not leaving my family behind. The memories of what we witnessed on this trip were coming home with us. Almost 57 years have passed, and not much has changed. Could it ever change in my lifetime? I don't know. As the sun set in the West, and before I got ready for drinks and dinner, I looked at the shoreline of Cuba. I waved goodbye to an imaginary group of Cubans standing on the imaginary observation deck of the imaginary airport terminal. Perhaps I will return again someday; maybe it will be a different Cuba.

It was now time for our final visit to the martini bar to say goodbye to the new friends we met on this trip and to enjoy a nice farewell dinner in the main dining room with our friends, Stephen and Allen.

CHAPTER 34

Happy New Year
1964

After the reunion celebrations and the media blitz faded away, reality stepped in - it was time to focus on beginning a new life as a family in Waterbury. It was time to rebuild a new household. Time to let go of possessions left behind and start over again. But we would never forget family members that remained in Cuba.

It was important to find a new job for my father and to build business relationships within our new community. It was time to get acclimated to our new surroundings in hopes that this time it would be a permanent move. For me, it was time to do the best I could in school and continue to improve my knowledge of English. It was time to look forward, but I'd never forget how we got here.

Father Blackall introduced my father to various community and business leaders in town. Within a few days, he was fortunate to get a job as a staff accountant at a local accounting firm in Waterbury. We found an apartment in the downtown district. With help from St. Cecilia's Church and other generous resources, we were able to acquire some basic household furniture from the local thrift store. Three single beds, a double bed, two dressers, a kitchen table with six chairs, a stove, a refrigerator, and an old wringer washing machine: That was the extent of our initial furnishings. It was the minimum required to live in our new apartment. We didn't care that our home was half empty because having our own place was our priority. Over the next several months, we were able to furnish the living room, get a television, and buy drapes and other important household items.

School ended in late June 1963. Soon afterward, Segundito and I enrolled in summer school where we made many new local friendships and traveled around the state on school-sponsored field trips. These included visits to the beaches on the southern coast of Connecticut less than an hour away from Waterbury.

My parents were grateful for all the help St. Cecilia's Church provided our family. In return for their support, my father volunteered as the church accountant. He would go there once a week after his job at the accounting firm to work on the church's accounting records. St. Cecilia's and other donors continued with their generosity towards our community by hosting three other Cuban families during the summer months. My parents volunteered to help them all get settled into new apartments. A Cuban family network was beginning to get established in Waterbury. We all helped each other get acclimated to our new environment. In exchange, we developed long-term friendships with wonderful new friends.

During the middle of the summer, my father came home with a used 1962 Buick sedan he purchased from a client at the accounting firm. Now we could go out on Sunday rides and visit some of the recreational parks, lakes, and other spots that surrounded the city of Waterbury. Being able to get out of the apartment and visit areas of the city we could not reach on foot was a treat for us. Our

Happy New Year - 1964

new favorite place was Black Rock State Park in Thomaston. The park provided plenty of picnic tables and grills to barbecue. In the center, there was a large lake with a sandy beach surrounded by the Litchfield Hills, the park had many walking trails that would reach the highest point. We spent a lot of time getting lost exploring the trails that summer.

****

Segundito and I were still under 16 and not able to work part-time after school. Delivering the local newspaper to households in the neighborhood was allowed at our age. So, during the summer, we got two morning paper routes that provided us with a few dollars we would both share equally. A portion of our profit would be given to our father for savings. The remainder we would use as our personal spending money. It was a tough job getting up at 5:30 a.m. to deliver newspapers. When school began in September, we would come home after delivering the newspapers to bathe and dress so we could be in school by 8:30 a.m. As the winter got closer, the paper route got harder to manage at that hour of the morning. The snowfall made it twice as difficult but we got used to getting up early and continued with it all year round.

****

In mid-summer 1963 and throughout the remainder of the year, Cubans continued to talk about the eventual assassination of Fidel Castro by the C.I.A. or perhaps an exile militia group hiding in the mountains of Cuba. One Cuban radio station based out of New York City had predicted the day Castro would be assassinated. Every day the show aired on the radio, they claimed it was one day closer to assassination day. Operation Mongoose technically ended after the Cuban Missile Crisis but many Cubans felt the C.I.A. was secretly continuing privately, at the request of President

Happy New Year - 1964

Kennedy, with a mission to remove key political leaders in Cuba. We were able to receive several Cuban radio stations based in New York City and northern New Jersey. Some claimed to have specific insider news about relations between the U.S. and Cuba and activities happening inside Cuba. Cubans in Waterbury were always glued to the radio when certain news programs aired. It was public knowledge that after the Cuban Missile Crisis, Kennedy wanted to have a relationship with Castro that would keep The Soviet Union out of the Western Hemisphere. At the same time, Castro knew that C.I.A.-sponsored terrorist attacks in Cuba were continuing, and their ultimate goal was his assassination.

****

The start of the school year arrived. It was the Wednesday after Labor Day in 1963. Now, all three of us would be attending St. Anne's school. Segundito was going to the eighth grade, Jorge began in the second grade, and I entered the fifth grade. Catholic school uniforms for three boys must have been an expensive purchase. The morning of that first day was a mad scene at our house. After delivering the early morning papers, we rushed home, took our turn in the only bathroom in the apartment, and got dressed for school. My mother returned to her classic inspection position by the door. After she made sure we picked up our lunch bags, she would give us one final look to check our hair was combed properly, our shoes were polished, and our shirts were tucked inside our pants. If anything was not to her liking, we had to go back and fix it or she would fix it for us. Once we passed inspection, she kissed us goodbye and we were out the door with a relieved feeling of accomplishment.

****

In September 1963, during a speech at the Brazilian Embassy, Castro warned American leaders:

Happy New Year - 1964

*... [If they are] aiding terrorist plans to eliminate
Cuban leaders, then they themselves will not be
safe ...*

Monday evening, November 18, 1963, in a hotel in Miami
Beach, President Kennedy told the Inter-American Press
Association that only one issue separated the U.S. from Castro's
Cuba. Castro's leadership had handed Cuban sovereignty to The
Soviet Union, which used Cuba to subvert other nations in Latin
America. President Kennedy said:

*As long as this is true, nothing is possible.
Without it, everything is possible.*

The following day, Tuesday, November 19, 1963, the C.I.A.
covert team brought President Kennedy evidence that Castro was
trying to stir a revolution throughout Latin America. Kennedy was
informed of an arms stockpile left by Cuban terrorists on a beach in
Venezuela, with a plan to seize control of that country by stopping
Venezuelan elections scheduled in less than two weeks. Disrupting
elections or falsely claiming fraud during the voting process is a
common tactic used by dictators and "dictators-in-training" to seek
control of a country. The C.I.A. knew that President Kennedy was
not going to authorize an invasion of Cuba but instead, he wanted
to step up efforts towards covert actions.

Three days later, on November 22, 1963, President John F.
Kennedy was assassinated in Dallas, Texas. If he had survived,
perhaps there could have been some historic improvement in the
relationship between the two countries. Perhaps the increased
activity of covert actions would have finally sparked the internal
revolution U.S. officials were always hoping to develop. Instead,
the assassination of President Kennedy changed the path of Cuban
history.

Happy New Year - 1964

President Kennedy's death was a shock to our newly established Cuban community in Waterbury. Many of us remember the date, the time, and the place we were when we heard the news. It was a huge loss to the Cuban immigrant population. Even though many felt betrayed by what happened at the Bay of Pigs, most Cubans still supported President Kennedy's policies towards Cuba.

Many Cubans in our local community were convinced that Fidel Castro and The Soviet Union were directly responsible for Kennedy's assassination. So much has been written about this theory after The Warren Commission's report stated that Kennedy's assassin, Lee Harvey Oswald, was the only person responsible for the assassination. We will never know the whole truth but we are certain that Kennedy's assassination truly changed the course of U.S., Cuba and Soviet Union relations.

****

We approached our first Thanksgiving together as a family in 1963. The sadness of President Kennedy's assassination still lingered. Not sure of the American menu traditions, my mother got advice from several of our neighbors and was ready to go shopping at the supermarket a few blocks away. I was always selected to go with her to help carry the bags since my father was still at work. Segundito stayed home to watch Jorge. Just before we left, there was a knock on our front door. A group of high school students with bags of groceries stood there in front of us wishing us a Happy Thanksgiving. Arranged by the local Catholic churches, about 15-20 students came to our building, and every Cuban family received a large turkey and six or seven grocery bags filled to the top with food items for our Thanksgiving meal. All the bags were brought inside the house and placed at our kitchen table. My mother was in shock. How could she thank these kids and the donors? She shed a few tears of joy in front of the high school kids. They recognized the impact they made on my family, and each of them gave my mother a hug on the way out. All the other Cuban families in the

Happy New Year - 1964

building received the same, and all of them were buzzing with joy and gratitude. It was a memorable Thanksgiving Day for us. A day to truly give thanks for the gifts we had around us, especially the gift of being together again.

Celebrating holidays during the first year after my parents arrived was difficult at times for them. They were relieved we were together and always demonstrated positive attitudes in front of us. But the memories of their brothers, sisters, Abuela Teresa, and other family members left behind in Cuba remained in their minds. I knew they thought of them often and shared their sadness with each other privately. Christmas was approaching, and we were able to afford and decorate a small live Christmas tree in our living room. Presents under the tree were minimal but we didn't care. Most of them were for Jorge since he was the youngest. My father was able to make several calls to Cuba the week before Christmas to speak with relatives and especially Abuela Teresa. We all took turns on the phone. My mother was thrilled to be on the phone with them but I will never forget the sad look on her face every time the calls ended. I knew what was going through her mind, but she refused to acknowledge her grief in front of anyone.

I remember the week before Christmas in school, the nuns at St. Anne's were excited that the popular group, The Singing Nuns, came out with a hit record, "Dominique". It was not our favorite – We were listening to other hits like, "I Wanna Hold Your Hand," by The Beatles. My parents were more interested in Perry Como, Frank Sinatra, and Big Crosby, and would always watch "The Lawrence Welk Show" on Saturday nights. We all had different preferences for television shows. With only one television in the house, that usually caused problems that were always resolved by my mother who played the role of judge and jury.

On Christmas Eve, Tia Maria Luisa, Tio Mario, and Juan joined us for a traditional Cuban Christmas Eve dinner at home with *lechon asado* (roast pig) and enough side dishes to feed the entire building. That night, after a long dinner, we walked to St. Cecilia's Church for the traditional midnight mass. My mother and

Happy New Year - 1964

Tia Maria Luisa sat next to each other during the mass and held each other's hand. I am sure they were both thinking of and praying for Abuela Teresa and the rest of their family left behind in Cuba.

****

The day after Christmas, the Cuban families in Waterbury got together and decided to have a small party to celebrate New Year's Eve. For most of them, this would be their first New Year's Eve in the U.S. My parents agreed to host the party at our house since we had the largest living room. Everyone was excited about the party and dressed up that evening as if they were going to dinner at Rancho Luna in the Wajay neighborhood in La Habana. The women styled each other's hair that afternoon, and we decorated our living room with streamers and balloons. Everyone brought their favorite plate of Cuban food to share. There was so much food, we could have fed many of the people we saw on television standing in Times Square at midnight. It was an elegant, fun, and festive New Year's Eve at our household.

A couple of hours after midnight would be precisely the fifth anniversary of Fulgencio Batista fleeing Cuba and the beginning of everyone's new life in Cuba with Fidel Castro. Back in the early hours of January 1, 1959, this group could not have imagined that in five years, they would be celebrating the same holiday 1,500 miles away from their homeland. In just five short years, their lives were turned upside down and the decisions they were forced to make tore apart their families and friendships that were meant to last for generations to come. They all lost their savings, their homes, and their possessions but not their memories nor their pride. Many of them did not want to discuss the past during the party and only looked to the future. The pain they experienced was difficult to re-live. Their memories were recent and still too vivid. I remembered that early morning of January 1, 1959, the street demonstrations and the sounds of people yelling and glass breaking, followed by my parents arriving home after a frightening drive from Rancho

Happy New Year - 1964

Luna. I was very young but knew that the noises I was hearing were not normal.

Five years later, I was only 10 years old and, as always, eavesdropping on some of the adult conversations as I walked around the room. Many were talking about where they were five years ago, never expecting to be here five years later. All of them were proud of their decision to leave their country. Many still talked about *"en esos días"* ("back in those days") in La Habana. They left their lives behind and everything they worked hard to build. Many left their professions behind and were forced to seek other means of employment in the U.S. Some of our new neighbors started to re-educate themselves in night school so they could maintain a higher-level job similar to what they held back in Cuba. The only regret in that room on New Year's Eve 1963 was not being with the rest of their families and close friends left behind.

The party was a great escape for many of the Cuban families. It was a time to be together, a time to heal, a time to give thanks, and to begin a new life and new friendships in a new country. It was also a time to look back at the past and hopefully learn from the experiences. History often repeats itself. Perhaps an occasional view of how and why we got where we are today will help us avoid replicating painful events.

It's always good to look to the future, plan for the future, and be of the future. But that occasional look at the past reminds us of the many lessons we should never forget. I will not forget. Happy New Year, 1964.

Happy New Year - 1964

Epilogue

After we celebrated the New Year 1964, our day-to-day life in Waterbury did not change significantly except that, as the years passed, we all got older, smarter, and wiser. Segundito and I continued delivering newspapers. After finishing grammar school, I moved to J.F. Kennedy High School. When I turned 16, I gave up my paper route and got an after-school part-time job at a local department store in downtown Waterbury. That's where I met my husband in May of 1969. I was 16 years old. Arthur was only three months older, attended a different high school, and lived in a different neighborhood. We were not romantically involved until we both came out to each other one year later on May 8, 1970.

I graduated from Central Connecticut State University with an accounting degree in 1976, and eventually passed my C.P.A. (Certified Public Accountant) exam. During and after college days, Arthur and I lived together in Waterbury; Hartford, Connecticut; Boston; New York City; and Stamford, Connecticut. I was an experienced mover, so we moved for better job positions during our younger days. Today, 51 years later, we are still together, retired, and living in South Florida.

During his school days in Waterbury, Segundito changed his nickname to "Jerry," which was much shorter and more American sounding. He also left the paper route when he turned 16 and got a part-time job at a retail store after school. He attended college, earned his M.B.A., married, raised two beautiful girls, and became an executive of a major West Coast utility company. Today, he is retired with his wife and enjoying visits from his family, especially his three grandchildren.

****

On Saturday, June 8, 1963, the day may parents and Jorge left Miami and began their journey to reunite with Segundito and me in Waterbury, President John F. Kennedy gave his famous "Ich bin ein Berliner" (I am a Berliner) speech, delivered from a platform overlooking the new wall dividing East and West Berlin.

> *Two thousand years ago, the proudest boast was 'Civis Romanus sum,' (I am a Roman Citizen)"*
> *he proclaimed. "Today, in the world of freedom, the proudest boast is 'Ich bin ein Berliner!'(I am a Berliner)*

The words touched the hearts of thousands of people who were there and the millions around the world who saw the speech captured on film. Everyone felt a sense of belonging to their country of birth or their adoptive country, *"Soy Cubano-Americano"* (I am a Cuban-American).

****

My mother wanted to contribute financially to our household budget while still maintaining a home for all of us. She decided to get a job at a local factory making ties for fashion designers. The additional income was helpful. She kept this job for more than 20 years and retired with a small pension in the mid-1980s. In 1989, when she was 66 years old, she was diagnosed with a benign brain tumor, and had it removed at Yale New Haven Hospital. It was a very serious operation, and we all hoped for the best. She survived the operation and the recovery period. She went on to live another 30 years until her recent death at the age of 96.

****

Epilogue

My father continued with his accounting work at a local accounting firm in Waterbury. He did not share much about the difficulties in Cuba while we lived there nor the time he was sent to jail after the Bay of Pigs Invasion. Unfortunately, we lost our father in 1997 after a long battle with leukemia. During his illness, my mother was there for him every hour of the day. Unfortunately, Segundito was married and living with his wife and two daughters in San Jose, California. I lived in Stamford, Connecticut with Arthur and we both worked in New York City. Jorge was still living in Waterbury with his wife and two children. We were all limited as to what we could have done to make him feel better. The night he died, the three of us and my mother came together and stayed with him around his hospital bed until he stopped breathing.

Many years after his death, my brother Jerry showed me a copy of a speech my father delivered to the Chamber of Commerce in Waterbury, Connecticut about his experiences under the Castro regime. I had never seen that speech and was surprised by its content. In a section of that speech, my father described the conditions of his incarceration after the Bay of Pigs Invasion. I had never heard him talk about this in front of our family or anyone. I was truly surprised to know this document existed:

... they locked me in a cell shaped like a tunnel in a deep basement of an old Spanish castle. The place was so small that we had to take turns lying on the floor to try to sleep. We did not see the sun at all, and we could only see each other with the few lights we had. We remained locked in that cell without any contact with the outside world for two nights and three days with no food. Water was the only thing we had. We saw three men die, who could not endure this torment. At the end of the third day, they brought us milk, but it was not enough to share, as well as some rotten rice and beans. At the end of the sixth day

Epilogue

of what I called purgatory, they took us out in the open to identify us and take our fingerprints. A few days later, we were called one by one, and they let us go home.

To this moment, I still do not know why they arrested me. Over those few days, I never changed or even took my shoes off. I could not sleep because of nervous tension. We had to take care of the basic human necessities on the same floor where we were sleeping. I saw men cry like babies. That was their only consolation. They could do nothing else.

I was desperate thinking of my family because they did not know where I was until they saw me coming home in my same dirty clothes. They were so filthy, I could never wear them again ...

****

Tia Nena played an important role in getting all of us and many of her friends out of Cuba. She had plenty of connections and was instrumental in using her influence to get us on a list to exit Cuba. After Abuela Balbina died in the summer of 1962, Tia Nena married a man she dated for many years.

A few years after the Cuban Missile Crisis, an agreement between the U.S. and Cuban governments resulted in *"Los Vuelos de la Libertad"* (Freedom Flights), which transported Cubans to Miami twice daily, five times per week, from 1965 to 1973. Tia Nena and her new husband, Tio Amado, were able to leave the country before the flights ended and join us in Waterbury. She worked very hard with my mother at the same factory making designer ties. She eventually retired. Several years after Tio Amado died, she moved to Florida where she died peacefully at the age of 94.

Epilogue

****

The demolition of the above-ground portion of the architectural splendor of Penn Station began on October 28, 1963, approximately six months after I walked into that station for my first and only time. I remember reading about the demolition and could not understand why anyone would want to destroy this impressive and massive structure.

****

Tia Maria Luisa, Tio Mario, and Juan were never comfortable in Waterbury because of the long, cold winters and snow. During the summer of 1964, they packed their bags and drove to Los Angeles, California, to start a new life.

The day we arrived in Waterbury with them, April 16, 1963, was the historic day that Martin Luther King, Jr. wrote an open letter known today as the "Letter from Birmingham Jail." The letter was in response to a "Call for Unity," suggesting a cease to the fight for equality and freedom to allow justice to take control. Martin Luther King, Jr. wrote the following in his letter on that date:

> *We know through painful experience that freedom is never voluntarily given by the oppressor; it must be demanded by the oppressed. Frankly, I have yet to engage in a direct-action campaign that was 'well timed' in the view of those who have not suffered unduly from the disease of segregation. For years now I have heard the word 'Wait!' It rings in the ear of every Negro with piercing familiarity. This 'Wait' has almost always meant 'Never.' We must come to see, with one of our distinguished jurists, that justice too long delayed is justice denied.*

Epilogue

****

In 1989, Tio Orlando and Tia Asuncion were able to obtain a one-month visitor's visa to come to Waterbury. Unfortunately, several years after their visit, Tio Orlando died in La Habana from a brief illness. Tia Asuncion returned for another visit with her eldest daughter, Asun, and stayed permanently in 1995. They worked very hard to get the rest of their family, including Asun's husband and daughter, and her sister Milagros and her family, out of Cuba. Today, everyone in the family owns their own home and are employed in professional jobs in South Florida.

****

Tio Alberto, Tio Yayo, and their families did not wish to leave Cuba. They had hoped the Castro regime would end soon. Both Tios died during the 1990s after long illnesses.

Tia Vivina and Tio Frank also stayed behind. Frank was still convinced that Castro was the best leader for Cuba. He was never a favorite relative within the family. Both were able to obtain visitor's visas during the early 1990s and came to stay with my parents in Waterbury. My father was not a happy person to have Tio Frank staying with him but knew that my mother was enjoying the visit from her youngest sister. Tio Frank died in Cuba after a brief illness in 2001.

****

Abuela Teresa died exactly one year after my parents and Jorge arrived in Waterbury. It was a very sad moment in our home. My mother was always very close to her mother, and not being able to comfort her during her last days was extremely difficult for her. She tried to hide her emotions and continued to maintain her normal schedule around the house. One night after dinner, we were all sitting there talking about the fun times we had with Abuela

Teresa. Suddenly, my mother broke down and cried. We got out of our chairs, approached her, and hugged her.

****

During the summer of 2002, while living in Stamford, Connecticut, Arthur and I decided to take a Sunday drive to St. Agnes orphanage in Sparkill, New York, about a 40-minute drive from our home in Stamford. When we reached the property, I was not surprised to find most of it torn down and new structures developed into commercial real estate. Several years later, I found the following article from "The New York Times," February 28, 1977, on the Internet:

> *SPARKILL, N.Y.—The St. Agnes Home and School for Children has announced it will soon close its doors after caring for troubled youngsters—most of them teenage boys from New York City—for more than 100 years. The Rockland County institution had given a home to thousands of orphans and young people from broken families since it was started in New York City by the Dominican Sisters in 1876 ...*

St. Agnes Home and School for Boys was home to several Pedro Pan boys in the 1960s. It closed its doors in 1977. By 1980, its new owner had razed nearly all the structures from the grounds. Today, only the church and pond remain.

****

On June 29, 2007, Jorge died from a self-inflicted gunshot wound. I had the difficult responsibility to tell my mother that her youngest son had committed suicide. My older brother Jerry was

Epilogue

traveling with his wife in Europe, and I also reached out to him that afternoon to tell him the unfortunate news. It was a sad day for all of us. Depression is a very serious illness. I only wish there was something I could have done to prevent this horrific day from happening.

****

Arthur and I recently tried to visit the campus where Jerry and I lived in Florida City, and we could not find it. My memory of the exact location was sketchy. In early 2021, while surfing through the Internet, I found the following portion of an article from November 3, 2012, in the "South Dade News Leader," a local newspaper:

> *... There were numerous camps in Florida for the children to reside in, but the Florida City camp, which used to be located on NW 2nd Ave., between NW 14th and 16th Streets, has received special recognition. This month it will become the home to a historical marker identifying the significance of the area and explaining some of its history ...*

I am looking forward to a return visit to Florida City.

****

On November 25, 2016, at the age of 90, Fidel Castro died. During his leadership, he was responsible for transforming Cuba from one of the richest countries in the Western Hemisphere to one of the poorest. The headlines in the "Miami Herald" the following morning were simple:

Epilogue

CASTRO
DEAD

****

More than 14,000 Pedro Pan children experienced events similar to those described in my book – some better, some worse. My story is not unique. History should always have an important place in our education. Without that base, we have no platform from which to leap ahead to the future. Roads others have paved in the past should be used to determine our future paths and avoid the repeat of previous mistakes.

****

Decisions that we make or that are made for us during our childhood, no matter how minor, affect us the rest of our lives. They impact our life experiences and are absorbed in our souls and in our culture. They help develop and mold us into the person we become. Events I experienced during the five years described in this book have given me the strength to deal with life's adversities. Many of our Pedro Pan brothers and sisters did not experience a happy ending to their story. We were the fortunate ones.

****

I can see traces of my father and mother in me today. I have learned from them the importance of honesty, hard work, determination, and strength. Our separation was a traumatic and heroic act. They made a very difficult choice to send us ahead of them, and I was not convinced that I would ever see them again, even though they assured us that the separation would be very

Epilogue

short-term. It was obviously a difficult time for my brother and me and many other Pedro Pan children – a new country, a new language, new friends, and new people looking after us. It was a new life without our parents as everyone navigated their exit under the rule of an irrational and vindictive dictator. All of it was unreal. I know the lessons my parents taught me prior to our separation helped me survive being without them.

These experiences as a child made me grow up faster than most children. I never regretted my parents' decision. In fact, I am thankful to them, especially after I experienced the Cuba of today from our cruise in 2018, almost 60 years from the start of this book.

Today, when I look back on how life has turned out for me and my family, I can only say I am …

… forever grateful.

Epilogue

Note from the Author

Throughout the book, I used, in most cases, pseudonyms for characters who were not family members. I did it to protect their privacy in some cases and in others because I did not recall their names. My apologies to those whose names I did not recall. Descriptions of specific locations, events, and dates are based on my recollections and family photographs. Family members and others who will read this book may have a different memory of the scenes I described. Again, I apologize for any (if any) differences and errors in advance – My story remains the same.

PHOTOS

New Year's Eve, December 31, 1958 - Rosa and Segundo seated on the right with friends at Rancho Luna Restaurant shortly before Batista fled the country.

Rosa and Segundo in 1958

Photos

Rosa and the boys in La Habana 1959

One of my Birthday parties in La Habana. (Date unknown)

Photos

First day of school in Connecticut (1963) First day of school in La Habana (1960)

1961 - Family gathering in La Habana with Abuela Balbina (left photo) and 1958 with Abuela Teresa (right photo)

Photos

St. Agnes in Sparkill, NY (April 1962)
Above: Tony is standing in the center of the photo, Segundito on his left.
Below: Tony is in the center, Segundito behind him (the six spiks)

Photos

Above: December 2018 - Outside at Calle J.H. Goss (my home) in Santo
Suarez, La Habana with (Left to right) Tony, Arthur, Allen and Stephen

Below: December 2018 - Outside of the remains of Abuela Balbina's home on
Callle Amargura in La Habana Vieja

Photos

Above: December 2018 - Aerobic dancers on the plaza in Santiago de Cuba

Below: December 2018 - Young boy roasting a "cochinito" for Christmas Eve in Trinidad

Photos

Above: 1960 - A gathering in our living room on Calle J.H.Goss of cousins and neighborhood friends (Tony is in the center with checkered shirt)

Below: 1960 - Valmana school photo with all the boys and teacher. (Tony is in the top row fifth from the right)

Photos

Together Again

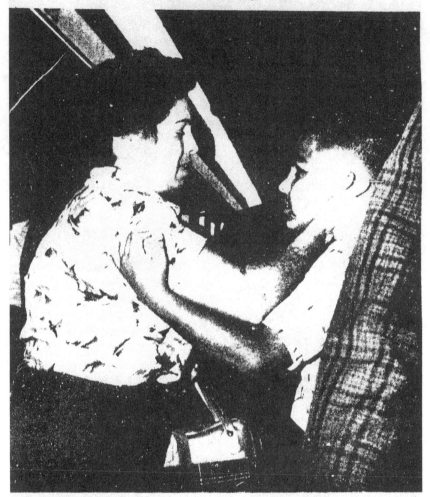

MRS. ROSA TIMIRAOS, a Cuban refugee, yesterday tearfully embraced her 10-year-old son, Antonio, at the Waterbury railroad station. She had not seen her son for more than a year as they were separated because of the Cuban crisis. Mrs. Timiraos, her husband, and their sons have been resettled in Waterbury with the help of the Spanish-Speaking Center of St. Cecilia's Parish, which is participating in the National Catholic W e l f a r e Conference's resettlenent program for Cuban refugees.—Marens Photo.

Above: Front page photo of the Waterbury Republican American newspaper on Monday, June 10, 1963.

Photos

Above: January 1961 - The wedding of Tia Vivina and Tio Frank. (Left to right) Abuela Teresa, (flower girl), Tia Vivina, Tio Frank, Tony and Frank Sr.

Left: 1958 - Tia Nena with Segundito, Tony, Jorge (on Tia Nena's lap) and Cousin Asun.

Photos

Above: Family portrait taken in 1961

Below: Family portrait taken on the 50th wedding anniversary of Segundo and Rosa - 1993

Photos

You must do the thing you think you cannot do.

- ELEANOR ROOSEVELT

CPSIA information can be obtained
at www.ICGtesting.com
Printed in the USA
BVHW060746151021
618952BV00006B/365/J